Promises To Keep

Promises To Keep

by Ernest W. Michel

Foreword by Leon Uris

BARRICADE BOOKS

NEW YORK

Published by Barricade Books Inc.
61 Fourth Avenue
New York, NY 10003

Distributed by Publishers Group West
4065 Hollis
Emeryville, CA 94608

Printed in the United States of America

Library of Congress Cataloging-in-Publication Data

Michel, Ernest, 1923-
        Promises to keep / by Ernest Michel.
                p. cm.
        ISBN 0-9623032-4-0 : $22.00
        1. Michel, Ernest, 1923-   . 2. Holocaust survivors—United State—
Biography. 3. Holocaust, Jewish (1939-1945)—Personal narratives. 4. Auschwitz
(Poland: Concentration camp) 5. Philanthropists—United States—Biography.
7. United Jewish Appeal—Federation of Jewish Philanthropies of New York.
I. Title.
E184. J5M535 1993
940.53'18'092--dc20   93-13550
                                        CIP

9 8 7 6 5 4 3 2 1

This book is dedicated to the blessed memory of my parents, Otto and Frieda Michel, who were killed in Auschwitz in August, 1942.

My life's greatest regret is that they died without knowing that their two children, my sister Lotte and I, would survive the Holocaust. Between us we have seven children and nineteen grandchildren, sixteen of them in Israel.

This book is also dedicated to my children, Lauren Shachar, Joel Michel and Karen Daniels, and to my six grandchildren, Noga, Yair, Rachel, Nesia, Gil and Evan. I hope and pray that they and their descendants shall remember my miraculous survival as proof of the strength and continuity of our people.

Last, but not least, part of this dedication belongs to my wife, Amy, who has given me a new life.

Acknowledgements

I HAVE ALWAYS BEEN an avid reader. When I was a kid, I loved books so much, I would take a flashlight under the blanket so that I could read and my parents wouldn't catch me staying up past my bedtime. I still love to read anything I can get my hands on.

Most books carry acknowledgements. For a long time, I couldn't understand why the author had so many people to thank. Now I know. This book would never have seen the light of day if not for the support, encouragement and hard work of individuals I must acknowledge. Without them, I couldn't have done it.

First, my thanks to Ludwig Jesselson, Burton Resnick and William Wishnick, with whom I worked closely during my years at UJA-Federation, and who have become personal friends. They encouraged me to tell my story and undertook the effort to get my memoirs published. I also want to thank my friends and colleagues, Irving Bernstein, Brian Lurie and Stephen D. Solender for their unflagging support.

I'm deeply indebted to many individuals, all long-term UJA-Federation contributors who have made the publication of this book possible. It is because of their generosity that I am able to relinquish all financial gain from the sales of this book. Any profits are going to UJA-Federation, the organization that brought me out of Europe and was the focal point of my professional life.

I also want to thank my agents Pam Bernstein of Pam Bernstein Associates and Mel Berger of William Morris, who were always ready with honest professional advice, clear judgement and valid criticism. No writer could find better pros. A very special thank you is due my editor, Jeanette Friedman. Out of sentences, she made a chapter; out of chapters she made sense. And out of my manuscript, she made a book.

I want to express my thanks and appreciation to Carole and Lyle Stuart and the members of their staff, for helping to make the publication of this book possible.

I am grateful to Beverly Abramowitz, Ruth Greenfield, David Mark, Libby Peppersberg and Sue Wolfson. Their daily dedication to my project went above and beyond the call of duty.

Leon Uris, one of the great writers of our generation, has been my close friend for thirty years. He readily agreed to write the foreword. Lee, I thank you.

A special word of appreciation must go to Chaim Herzog, President of the State of Israel. Despite his busy schedule, he was kind enough to review the chapters dealing with our visit to Germany, the cornerstone of my story.

Finally, I must thank, with much love, my wife, Amy Goldberg. She suffered with me the ups and downs of the process of writing and getting into print. She was my toughest critic and my greatest supporter.

One last note. I started writing this book in 1945, when I was a reporter at the Nuremberg Trials. I wrote it in German and put it aside. I didn't look at it again until 1988, when I returned from the German trip on the 50th anniversary of Kristallnacht. My notes from that period formed the basis for the first part of this book.

New York
April, 1993

Patrons

I want to acknowledge with thanks and gratitude, the many individuals who made the publication of this book possible. Because of their support, all benefits from the sale of this book will go to UJA-Federation, the organization which has been the focal point of my life since my arrival in this country in 1946.

S. Daniel Abraham
Albert Adelman
Diane and Arthur B. Belfer*
Stanley M. Bogen
Joel Boyarsky
Ludwig Bravman
Jacob Burns
Simona and Jerome A. Chazen
I.N. Claremon
Leonard Davis
Mel Dubin
Melvin Dubinsky
Benjamin Duhl
Alvin H. Einbender
Irwin S. Field
Ronald Gallatin
Victor Gelb
Eugen Gluck
Eugene Goldfarb
Frederic H. Gould
Eugene M. Grant
Alan C. Greenberg

Bernard Greenman
Gerry Grinberg
Jerome J. Grossbardt
Stanley Hirsh
Irwin Hochberg
Ludwig Jesselson*
Stanley Katz
Gershon Kekst
Martin Kimmel
George Klein
Morton Kornreich
Ronald S. Lauder
Carl Leff
Morris L. Levinson
Leon Levy
David S. Mack
Robert A. Meister
Ursula and Hermann Merkin
Harold L. Oshry
Henry Pearce
Stephen M. Peck
Burton P. Resnick
Meshulam Riklis

Stephen Robert
Irving Rosenbaum
William Rosenwald
Robert de Rothschild
Selma and Lawrence Ruben
Bernice Rudnick
Irving Schaffer
Albert Schussler
Romie Shapiro
Irving Schneider
Lowell M. Schulman
J.D. Shane
Herbert M. Singer
John Slade
Meyer Steinberg
Saul P. Steinberg
Leonard N. Stern
Herbert Tenzer*
Alan and Peggy Tishman
James L. Weinberg
William Wishnick
Martin J. Zimet

---

*Ludwig Jesselson, who served as UJA-Federation Chairman during my tenure in New York, died unexpectedly on the eve of Passover, 1993, in Jerusalem. He was among those who encouraged me to write this book. He was one of the finest men I have ever met, and his memory will be with me as long as I live.

Within a few weeks two other giants of the New York Jewish community, both friends and UJA-Federation leaders, Arthur Belfer and Herbert Tenzer, died. Both had become good friends. They are sorely missed.

Table of Contents

Foreword

THE WORD 'SURVIVOR' has gained an extended meaning in the
Jewish and much of the world's lexicon. It implies a European Jew
who outlived the Nazi Holocaust and most likely one who endured
a concentration or extermination camp, as well. These men and
women are to be looked upon with wonderment.

My dear friend, Ernie Michel, is such a man.

For every survivor there is a tale that sears the soul. A half century after the event, it is still impossible to fully comprehend.

Each person who escaped Hitler's death machinery brought
with him a slightly different version of his or her personal story of
survival. Yet all stories had a convergence of common factors.

To have lived through this, the darkest pit of man's depravity,
he or she had to be untouched by an unseen golden hand. Call it
fate, luck, divine intervention or a miracle. Every survivor will
relate to you his or her particular miracle or miracles. Ernie
Michel is no exception. He was chosen to live by a force beyond
his own power.

Not everyone so blessed got through. In addition to that
moment of fate or luck, he or she had to have supreme will-power
and the presence of mind to impose it.

It is a glory to the Jewish people that those who survived came
through with their human dignity intact and many went on to live
prominent and useful lives.

I first met Ernie Michel in the late 1950's, when the revelation of the Holocaust first staggered the imagination (as indeed it still does).

At the time I was living in the San Fernando Valley and researching and writing my novel *Exodus*. Ernie Michel worked for the United Jewish Appeal in Los Angeles. We became fast friends almost immediately and although we have spent most of our friendship living in different places, we always stayed in communication.

I left for Hollywood and Ernie eventually went to Paris to help establish a prototype of the UJA in France. Later, he returned to New York and spent over two decades as head of that organization for the city. His tenure was truly distinguished and marked by enormous love and affection from the community he served.

I caught up with Ernie about five years ago when I moved to New York and re-established our relationship. Ernie was now retired and donating his time to help build a Holocaust Museum in New York City. Nonetheless, the UJA would not entirely let him go. He retained his office using his skills and devotion to do whatever might be asked of him. One of Ernie's vows in the camp was to bear witness. In keeping that promise he agreed to lead a UJA Mission to Warsaw and Auschwitz. I wondered, how did the man have the courage to return to that, the most hideous piece of ground on the planet? As you will read, few human beings among us have ever suffered more profoundly. Only if you know of Ernie Michel's courage and of his devotion to his people, can you realize an answer.

In my own years of research, I had visited several extermination camps; Maidanek, Dachau, Munthausen. I had interviewed dozens of survivors.

I had also stood the longest libel trial in British history. In the pages of *Exodus* was a passage referring to a Dr. Dering who had performed experimental surgery on Jewish men and women in Auschwitz in a grotesque scheme to sterilize the Jewish race and use them as neutered slave laborers. Only the strongest of the stock would be spared for the purpose of breeding new slaves.

I knew that Dr. Dering had been indicted but never tried as a war criminal. What I did not know was that he was not German, but Polish and a prisoner himself—one who willingly performed castrations and ovariectomies on Jews.

Lo and behold, Dr. Dering had escaped extradition to Poland, fled to a British colony and years later was knighted on the Queen's birthday . . . after which he returned to London and eventually brought suit against me.

I could not prove the numbers of my charges and I admitted openly that I had libeled him. I decided to defend the case on the premise that he was not entitled to damages because his character was worth nothing. After a short deliberation, the jury agreed with me. Dr. Dering was awarded a half-penny . . . the value of his character, in contemptuous damages.

The trial became the basis of my novel, *Q.B. VII*. In the charged moments of the trial, none was more electrifying than when my barrister arose to argue the jury. Lord Gerald Gardiner was a consummate Englishman, a brilliant legal mind who later went on to become the Lord Chancellor.

He was a Quaker, absolved of combat duty in the war, but he was in command of a medical unit which was part of the liberation of Bergen-Belsen. He never forgot what he witnessed.

He faced the jury and he said, "When the history of mankind is writ, there will be no darker chapter than what an advanced, civilized, Western, Christian nation did to the Jews in the middle of the twentieth century."

When Ernie Michel recently asked me to join an upcoming UJA mission to Warsaw and Auschwitz, I agreed. In addition to the meaning of the mission itself, I felt a need to resolve my own experience with Dr. Dering and the London trial.

Auschwitz is now one of the major tourist attractions in Europe with lines of tour buses from all over the continent. And I wondered: Do they come in curiosity?

Block X, where Dr. Dering performed brutal surgery on Jewish men and women, was shuttered, but one did not have to listen hard to hear the ghosts; the echoes of their screams. Between Block X and the next barrack, the SS torture chambers, was an execution yard.

I had satisfied my curiosity to come to Auschwitz.

As I wrote earlier, I had been to many concentration camps, but I had never been in the company of one who had been a prisoner there. Ernie Michel then took us to nearby Birkenau where inside one of the few remaining wooden barracks, he told us what day to day life was like. Herein, lies his remarkable story.

Back in Warsaw the Mission was to go to the monument to the Warsaw Ghetto Uprising, a few blocks from Mila 18, the headquarters of the Jewish fighters.

I was to give a short presentation, which I wrote out on stationery from the Warsaw Holiday Inn. By the time it became my turn to speak, it had grown dark and I could not see my notes.

A number of those present lit torches and formed a semi-circle behind me. The light and shadows of their flames cast an eerie background against the monument.

I had read a passage from my novel, *Mila 18*, in which a young Jewish boy is spirited out of the ghetto and into hiding because it was deemed that he had the best chance to survive because of his strength.

His uncle, Andrew Androfski, A leader of the Jewish fighters, commands him to survive . . . to survive and to live for a hundred thousand children who will not survive . . . who will be murdered in Treblinka. The boy vows he will survive.

At that instant, I felt something hot fall on my hand and then little red blobs fell on my notes. At first it appeared to be blood. As it congealed I realized it was wax that had dropped from someone's torch. I looked over my shoulder. It was falling from Ernie Michel's torch.

I was flushed with a tremendous moment of revelation. The boy I was reading about from *Mila 18* could have been . . . may have been, Ernie Michel being ordered to survive.

We Jews have survived through conquest. Not the conquest of armies but the conquest of ideas given to mankind as mankind groped for the moral definition of humanity. We have survived because we are family and each generation of Jews has done what was necessary in his lifetime, required for that survival.

We have survived because of men and women like Ernie Michel. This is the story of his survival and of his triumphant return to human dignity.

—Leon Uris

Prologue

IT WAS A CLEAR, blue, sunny November morning. Our group of twelve men and women, Americans all, stood talking in subdued tones in the lobby of the Steigenberger Hotel in Bonn. We were waiting for the minibus that would take us to Villa Hammerschmitt to meet with the President of the German Federal Republic, Richard von Weizsaecker. It was one of the controversial aspects of our Kristallnacht Memorial trip.

We would be received by the President and we would shake his hand. It was a "photo opportunity" that would go over the newswires to newspapers throughout the world. The caption would read "Delegation of New York Jews, including a Holocaust survivor, greeted by West German President." News stories would explain the purpose of our visit—the 50th anniversary of Kristallnacht—one of the darkest nights in all Jewish history, the night of November 9-10, 1938, the prelude to the Holocaust.

We wanted the story to be told in Germany. We wanted to make certain that Kristallnacht, named for the shattered glass of the Jewish synagogues and shops destroyed that night, would not be consigned to history and forgotten. We came to see the President of West Germany to commemorate that event in Germany, to keep it within the memory and conscience of Germany, the world and for the Jews, as well. It was a story we felt we had to tell.

I knew, ever since the plans were made, that this would be a tough trip for me. As a Holocaust survivor and then as Executive

1

Vice President of New York's UJA/Federation, the largest philanthropic organization in the United States, I met with Presidents
Eisenhower, Johnson and Carter and every Israeli president and
prime minister since the founding of the State in 1948. But this
was different. Very different. I was going to confront my personal
past.

The minibus slowed to a stop outside the hotel entrance, and
we edged to the door. My feet dragged reluctantly. We were all
quiet, our faces somber. I was sure I was pale and drawn. Why was
my anticipation dampened? Why didn't I feel vindicated? Why was
I so uncomfortable?

We were going to meet the President of Germany on the 50th
anniversary of the day that his countrymen began the systematic
killing of Jews, a systematic killing that resulted in the greatest
mass murder in history. That systematic killing was designed to
wipe me, my parents, friends and relatives, all the Jewish people,
off the face of the earth. I was about to meet the President of a
people who built a macabre museum during the Nazi era, a
museum of relics and religious items "of an extinct race." I was
going to meet the President of the nation that robbed me of my
education, violated my youth and murdered my parents. He was
the President of a country whose land seemed soaked beneath my
feet, because it was soaked with the blood of those I loved.

"What am I doing here?" I wondered. Was I being presump-
tuous? What right did I have to be here? Was I doing the right
thing? It was half a century, to the day, since the Gestapo agent
punched my mother in the face. It was fifty years, to the day, since
my father's arrest. My home, my innocence, and simple happiness
died that day, 50 years ago. 50 years ago, today, I wondered where
my father was. I saw my mother's bruised face. I watched my
grandmother collapse and my community die. Fifty years ago, I
felt my life was over.

We had just lunched with the Israeli Ambassador to West
Germany, a native of Austria. As he told us how significant and
vital our presence in Germany was on that day, I thought about
thin potato soup and sawdust bread, about cattle cars and lice.
About Jews dying. And I thought of my friend, Walter. I was

thinking about escape and close calls, about lies and fate and about friends, those who died and those who didn't. I was thinking about my life and its worth.

So here I sat, in an efficient minivan, with a group of my American peers, on our way to see the President of Germany. I was thoroughly disoriented. Did I have the right to come back to the country that destroyed nearly six million of my fellow Jews and their 1400 synagogues?

Instead of the neat, post-war streets of Bonn, I was seeing instead, in my mind's eye, that bitterly cold night so long ago. I saw the flaming synagogue. I heard the sirens. I ran back to the cardboard factory, to our shattered apartment, to my worn-out Papi, the friends who died in my arms, and the brutal medical experiments. I returned to the trucks and the ovens and the trains. I looked out the minivan window and saw Auschwitz.

I saw my father's sad face, drained of all hope, on the morning I was deported.

I saw my sister Lotte, age 10, put on a brave face on the night my father put her on a train to France—and none of us knew if she would get there.

I saw my dear friend Walter's ashen face as he died, totally emaciated, in my arms at Auschwitz.

I felt the weight of thousands of corpses I carried in my arms and loaded into trucks during my 22 months in the death camps.

I remembered running through the woods, shoulders hunched, as Honzo, Felix and I made a desperate dash for life.

At the entrance to the Presidential Compound, the German police, prim in their immaculate green uniforms stopped us, checked our names and waved us in. The minibus halted in front of the President's villa, a sturdy, impressive building.

"What am I doing here?" I asked myself. I stepped off the van and waited for the others. My sense of disorientation grew stronger; I felt trapped. Why did I allow myself to enter yet another compound under German authority?

The President's young, well-dressed personal assistant, Berthold von Pfeffen Arnbach, greeted us. "Welcome to the President's home."

I made the introductions. We entered the villa and the door closed behind us. I was prepared, but I also dreaded this moment. I was about to come face to face with the President of Germany, a direct successor of Adolf Hitler. I was shivering, just as I shivered in my nightclothes, fifty years ago to the day, when I woke suddenly, looked out the window and saw the wild, ominous flames.

I

Kristallnacht—Germany

I KNEW THE SYNAGOGUE was lighting up the darkness on that cold November morning in 1938. I knew it immediately. It was the logical target for what the Nazis called their counterattack. It was their revenge for the death, three days before, of a minor German consular official. He was shot at point blank range in the German Embassy in Paris by a young Jew, Herschel Grynzpan.

Last night, the radio blared out the ominous words: "The international Jewish conspiracy will find out once and for all what will happen when they attack an innocent German official. The full wrath of the German people will be felt soon."

Now, hours later, our synagogue in Mannheim was aflame. That couldn't be... It was too far away. Mutti and Papi must be awake also. They would know what...

I turned and started toward the door before I realized I wasn't in my own bedroom in Mannheim. I was in my rented room in Bruchsal, some 20 miles away, where I lived and worked as an apprentice in a cardboard factory.

Fully awake now, I fought off a 15 year-old's sharp pang of panic at being far from home at a moment of great danger, unprotected and unable to protect those I loved most dearly. I hurried back to the window. Sadly, the light came from the right direction—it had to be the synagogue blazing out there. I dressed quickly and ran out into the street.

I raced toward the flames, now shooting high up into the sky. Others were running alongside me, but I failed to recognize any of them. I got the impression of wide eyes all around me, filled with excitement or concern. Why were they running? To help? To gloat?

Suddenly, it was just in front of me. The entire building was engulfed. The brownshirts of the SA had taken out the prayer-books, the prayer shawls, the Torah scrolls, everything they could get their hands on. They'd dumped them in a pile on the street and, laughing boisterously, were trampling on them, enjoying themselves. I could see little specks of spittle coming out of the corners of their mouths.

"Burn the Jews!" they kept chanting. "Burn the Jews! Burn the Jews!"

Within a few minutes, fire engines arrived to protect the neighboring buildings. They made no effort to save the synagogue. Small children ran shouting happily through the crowd, fascinated by the fire, turning the disaster into a carnival. Men and women stood watching, talking in little groups. Some of the faces were deeply flushed, looking almost joyful. Despite the heat from the fire, the scene sent chills through me, and I turned away.

Nobody made a move to help. Or to protest.

There was a low rumbling. The walls of the synagogue had begun to crack apart. Parents snatched up their children and we all stepped back as far as we could before the entire structure came tumbling down. A large cloud of smoke and dust, with flaring flames at the center, shot up toward the sky. Slowly the flames died down and the cloud of smoke became a sprinkling of dust over smoldering ashes.

With the fire dying, the early morning cold penetrated my hastily thrown-on clothing. The onlookers withdrew, their faces now drained of excitement or shock. It was quiet. Even the children were completely silent.

I don't remember how long I stood there. There was nothing left of the synagogue. Where the entrance gate had been was a gaping hole. Strangely, only a stone altar showing the Star of David, remained. Everything else was smoking rubble. Pinpoints of flame spurted up, only to die down again. Dawn's gray light cast a chilling pallor over the scene.

The SA men were standing in a little knot, talking. I thought they looked over at me and the handful of others still clustered near the scene, so I walked away.

The sun was coming up. I went to my room to change, then decided to go to the cardboard factory.

Mr. Kaufman, the owner, was ashen-faced and unshaven. Standing close beside him were his son Franz and his daughter-in-law Lisa. The building heat had not yet come on, and they were wearing their coats. They looked as if they huddled together for warmth, but they were really huddled against something terrible that had been unleashed in the night. We were panic stricken, wondering what would happen next. We didn't have long to wait.

The radio commentator was calling it an act of justice and revenge. It was carried out in Germany and Austria, and there was already a name for it. *Kristallnacht*. Crystal Night. The night of the shattered glass.

The synagogue was not the only Jewish building to "feel the full wrath of the German people." The few stores in Bruchsal whose owners were Jewish had been demolished, looted, and torched. People had been beaten, jailed, and worse.

As we shivered in that cold office, I decided to get to Mannheim as fast as I could. I made a conscious effort not to think about what I would find when I got there.

Suddenly, the door burst open and three men, obviously Gestapo, stamped in. They wore long, black leather trench coats with swastika buttons on the lapel. One was tall, the other two were stocky, and all were unshaven. One stepped toward Mr. Kaufman, his gun drawn, his jaw set, and his eyes gleaming.

"Jew Kaufman, this place is taken over by order of the Gestapo. You are under arrest!" he barked. He sounded exhilarated.

"Can I call...?"

"Shut up!" and turning to Franz Kaufman, he spat, "You are under arrest too!"

The other Gestapo men moved swiftly. One grabbed Mr. Kaufman's arm, the other pulled Franz. Roughly, they shoved them into a corner. The man with the gun slipped it back in its holster and turned to me. I stood next to Lisa Kaufman, shaking with fear.

"You! How old are you?" he shouted.

"Fifteen."

Without a word, he turned away.

Franz tried to say something to Lisa, but the guards stepped between them and thrust Franz and his father through the open door. We heard their footsteps, two men firmly treading, two men stumbling and scurrying, echoing down the stairwell until they were out of ear shot.

The remaining Gestapo man turned to Lisa.

"You! Jew pig! Hand over the keys!"

Lisa started to say something, thought better of it, and reached silently into a desk drawer and brought out the keys. He snatched them away and pounded strongly on the desk with the keys clenched in his fist. "Now get out! This place does not belong to you any more! Out! You're lucky I don't kill you!"

We grabbed our coats and left. We had no choice. Lisa bit her lip, trying not to cry in front of me. I didn't know what to say. "You better get home to your family," she said softly. "I'll go to our apartment." I tried to comfort her with a hug, then bid her farewell. I ran all the way to the railroad station, arriving just in time to catch the train.

I dug my shoulder into a far corner seat, turning away from the welter of voices thickening the air like smoke. Whispering voices.

Loud voices. Gloating voices. Laughing voices. Full of talk about *Kristallnacht*.

"They finally got what was coming to them!"

What would I find in Mannheim? I couldn't erase five years of Hitler hatred and imagine it would be without change. I couldn't pretend it was a nightmare and I would wake up knowing that things would be all right.

It was too real. To be a Jew under the Nazis after 1933 was deadly and dangerous. And it didn't matter that my father's family had lived in Germany for more than 300 years. It didn't matter that my father served his country bravely in the first World War and was always as proud to be a German as he was to be a Jew. It didn't matter that my grandfather, now dead, had been a dashing, mustachioed cavalry officer in the 1870 Franco-Prussian War and a communal and Jewish leader in his native town of Norden. It didn't matter that two of my closest friends in Mannheim were Kurt Hess and Heinz Manz, both non-Jews. We were inseparable—we were in the same class, belonged to the same sports club, played soccer on the same team.

None of that mattered once Hitler came to power in 1933. I first felt the change on the playground. My once inseparable buddies joined the Hitler Youth Movement and turned their backs on me, and so did all the other non-Jewish children. When sides were selected for a game, I was the invisible man.

It hit home and hit hard. My father's cigar business was Aryanized, taken over by non-Jews. What they paid him didn't last long. Our food became plainer, less plentiful. Little treats for my younger sister Lotte and me became rare and finally disappeared. Mutti and Papi seldom smiled. Our grandmother—we called her Oma—was a beautiful white haired lady in her eighties, who was frightened and unable to understand what was happening around her.

On the radio, tirades against Jews by Hitler, Goebbels, Streicher—wave after endless wave of them—became more and more strident. Signs were posted at entrances to parks and playgrounds that said "Dogs and Jews Not Allowed." Jews were barred from local cinemas and theaters. One day I was told I could no longer play on the school soccer team. The team must be *Judenrein*, free of Jews. It was the biggest blow of my young life. I was 13 years old.

To feed the family, my mother sold some of her jewelry and my father parted with prize stamps from his large and valuable collection. The talk in the house, and anywhere Jews met in Mannheim, turned to ways of getting out of Germany. A visa became the most precious commodity in the world. I shared my grandmother's room because mine was taken over by a young couple from another town who were forced to give up all their belongings and were waiting for their visas.

The last thing I saw each night before I went to bed was a framed photo of my grandfather sitting proudly on his cavalry horse. I wondered what he, a proud German, would think about what was happening. I was glad that he didn't live to see it.

In 1937, a new edict was issued: Jewish children could no longer attend public school. I was in the seventh grade, and the attempt to organize a special school for Jewish children didn't last very long. With children from all grades thrown together, classrooms were chaotic and learning became impossible.

When the Jewish school dissolved, life seemed to come to a complete halt. It was unbearable for me to sit at home with nothing to do. When I did go out, I was, at best, ignored by our non-Jewish neighbors. More often they jeered at me. Buerkel, a man who lived in our building, was always strutting around in his SA uniform, snooping around with sharp, sinister eyes. I was always afraid to run into him.

The only pleasant moments I remember from those days were the times I spent with my close friend, Maxi, and the times Walter came to see us. Maxi lived just down the street. Born with one foot slightly shorter than the other, he walked with a decided limp. In the days before Hitler, he'd come to watch us play soccer and other games in the playground. Now he was never seen limping through the streets to the playground or anywhere else. Those streets, with bands of Hitler Youth in their uniforms and swastika armbands swaggering around, were no place for Maxi, Jew-boy and cripple. He was a perfect target for attack, so he stayed home all the time, and when I visited him, it was to exchange one cage for another.

We read books and magazines, talked about the good old days (imagine, at 14!), and played the only game young German Jews were allowed to play—fantasizing what it would be like to live in a free country—England, America, or Australia.

Another close friend was Walter, a boy of incredible strength. Orphaned at infancy, with no home of his own, he was always welcome when he came to visit, which was often.

"Walter, do your trick," Lotte and I would plead with him.

He didn't need much encouragement. He'd take a sizable table, rest it on his chin and balance it for several seconds. We stood there in total awe of his strength and dexterity. He was a sports fanatic who excelled in everything. When anything needed to be fixed—a bike, a radio—it was always, "Call Walter." And Walter would come and fix it.

After we were expelled from school, he took a job as a mechanic for a non-Jewish shop, but when Jews were no longer permitted to work and the orphanage where he lived closed, Walter left town. When he came to say good-bye, I felt as though I was losing a brother. I didn't know if I'd ever see him again.

Some of our friends were getting out of Mannheim, alone or with their families. As 1938 began, we heard news that my friend Robert Suess and his family were about to get their visas. Robert was a boy more seriously handicapped than Maxi. Paralyzed from birth, he used a small motorized vehicle to propel himself through the streets. Now, of course, it was safer for him to stay home. Unable to walk at all, Robert was the most severely imprisoned of us all. But I was jealous. If he could get out, why couldn't I?

My parents tried everything they knew to get Lotte and me out of the country. To obtain an affidavit, we needed someone in another country to guarantee our stay, but the only relatives we knew abroad were those who had managed to emigrate in the last year or two, and they weren't in a position to help us.

With more and more of my friends gone, the chances of my being able to leave Germany became slimmer and slimmer and I was becoming desperate. I kept after my father to try and find something for me to do, anything, although we all knew how difficult that was. His persistence brought results when he succeeded in locating one of the few businesses in our part of Germany still in Jewish hands. The Kaufman Kartonagenfabrik, a cardboard-box plant in Bruchsal, was not far from Mannheim.

I started work on January 2, 1938, and found room and board with a very nice elderly widow. It wasn't easy to get used to being away from home for the first time and in strange surroundings, but at least I now had something to do. The factory wasn't big, but Mr. Kaufman ran it well, with help from his son, Franz, and Lisa, Franz's wife. The workmen all respected him. I wasn't earning much, but it was enough to pay for my room and board with a little to spare.

Every other week, I went home to Mannheim. More and more Jewish families were leaving for America, Indonesia, Shanghai or South America. There was a chance that Lotte and I could get out separately. A children's refugee program in France just might open up for her.

One day I came home to hear the shocking news of Robert Suess' suicide. He had sat in his room, in his motorized chair, put his father's service revolver to his head and fired. Robert left a note. He was sure his condition was the reason his family was being denied their long-awaited visa. He was putting himself out of the way. Robert was just fourteen.

In October, 1938, a new regulation came into effect. All Polish-born Jews living in Germany would be deported to Poland. Overnight. No exceptions. Among them was a family named Grynzpan. Their only son Herschel, 18 years old, was living in Paris at that time. It was his act of rage and retaliation at the German consulate in Paris that gave the Nazis an instant martyr— and the excuse they wanted to launch *Kristallnacht*...

These were my thoughts on the short ride home. I was afraid of what I would find. As soon as the train slowed down enough, I swung off and ran toward home. On the way, I saw some of the few remaining Jewish shops in ruins, shattered glass all around, crates and boxes opened and rifled clean. Brownshirts were everywhere. Most of them were flushed and grinning.

I dreaded to see our apartment. The sidewalk in front of our building was littered with broken furniture and a layer of broken glass from smashed windows. The door to our apartment had been battered down. I looked around but I didn't see anyone.

"Mutti! Where are you?" My heart was pounding furiously.

I heard sobbing from the bedroom.

My mother was lying on the bed, her face swollen, holding my grandmother, who was sobbing uncontrollably.

"Mutti, are you all right? What happened?"

She got up and put her arms around me. She was bloody, her dress was torn. She was shaking.

"Ernst, Ernst..." She looked up at me with the saddest, most stunned look I had ever seen in her eyes. "They came in this morning... broke in... Buerkel smashed open the door..."

"Where is Papi?"

"They took him. I don't know where to." She wasn't shaking any more, but now her voice began to tremble. "Before that, they forced him to open the safe where he keeps his stamps. They took the whole collection, threw it out in the street and burned it. Papi couldn't stop them, two big SA men were holding him. I tried and one of the men hit me in the face. That's when they took Papi away. Oma became hysterical and I had to hold her. Buerkel, the SA man who lived in our building, brought some more of them in, with clubs and guns. They went through the apartment, destroyed it piece by piece..."

Her voice had fallen to a whisper. Now fatigue overwhelmed her and she sank down on the bed. Oma was moaning.

"Mutti—where's Lotte?"

"I sent her to one of her friends. I thought she would be safer there. Not so many Jewish families in that building." She looked at my anxious face and managed a feeble smile. "Don't worry. She called. She got there safely. She's all right..."

I stumbled through what had been our apartment. Broken dishes, pictures, silverware were scattered all over the floor. Chairs were broken. Mirrors were smashed. Nothing had been left untouched. The apartment was a shambles.

"Mutti—the synagogue...?"

She shook her head. "That was the first to go. I heard on the radio that most synagogues in Germany were destroyed last night. It's a pogrom, just like the ones in Russia and Poland. And we thought it couldn't happen here."

Mutti was calming down. Oma, exhausted, had fallen into fitful sleep. Mutti put her finger to her lips, got up and we tiptoed out of the bedroom. When I saw her looking around at the devastation and then bend down to pick up the pieces, I knew she would be all right...

I went to see my friend Maxi and found him and his mother pale and shaken, but their apartment was intact. We didn't know then, and will never know, why some Jewish homes and apartments were selected for destruction while others went untouched. Maxi's father, like mine, had been arrested. His mother was on the telephone with another woman whose husband had been taken. There was no way of knowing where they were, or what was in store for them. The report was that all Jewish men over 16 were being rounded up...

The walk to the synagogue took me through side streets where every Jewish store had been demolished. Primitive signs were painted on doors and over windows: JUDE VERRECKE (JEW DIE). The Nazi assault on Jewish businesses had been less random than the attack on Jewish homes. Not a single Jewish store was left intact.

Police and the SA had cordoned off the street around the synagogue. Hundreds of people were still milling around. There was nothing left of the synagogue except the bare four walls. Exactly like the synagogue in Bruchsal, everything collapsed into a charred pile of smoldering rubble. The benches, the books, the Torah Scrolls, the Holy Ark. All reduced to ashes. All gone. I stood there, transfixed.

I was in tears when I got back to the apartment. Mutti was still trying to clean up. Her mouth was set firmly. Her face was still swollen.

I don't know how we got through the night.

Two days later there was a knock at the door. It was Papi, but I hardly recognized him. He had aged years. There was an empty look in his eyes, as if the life had gone from them. Mutti rushed into his arms. His suit was dirty, he was unshaven, gaunt.

"What happened to you? Where were you?"

"Let me have a bath and something to eat. Then I need some sleep. I haven't slept since it happened."

Mutti took him to the bathroom, helped him undress, tossed his suit into a heap in the corner of the room, and let him get some sleep. After he ate, we walked around the apartment on tip toes as he slept.

The next day Papi told us he was taken to Gestapo headquarters, where there were hundreds of Jewish men of all ages. They were lined up in the courtyard and left standing for hours. Some of the younger men were taken away. Nobody knew where to.

Nobody was allowed to call home. There was no food. Permission was required to go to the bathroom. At night, they were transported by truck to a large hall, where they slept on the floor.

The next day there was another line up. The prisoners were interrogated. Name. Address. What bank accounts do you have? What property do you own? What insurance? The selections continued, seemingly at random. Nobody knew why some were picked and some were not.

The prisoners received some coffee and a piece of bread. Nothing else. By the second morning, less than one third of the original group remained. A Gestapo man came to the room and told them to go home and wait for instructions. Papi had no idea why he was not sent away. There was no explanation.

Slowly, we picked up the pieces of our lives and put the apartment back in order.

A few days later I returned to Bruchsal to get my belongings.

I visited Lisa at her apartment and hardly recognized her. She looked years older, drawn, with dark shadows under her eyes. She paced back and forth in the empty apartment. She was alone, with no word from her husband or her father-in-law. Together with most Jewish men from Bruchsal, they had been sent to a concentration camp called Dachau... We talked for a while and I tried to comfort her, but there was nothing I could do. I went back to Mannheim.

I had no job, nothing to do but stay home and watch my parents suffer, my grandmother deteriorate and sense the hopelessness growing in Lotte. Weeks went by with no word of how we could get her out of Germany. There was nowhere to go.

The results of that tragic night, undoubtedly one of the most horrendous in all of Jewish history:

More than 1,400 synagogues in Germany and Austria were totally destroyed.

30,000 Jewish men were arrested and sent to concentration camps.

Hundreds committed suicide.

Unknown numbers died in the camps. The bodies were shipped home with explicit orders not to open the coffins.

50 Jews were killed in the streets.

7,500 Jewish businesses were destroyed.

Thousands of Jewish homes were vandalized.

German Jewry was fined 1 billion marks.

All Jewish businesses were closed. Property was transferred to non-Jews.

Jews were forbidden to be employed.

Kristallnacht, November 9-10, 1938 was the foreshadowing of the Holocaust.

At the age of 15, my life was in suspended animation.

I had only one faint hope for a way out. It lodged with a kind stranger from America—a non-Jew I met for one brief moment in the summer of 1937...

The Lindsay Family
from Wilmington, Delaware
PART I

IT WAS SUMMER, 1937. I was riding my bicycle to the weekly afternoon Hebrew lessons at the synagogue. On my way, I stared in astonishment at a foreign automobile. It was larger than any European car I had ever seen. The men standing next to it were foreigners who consulted a large open road map, pointing and looking up in several directions, shaking their heads...

I got off my bicycle and moved closer. They were speaking English. Not really confident that my school English would be good enough, I took a deep breath and walked over.

"Can I help you?" I asked.

The men smiled with relief at hearing English. One of them, a tall, distinguished looking man of about 60, said: "We want to go to Heidelberg. We're lost. Do you know the way?"

"That's easy," I said. "Turn the car around and drive until you see a sign to the Autobahn. That will take you directly to Heidelberg."

The man thanked me and asked where I learned to speak English.

"I study in school and my father taught me a little," I replied.

He asked my name and how old I was. When I told him I was 14, his face lit up. After they climbed back into the car, he turned to me and said, "I have a son your age. How would you like to write to him? His name is Bob. We live in Wilmington, in a state called Delaware, in the United States, and I know he would like to get a letter from you. Would you like that?"

I nodded eagerly. A pen pal in the United States—wouldn't that be great! The man took a scrap of paper from his briefcase and wrote the name Robert Lindsay and his address in Wilmington on it.

"Go ahead, young fellow, and write to Bob. Thanks again for your help."

It took me some weeks to get up enough courage to sit down and write the first letter. When I mailed it, I knew it was filled with mistakes. I could speak some English, but writing was something else. My grammar and spelling left much to be desired.

Years later, when I finally met Bob in the United States, he showed me the letters (he kept every one of them), and we had a few good laughs. We particularly enjoyed this paragraph from my first letter:

"*A girl friend of me is also in U.S.A. in Franklin, Michigan. Do you know that? Do you like any sport? I play very likely football, I swim, play table-tennis, drive bicycle and so on. I have looked at the map where is lying Wilmington. Mannheim is lying on the Ryne. It is built 1600 and has 300,000 inhabitants. It is in South Germany near Frenche. We have no highscreaper, and our largest house has 13 stories. I very like to read, at most criminal-romanses. Our oculist has forbided me to read so much.*"

Throughout our correspondence in 1937 and later in 1938, I wrote at night in my rented room in Bruchsal with a German-English dictionary at my fingertips. I worked hard to improve my English, and Bob assured me I was making fewer and fewer mistakes. I was glad because I decided to write one particular letter. It would have to be perfect. It would be the letter, I dreamed, that would get me out of Germany.

Soon after my 15th birthday, July 1, 1938, I sat at my father's typewriter in the bedroom I shared with my grandmother, whenever I came home, and pecked out my "Freedom Letter." I typed it over and over again, until the English was perfect. There were five letters, all the same and I still remember the text, word for word.

"To the President of the United States, Washington, D.C.
Dear President Roosevelt:

To the King of England
Buckingham Palace
London, England
Your Majesty:

To the Prime Minister of Canada
Montreal, Canada
Your Excellency:

To the Prime Minister of Australia
Sydney, Australia
Your Excellency:

To the Prime Minister of South Africa
Johannesburg, South Africa
Your Excellency:

I am a young Jewish boy. I am 15 years old and I live in Mannheim, Germany.
I am desperate, trying to emigrate. I can no longer go to school. My parents have difficulties feeding the family. I am healthy. I will do any work.
We have no relatives outside of Germany to guarantee us. Sir, please help me to leave here before things get worse.
I hope you will help me. Thank you."

I was so naive.

There were no replies. Perhaps my letters were intercepted by the Gestapo and never reached their destinations. If they did, maybe they were ignored. I don't know. I only knew that all attempts to get out got me nowhere.

In desperation, after coming home from his arrest on *Kristallnacht*, my father wrote to the one person in America who could possibly help, Mr. Lindsay of Wilmington, Delaware. He wrote from the heart, one father to another. He wrote as a Jew who urgently sought to save his son from certain danger in Germany. Although they never met, although he knew nothing about Mr. Lindsay, in his best English, he appealed to a Christian, an ocean away.

It wasn't a long letter. It was clear, direct and did not waste words.

"I am the father of the young boy you met on the street in Mannheim last year," it began. "As you know, we are Jewish. You also are aware of what is happening to Jews in Germany."

My father, who led a life of total pride and quiet dignity, went on to do something he had never done before. He asked a favor of a stranger—could Mr. Lindsay put us in touch with a Jewish family in Wilmington who might be willing to provide an affidavit enabling his son to get permission to come to the United States?

The next morning, I mailed the letter at the local post office. I remember standing there, pasting on the necessary postage stamps. With the envelope went my hopes and my prayers.

Weeks went by. A month. No answer. It was too much to hope for a response. And yet, every day, I anxiously waited for the mailman. Finally, after two months, on a Saturday morning, a letter arrived. It was addressed to my father and came from Mr. Herbert V. Lindsay, Wilmington, Delaware, USA.

Papi was careful not to tear the stamp even as he ripped open the envelope. Lotte, Mutti, Oma and I gathered around, and Papi read it out loud. Although I could not understand every word, I got the gist.

Mr. Lindsay wrote:

"I received your letter and read it with great feeling. Indeed, I remember your son, and I can tell you how much Bob enjoys reading the letters from his pen pal Ernst. You should know that

the letters are read by everyone in our family. We think we know all of you."

Then he went on—it was good news: Mr. Lindsay had arranged through his attorney and the appropriate office of something called the U.S. Department of State, to arrange for an affidavit on my behalf. I was going to get out! I was going to America!

Papers were being sent to the U.S. Consulate in Stuttgart, Germany and we would be informed when and where to appear to fill out the necessary forms.

The letter concluded:

"It is our hope that Ernst will be able to come to the U.S. quickly. He will stay in our house and go to school with Bob. With his knowledge of English, it should not take him long to adjust to life in the United States.

"Looking beyond his expected arrival, we would also hope to assist you, your wife and Ernst's sister to join him eventually. I have been in touch with people in the Wilmington Jewish community who want to be of assistance. Our family prays for your well-being, and we hope that with God's help you can begin a new life in our country."

After the letter was read aloud, we were speechless. My father had tears in his eyes. My mother read the letter a second time and started sobbing. My grandmother kissed me and stood there looking at me and nodding her head.

I was dumbfounded. A total stranger, who knew me only from correspondence with his son, was providing a lifeline for me and my family. Living with Bob! Going to school! In America!

We had a family celebration that evening, the first in many years. Papi and Mutti exchanged smiles. I couldn't remember the last time I had seen such happiness on their faces.

We were euphoric for several days. Then, as always, there came the waiting that went on too long, the letdown, the disappointment. There was no word from Stuttgart.

Every German Jew was given an additional middle name by Nazi edict. Males were called Israel; females, Sara. My name was now Ernst Wolfgang Israel Michel. My sister was Lotte Bertha Sara Michel.

Special ration cards for Jews were distributed. We were denied butter, we were permitted a little milk and meat once a week. Potatoes and bread were severely rationed. The laws banning Jews from employment and from any contact with non-Jews would be strictly enforced.

To keep the family going, my father resorted to the one item of value he had left, the remnants of his stamp collection. Although Buerkel had stolen and destroyed most of the collection during *Kristallnacht*, some of the stamps had been out on consignment. As he got them back, Papi was able to sell a few at a time, bringing in barely enough to feed the family. I earned a few marks working at the Jewish cemetery. I had no idea how long we could last. Neither did my father.

He, however, was determined to last long enough to get me to Wilmington. He called the U.S. Consulate in Stuttgart, again and again. Each time he got the same answer. No. No affidavit had been received. They were swamped with applications and it takes time to process the papers. When the papers were received, we would be informed by mail and told when to appear.

How long would that take? The man at the Consulate couldn't say. It all depended. On what? The papers had to be properly filled out, the guarantees adequate. There was the quota to take into consideration. Quota? What was that? The number of German citizens permitted to emigrate to the U.S. annually under U.S. law was limited.

I tried not to lose all hope. In March, 1939 I wrote to Bob:

"I hope I can come in the shortest time to the U.S.A. But I don't know how long I have to wait till my number at the Consulate in Stuttgart is called. And who knows what will happen in this time? I have written to a cousin of mine, which is living in England, and she tries to find a situation for myself, that I can come to England, till I can come to the United States. But there

is the great question, who will pay my living there in England?
And I think, on this question, this fine scheme wrecks. But I wait
for a chance, and I do hope it will come."

In the spring of 1939, there was talk of war. "Soon, it will break out," everybody said, "very soon." Once it did, we knew there would be no hope of getting out at all.

The strain began to tell on my father. One night he said something very strange. He told me to take lessons in calligraphy.

"Lessons in what?!" I was astonished.

My father was serious. Calligraphy was the ancient art of producing hand written lettering for clarity and beauty. There was a Jewish art teacher who was giving calligraphy lessons to get by. He wasn't charging much and so we could afford it.

"But why calligraphy, Papi?"

"You never know when it might come in handy," he replied. "Besides, it will give you something to do."

At first I went to the weekly lessons just to please Papi. Then I got to like it, and I became good at it. Besides, it got me out of the apartment once a week. I could walk somewhere with something to do. It was my little escape, although I had to look around carefully whenever I left the apartment.

One day there was a phone call. Good news. A French-Jewish relief organization was ready to accept my younger sister Lotte. I wasn't eligible. At 15, I was too old for a children's transport. Too old!

Papi and Mutti were torn between their desire to see at least one of us leave Germany and their concern about letting Lotte, at 10, travel alone to a foreign country. But there was no choice. The handwriting was on the wall. We had to get her out while there was still a chance. No matter how difficult or dangerous it might be, the alternative was worse.

Lotte would take a night train. The only information my parents were given was that she would be met at the train station in the first French town across the border. They were given no names or addresses—nothing.

At dinner that evening—the last we would ever have together as a family—everyone was silent except Lotte herself. She was flushed, excited and restless.

My mother washed Lotte's hair, all the while giving her last minute instructions on what to do and what not to do. "Be a good Jewish girl, and remember to brush your teeth regularly."

"Yes, Mutti." Lotte sounded very confident and more than a little impatient with adult advice. "I am not a baby. I will be all right."

That night, I took a photo of my parents and Lotte. I don't know how, but somehow a print was preserved by a member of our family and came back to me after the war. Unmistakably, there is a look in my parents' eyes which speaks of the agony they felt that night.

"Lotte," my father kept saying over and over again, "you must let us know where you are as soon as you arrive."

"Yes, Papi, I know." Lotte sounded almost grown up. Papi took her hand. "It is important that we know where you are at all times," he cautioned her. "I still hope all of us can get to the United States. That's why we must always know where you are." He was trying very hard to sound confident. Maybe he even believed what he was saying.

Later that evening, we all went to the railroad station. Lotte carried a knapsack. I carried her suitcase, carefully packed so she could handle it herself. When she kissed Mutti goodbye, she clung to her for a long moment. She hugged me and I could feel the tremendous effort she was making not to cry.

The warning whistle blew and Lotte put on her bravest, most grown-up face, stepping quickly into the train. I handed Papi her suitcase and he followed her. I saw them through the window as they looked for a place to sit down. When the train started to gather speed, Lotte came to the window, tears running down her cheeks. She waved slowly with one hand and wiped her tears with the other. Mutti stood on the platform, motionless, staring at the train as it disappeared around the bend. Wordlessly, she hugged me and we made our way back to our apartment.

Papi did not come back till the next evening. He accompanied Lotte to the last station before the French border, and returned to Mannheim later the same night. He stayed at the station for twenty-four hours, pacing back and forth, looking for Lotte on every train coming back from the border, hoping that he would not see her, praying that she had made it safely across the border.

"It was the most difficult thing I ever had to do," Papi confided. "First Lotte did not want to let me go. 'I want to stay with you!' she kept crying. 'Don't leave me alone!' But we knew there was no choice. I just hope that we made the right decision."

Exhausted from his all night, all day vigil, Papi still could not rest. He sat down and wrote once again to Mr. Lindsay, thanking him once more for his magnificent gesture and describing the delay. Could Mr. Lindsay do anything to speed up the process?

More waiting followed. March. April. May. My father phoned Stuttgart every week.

Finally, at the end of May we received a reply. Yes, the affidavit was received. Yes, everything seemed in order. Yes, we could come to the Consulate to fill out the papers.

Early in June, 1939, Papi and I took the train to Stuttgart. We sat in a separate compartment. People stared at us, but nobody said a word. When we arrived, we walked to the Consulate because Papi was afraid to take a streetcar. At the Consulate, there were long lines of people waiting. They all had the same expression of fear and concern on their faces.

The line moved slowly. It took several hours before we were ushered into the office of a Consul of the government of the United States. He seemed harried and impatient.

"Yes," he said, "your affidavit seems to be in order... but I must tell you there is a long waiting list."

Now he looked at my father. "As you probably know, many German Jews want to leave for the United States, and all rules and regulations have to be observed."

He said something about making sure we were not Communists. I tried not to laugh. The few Communists in Mannheim were arrested immediately after Hitler came to power.

Besides, how could a Jewish 16 year old boy in Germany be a Communist?

We filled out all the papers, and then came the words I know I will never forget as long as I live. They were spoken softly, impersonally, but sounded like a death sentence.

"You will receive a number today," the Consul said. "If everything goes as expected, your number should be called some time in 1942."

Nineteen forty-two! In three years!

"Three years!" I jumped from the chair, tears streaming down my face. "But Mr. Lindsay wrote us..."

My father pulled me down on the chair. He, too, was choking. "Is there anything that can be done to speed it up?"

My father showed the American the letter from Mr. Lindsay saying I would be able to stay in his home and go to school. All the assurances were there.

"Why three years? How can we last for another three years? Don't you know what is happening to the Jews in Germany?"

Usually quiet and composed, my father had risen from his chair, his voice almost shrill. The Consul just sat there, unmoved. His reply was quiet and chilling. "You have to wait, just like everybody else. That's the way it is!"

My father got up from his chair and tried to grab the consul's arm. His action was meaningless. He stopped, realizing its futility. The interview was over.

Slowly we walked down the steps. My father held my hand. He was devastated. We took the train home, hardly exchanging a word.

Three months later, on September 1, 1939, Germany invaded Poland. England and France, honoring their commitment to Poland, declared war on Germany two days later. The Second World War had begun.

Despite the affidavit, despite Mr. Lindsay's offer, my hope for a new life, of freedom in America was over. I wouldn't be going to school with Bob in Wilmington.

It wasn't until many years later, when I studied the historical events leading to the Holocaust, that I became aware of the name

Breckenridge Long, undersecretary of State in the Roosevelt Administration. He was responsible for the issuance of visas under the quota system authorized by Congress.

Long, an anti-Communist and reputed anti-Semite, issued strict orders to limit immigration of German Jews to the United States. The result was that despite the desperate attempts by Jews to get out of Germany, the quota for visas was never filled. Between 1933 and 1938 over 129,000 slots were available. Only 27,000 were ever issued. Thousands of Jews with valid U.S. affidavits, including me, were thus prevented from reaching the shores of America. Most were eventually deported to the extermination camps and killed.

III

Gestapo Arrest

FOR THE FIRST two days of the war we were glued to the radio, tracking the onslaught of the German troops through Poland. I wondered what they did to the Jews in their path.

On September 3 came an unceremonious banging on the door. I knew it was the Gestapo before I opened the door.

"Ernst Israel Michel?" the man barked. He was short, heavy-set and wore ill-fitting civilian clothing. There was a large Swastika button on his lapel. His lisp blurred my name.

"Yes."

He shoved a piece of paper at me.

"Be at the train station at six in the morning! One suitcase, working clothes, 50 marks. That's all!"

"Where...?"

"Quiet, Jew boy," he hissed. "Don't ask questions."

Then he was gone.

I stood trembling. I couldn't focus on the piece of paper in my hand. Papi came to the door, gently took my arm, and led me back to Mutti in the living room. Her face was chalk-white. Thank God Oma was napping and hadn't experienced the Gestapo visit. She was so depressed, she slept almost all the time.

By order of the Mannheim Gestapo I was to follow all instructions in the letter. Any resistance or failure to obey any order would be severely punished.

29

I wrote one last letter to Bob Lindsay, to let him know what was happening. I entertained thoughts of escape, perhaps getting to the French border. I knew it was futile. My papers were stamped with the requisite "J" for Jew. There were checkpoints everywhere. Capture meant prison or worse.

My mother and I carefully chose what I would pack. All the things that told me I was me—my books, photos, clippings, my soccer ball, my board games, pages of calligraphy—stayed behind. I was saying good-bye to my childhood.

My mother made my favorite meal. I knew it would be my last full meal for a long time. The menu was my favorite: thick, rich mashed potatoes with lots of gravy, dumplings, pudding and a cake with whipped cream. I loved whipped cream and I often wonder what she bartered for that farewell treat.

We didn't talk much. What could we say? The air was permeated with exhausted silence. Mostly, we looked at each other. Mutti was close to tears. I tried to put on a good face, to be a man. None of us slept that night.

It was still dark when I rose from my bed. My suitcase was packed. Mutti had baked cookies and made sandwiches. As a last loving gesture, she added the bar of chocolate she had been saving for a special occasion. I held my Oma and murmured good-bye.

She reminded me to be a good boy. Her last words were, "Remember your Hebrew."

It was too early for the streetcar. Mutti and Papi slowly walked me to the station, savoring each step. Papi and I took turns carrying my suitcase. Our hearts were heavy and so was my bag. At the station, there were thirty of us in the same age group. I recognized some faces but we kept apart, in family clusters, saying little. Guards hurried us along to the station house. They checked off our names and ordered us through the door. They pushed our parents aside. I don't think full reality sank in until that moment of separation.

My father wore his gray, crumpled suit with a vest and his best tie. "Take care of yourself. Let us know where you are as soon as you can. Maybe we can still get you out." His hands shook. He looked at me, embraced me once and turned away to hide his tears.

My mother could not say anything. Neither could I. Finally, she blurted out: "Be a good Jewish boy, Ernst. Don't..." She couldn't finish. Everyone on the platform was going through the same torture. As I was pushed through the door, I turned my head and watched my parents disappear around a corner. I tried not to deal with my fear that I would never see them again. What would happen to them? They were alone, and so was I.

After our parents left, the Nazis kept us waiting. In late afternoon we were escorted, under heavy guard, to the train. We gave up exchanging guesses about where we were headed. After a night on the train, we arrived at Fuerstenwalde; a Nazi nobleman's estate. It wasn't far from Berlin. In exchange for harvesting his potatoes, we were served edible food and had lenient guards. When we finished the harvest, we cut trees in a forest, and after that we were sent to another estate to do spring planting. We were permitted to stay in touch with our parents by post and telephone.

My parents were barely surviving. They hadn't heard from Lotte after France declared war on Germany, and were deeply worried.

In late spring of 1940, a letter to my parents came back to me stamped "MOVED. NO FORWARDING ADDRESS."

That night I frantically called Mannheim, 40968 (after all these years I still remember our phone number). An operator answered, "The number you are calling has been disconnected." Click.

The next morning I learned that 30,000 Jews, including my parents, had been deported from southern Germany. They were given two hours notice and allowed fifty marks, one suitcase per person, and food for a few days. All other possessions were left behind and confiscated by the Gestapo.

I never heard from or saw my parents again. After the end of the war I learned they had been sent on a harrowing trip to Gurs, a concentration camp in the south of France, near the Pyrenées.

Oma, 85 years old, lived for a few months, then died of hunger and deprivation. Her grave still exists, not far from the camp. At least she was spared the fate of Mutti, Papi and thousands of others.

In August, 1942, Mutti and Papi were sent, via Drancy, to Auschwitz. In the meticulously kept Nazi files recently made public, I found the exact dates of the final deportation and their transport number. My father, Otto Israel Michel, born in Bad Kreuznach, Germany, age 64, arrived in Auschwitz on August 26, 1943. My mother, Frieda Sara Michel, née Wolf, born in Norden, Germany, age 55, arrived two days later.

I have never been able to find out why they didn't arrive on the same day. No one from these transports was found listed as an inmate of Auschwitz, so I assume that immediately upon arrival, they were sent to the gas chambers. The official Red Cross records read "Fuer Tod erklaert." Determined to be dead.

Seven months later, ignorant of my parents' fate and drained from dragging through half a dozen labor camps, I arrived at that place called Auschwitz.

IV

Arrival in Auschwitz

FEBRUARY, 1943.

Rtata... Rtata... Rtata...

The train slowly crawled through the night as one station after the other disappeared in the dark. We knew we were traveling east.

"Gleiwitz." A voice came from the slit on top of the cattle car.

The train stopped, as it had many times during the three days and nights since we left Paderborn. We were never permitted to get off the train.

"Perhaps we'll get something to drink. I can't take this thirst much longer," someone remarked at the far end of the car.

The train started to move again. Three nights in a cattle car. I worked in Paderborn for over a year, since the fall of 1941. Was it my sixth or seventh labor camp since the deportation from Mannheim in September, 1939? I lost count. It made no difference. One camp was like the other. Work. Never enough to eat. Sleep. With 10-15 men in one room, there was no privacy. No change of clothing. Day after day, week after week, it was the identical routine. We didn't work on Sundays only because the German guards wanted their day off.

Work in Paderborn was particularly difficult and distasteful. We were street cleaners, garbage collectors and canal sweepers. I spent my days standing in human excrement, cleaning the sewage

33

pipes with brushes. No matter how often I washed myself, I could not rid myself of the smell and I could never get used to it.

We were a *Kommando* of about 100 men and women, all Jews. We lived in four small wooden barracks, just outside the city. We wore our yellow stars at all times and in the evening, we were confined to the camp.

The only news we received was from the German radio, which proclaimed one victory after the other. We knew Jews were being deported to the East and there were rumors of mass killings in a place called Auschwitz.

We tried not to believe it, and continued our routine. We existed. Who knew for how long?

In late February, we were told the camp was closing and that we were to be deported. We were allowed to bring food for 3 days and one suitcase of clothing. Then, at midnight and under guard, we were marched through familiar and deserted streets to the train station. I suppose the authorities didn't want us to be seen by the local populace.

At the station the local police put fifty of us into two cattle cars, men and women together. The cars were totally barren— except for a small pail for waste. There was no straw. Nothing. The doors were locked. It was dark. After a long wait our two cars were hooked onto other cars. Suddenly, the train started and slowly, with its frightened human cargo, it began its journey.

After two days, whatever food we brought with us had been eaten. Only a few of us brought something to drink. We shared precious water and rationed it to a few drops for everyone in the cattle car. Soon there was none left.

More than 72 hours passed since we left Paderborn. A few of the older men were getting weak. The stench of urine and excrement in the car was unbearable. Privacy did not exist. We stood, we sat. There wasn't enough room to lie down. My bones ached. Sleep was impossible.

Those of us who had the strength, took turns climbing on top of each other in order to read the names of towns and cities we were passing through.

One of the women was in bad shape and needed medical attention. We made room for her, covered her, but there was nothing we could do. She soon slipped into a coma.

We were dirty, tired, cold. The wind whistled through the cracks. I found a place next to Ruth. We met in Paderborn shortly after my arrival. She was the first girl I was ever attracted to. She was my age, my height, very bright and very pretty. She came from Frankfurt, only a short distance from Mannheim. I had always liked her, and we spent a lot of time together. Now we sought each other out in the dank cattle car.

"They can't keep us like this much longer," she whispered to me. "Another day, and nobody will have any strength left. We'll die."

What could I say? She was right. I could hardly stand up. I was thirsty, hungry. I needed to sleep. "Let me just get out of here," was the non-stop refrain that pounded through my head in time with the wheels. I realized I was stuck. There was no way out.

Day 4.

Rtata... Rtata... Rtata...

One word gets whispered. "Auschwitz!"

Nobody remembers who said it first.

None of us knew very much about it. It's supposed to be the largest camp for Jews in Poland. That's all we knew.

"Beuthen!" someone called out. We were in eastern Germany.

By now it was clear that we were traveling into Poland. Slowly, I made my way through the car, trying not to step on any bodies. I found Gerd, who watched through the small slit as lights and silhouettes of chimneys and factories appeared and then quickly faded into the night.

Gerd was one of my friends from the Hachsharah group, which was assembled in an agriculture camp in 1940. The two of us had spent 1940-1941 together, preparing for Aliyah, immigration to Palestine.

"What do you make of this?" I asked him.

"Ernst. I have a strange feeling. This doesn't smell good. If the Germans are serious about us taking us to another labor camp, why did they lock us up? Why no food or water for four days?"

I could only nod.

"Do you remember the time we were stuck in the canal and the stream of shit almost drowned us?" he asked.

How well I remembered! It was probably one of the most horrifying moments in my entire life. We were some 25 feet below street level, in the bowels of the Paderborn canal system when suddenly without warning, we were hit by a stream of hot water, mud and excrement.

The canal was 5 feet in diameter. We were thrown by the force of the onslaught and almost drowned in it before we could fight back. We hung on to one another for dear life and slowly fought our way into one of the main canals. We were terrified of drowning in the excrement of the Paderborn canals. Totally exhausted and covered from top to bottom with stinking filth, we eventually made it to safety.

I tried to be cheerful. "Gerd, we got out of that mess. We'll get out of this one, too. After all, the war must end some time."

Rtata... Rtata... Rtata...

Two of the women died. One of the men was in a coma. Others weren't going to make it, either. No one knew how lucky they were.

One of the boys wrote a postcard to his mother.

"Dear Mom:
Don't worry about me. We are on our way to another labor camp. We'll see each other again soon.
Be strong.
Your loving son."

He threw it through one of the cracks as the train passed through a village, hoping that someone with a kind heart would find it and mail it.

At the next stop they threw open the door to our cattle car. Three SS men in black uniforms with the death head insignia on their collars stuck their heads in.

"We have three dead bodies in here. Is it possible..."

They didn't even listen. "Who threw a postcard out of the train?"

No answer. The commander yelled. "I'll count to three. If nobody comes forward. We'll shoot!"

We froze.

"One!"

Nobody moved.

"Two!"

The three SS men raised their revolvers.

"Don't!"

The boy who wrote the card raised his hand. One of the SS men took aim. One shot. Right through the head. The boy stumbled, then crashed to the floor, on top of some of those lying nearby. He was dead before the door closed.

"Don't worry, Mom. We will see each other soon!" We covered him, put him in the corner. We now had four dead.

Rtata... Rtata... Rtata...

Five nights.

We finished the last scraps of bread yesterday. More painful than hunger was thirst. There wasn't a drop of water to be had. It was difficult to swallow.

"When we arrive, let's stick together." Ludwig, one of the senior leaders in Paderborn, gave us instructions. He was tall, gangly, and very serious. He was always concerned about us and tried to ease our pain by keeping our hope alive.

We understood. We knew each other and could help one another. I was sure there would be a need for that.

"Bismarkhuette!" Gerd announced from his viewing post.

I couldn't keep my eyes open, and tried to find some place to lie down and get some sleep.

"Sosnowitz!" a voice woke me up.

"Isn't that Polish?"

After a while—I had no idea how long—I sensed that something was wrong. I heard voices yelling and the train had come to a halt. I heard dogs barking. Angry dogs. Dogs that meant trouble.

"The first thing I'll do is go to a hotel, take a long shower, real hot, then..."

The door was thrown open. There were SS men, dogs, and men in striped clothing.

"Out! Everyone out! Move! Move! Leave your baggage behind. Out!" I heard the word which would follow us every day. "Move!"

Everything was happening so quickly, I could hardly take it in. I saw barbed wire and rows of lights. "K.Z.! Concentration Camp! What did I tell you?" No one doubted it any longer.

"How about our luggage. What will we do without our luggage?"

We hesitated briefly. What would happen to the dead bodies in the car? The dogs were barking, baring their teeth.

"Out, I said. Out! Don't you hear well?"

The beatings began as we jumped from the train. Keeping a small bag under my arm, I jumped down, grabbed a fistful of snow, and shoved it into my mouth. It was the first liquid I tasted in over 36 hours. I wanted another fistful, but before I could reach for it, I received a blow on my back.

"Stick together!" Ludwig tried to keep some sense of control but his voice was drowned out by the screams and the barking dogs.

As far as I could see, there were cattle cars with hundreds, possibly thousands, of men, women and children looking around in total confusion and fear. I forgot my hunger and thirst as Gerd and I tried to stay together in the unfolding chaos.

Men in striped clothing were collecting the baggage from the cars. Others were throwing the dead bodies onto carts. As far as I could see, there were endless rows of cattle cars being emptied. The old, the infirm, men, women, children, babies, created a seething mass of humanity. It was mayhem. The SS beat those who did not move fast enough. There were bodies on the ground. We saw other prisoners, obviously camp inmates, herding people along.

The noise was like nothing I had ever experienced.

"Mom! Where are you?"

"Don't leave me, please."

"Hold on."

"Karl, Karl, here!"

It was a scene from Dante's Inferno. More and more people joined the procession, which slowly moved forward. I could not see where it was going. Men and women were searching for each other, crying and yelling. Then the SS loosed the dogs on the crowd. Some were bitten. More SS men beat us with their sticks.

"Let's go! Move! You can look for each other in hell!"

I lost Gerd in the commotion. Some others I knew were nearby. I stumbled over the body of an older man. Before I could help him up, the crowd pushed me forward. The only one I held on to was Ruth. She was as confused and as scared as I was. The hunger and fatigue were gone. This was strictly a matter of survival.

Adrenalin kept us moving.

More and more bodies littered the ground. What would happen to them? They were parents, children...The yelling and screaming died down. A sense of foreboding, of the inevitability of what this would lead to permeated the crowd. We were numb.

I passed a woman leaning against one of the now empty cattle cars. Her empty eyes stared ahead; "Please, let me go home. Please, let me go home." She repeated it incessantly. Then she disappeared in the swarm of humanity pushing forward.

Then I heard someone shouting: "Women... Men..."

I tried to raise my head but couldn't. Too many people were shoving around me. "What does this mean? Men... Women..."

Ruth looked at me. There was naked fear in her eyes. What could I answer? I did not know. Nobody did. Except those SS men in their long leather coats with whips in their hands.

We continued to move slowly forward and now we heard the order clearly.

"Women to the left. Men to the right! Women to the left! Men to the right!"

I swallowed hard. What did this mean?

If I thought the situation was helpless before, the next minutes were the worst I had ever experienced. We reached the point of separation, all of us shuddering with fear. Children were torn from their parents' arms. One little girl did not want to leave her father.

The SS men grabbed her and threw her to the ground, where she crumbled in a heap. Her father ran to her. Before he could reach her, a shot rang out and down he went, a few feet from his motionless daughter.

I had no time to absorb the scene when Ruth reached out to me one last time. We couldn't speak. I tried to grab her once more but then she was gone. There were now two columns, both moving slowly forward. Men on one side, women on the other.

Left and right. SS men held their snarling dogs on leashes. "Go! Go! Move!" Some spoke with Bavarian accents, and they were all young, well dressed and looked well fed.

Husbands held their wives. Brothers held sisters. Children clung to parents. I clenched my teeth to keep the tears in. Izzy shuffled next to me. He was the most charismatic, dependable leader in Paderborn. He was dynamic, optimistic, and always helpful. He was also strong as an ox. He had married Lilo in Paderborn a few weeks before we were deported. She was already on the other side. Tears were running down his face. I reached over to touch him. He only nodded.

No one spoke. The incessant screams and barking wore us down. It was bitter cold. I felt chilled. "Let's go. Stand straight. You can sleep later."

The SS men pointed to Ludwig. He was one of the oldest in our group.

"What is your job?"

"Teacher."

"You will answer 'Yes, sir,' stand at attention and take off your hat when you are addressed by an SS officer, understood?"

"Yes, sir." Ludwig did as ordered.

"Here, so you remember!" The SS man hit him in the face with the gun. Ludwig tried to keep from falling, blood pouring down his face. He managed to remain standing.

"Form single rows. Stand straight. Move!" We fell in line.

Gerd was next to me. He pointed to the left. "Look! Our girls!"

I saw them. They were already on trucks, pushed together, with hardly any breathing room. Then the trucks moved and disappeared in the dark. Our girls. Ruth... Lilo... Would we ever see them again?

At that moment I decided to take in every detail, every move of what was happening so that when this hell was all over, if I survived, I'd be able to remember it, maybe write about it. What I felt, what I saw. Everything. Whatever else it was, it was also history. Human history. Jewish history.

"Move!" The beatings continued.

What an idiot I am, I told myself. I think about writing of this when it's all over, but I didn't know if I'll be alive in half an hour.

As we slowly moved forward I heard first faintly, then louder, numbers being called out.

"Eighteen."

"Thirty-four."

"Nineteen."

We came face to face with a handsome, exquisitely dressed officer in a long gray coat, wearing leather gloves. His hat was cocked a bit to the left, and he was of medium height.

Now it was my turn. "How old?" He looked briefly at me.

"Twenty." In a split second his thumb pointed up. "Right." I followed the column to the right, not knowing that in that split second I was given a chance to live.

Gerd was behind me. "Twenty-one." Thumb up. "Right."

"Thirty four." Thumb down. "Left." What did this mean? Right? Left? Thumb up? Thumb down?

The line was now divided in two. I was in the column to the right. So was Gerd. Others were moving to the left. Ludwig was sent to the left. Most of our group was sent to the right. Most of us were in our twenties, Ludwig was older.

We had to do something. Things happened fast. After we passed the SS officer, one of our friends dropped his hat to the left, called out "Ludwig" and pointed to the cap. Ludwig got it, moved a step to the right to pick up the cap and immediately joined our column. The SS officer didn't see it. At least we were still together. I looked around and recognized most of our Paderborn group. A few were missing, but we expected they would catch up with us later.

Suddenly, I become aware of an unusual smell. It was sweet and yet unpleasant. I couldn't figure it out, and pushed it out of my mind. On the left, I saw a row of trucks. They were being loaded with older people and children. An old man didn't have the strength to climb on the truck. I saw him turn to one of the SS men and I could hear his plea. "...war injury... shot in the leg... I can't..."

"You can't!" the SS man mocked him. "I'll show you!"

He repeatedly hit the old man with his gun. When the old man fell down, the SS officer kicked him in the groin and then picked him up, and head first, threw him on the truck in the midst of all the other people. The truck took off. Another came forward.

There were bodies everywhere. Men, women, children. Some were dead. Some were moaning.

This wasn't a work camp. This was worse. It was something no one in his right mind could imagine. What would become of us?

I was freezing, so I rubbed my hands and stamped my feet to keep warm. "Stay still!" an officer screamed, touching his machine gun. Those nearest to him were clubbed.

I wondered what happened to my luggage and my warm sweater. The only clothes we had were on our backs. The empty trucks came, were loaded and carried away their human cargo. There was some commotion in front of us. We began to move again. I was totally numb from the cold, the hunger, and the fear. None of us had enough strength to talk.

"Come on, move! What do you think this is? A sanitarium?" Then he laughed, "You're lucky you're still alive!"

It was our turn to climb into a truck. SS men surrounded us, beating those of us who didn't move fast enough. One man just stood there. "I won't go. I don't care. Do what you want." One quick bullet in the head killed him instantly.

We were jammed in so tightly that I could hardly breathe. Gerd was nearby.

I tried to figure out how long we had been here since the train arrived. It was less than two hours. I looked around at the sea of humanity. Prisoners in striped uniforms were cleaning up the place. Some were picking up bodies, others were hauling suitcases.

The train with the now empty cars was leaving, making room for the next arrival. Our truck lurched forward. This was our welcome to Auschwitz-Birkenau.

First Day in Auschwitz

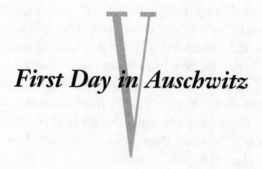

ONLY MY EYES moved freely. The rest of me was hemmed in against the others. They packed the truck so tightly, we couldn't even squirm. We rode through a little village, its outlines blurred in the pitch dark. Skeletons of half constructed, low buildings and darker shadows of heavy machinery were scattered along the route.

In a few minutes we saw lights, double rows of barbed wire and guard posts manned by soldiers with guns drawn. We drove through a wide gate and jolted to a halt. The gate slammed shut behind us. No doubt about it. We were in one of the feared concentration camps.

"Out. Move!" Did they really expect us to react? We were disoriented, hungry and weak. Did they think we would go up against their guns with our bare hands? Did they really believe their own lies about us? I jumped off the truck, almost fell and tried to get some circulation back into my limbs.

"Forward. March!"

We were in an open plaza, lit with kleig lights and enclosed by rows of wooden barracks. We were surrounded by SS and prisoners in striped blue and white uniforms. It seemed like days since our arrival, but it was only a few hours. We halted in front of one of the barracks. Most of the Paderborners were there and I had no idea where the others were. All of us were in our 20's or 30's.

Where were the thousands of other men, women, and children who entered the camp with us? As if to answer my question, one of the prisoners in the striped uniforms came over. "Welcome to Auschwitz-Buna! You are the lucky ones!"

"Why lucky?" one of our bolder comrades asked.

"Because the others already went up the chimney!" I didn't understand. What did he mean by "up the chimney"?

I looked at Gerd. He was as perplexed as I was. Before we could find out more, the SS guards pushed us into the barracks. Home. Plain wooden bunks lined the walls, three levels high with very little room between them. No mattresses. Just straw. Thin dirty blankets lay on top of the straw.

"Everyone undress. Everything. All clothing to be brought to the front!"

We looked at each other. This could not be real. Undress? Everything? Were we supposed to run around naked? In March? In frigid weather?

"I said undress and I mean undress!" the SS man shouted. "Do I have to show you?"

There was nothing to do but follow orders. Coat. Pants. Jacket. Sweater. Shirt. Underwear.

"Keep your shoes, belt and glasses. Everything else goes."

Some of the uniformed prisoners collected our things and carted them away. Izzy asked one of them about the girls and the others who came with us. The answer defied belief and word spread quickly.

"Dead. All of them. Gassed!"

Gassed? I remembered that peculiar, sweet smell as we got off the train. They were all dead? Those hundreds and thousands sent to the left at the selection were all dead? Not even the Nazis would do that, would they? I shuddered and remembered "You're the lucky ones! The others went up the chimney!"

Ruth, Lilo. The others. The enormity and monstrousness of our situation was overwhelming. Dazed as we were, we felt the horror. The Nazis were going to kill us all. It would take a little longer, but the end result would be the same—being snuffed out, just like that!

War was understandable. Deportation was understandable. Hard labor was understandable. But murder? Gassing? They were doing it, and my fellow Paderborners and I were living in the middle of a killing factory.

"Barbers up front!"

The command interrupted my thoughts. Barbers? What for? In less than an hour all our body hair was gone. We stared at each other, naked, bald, stripped of everything, holding our shoes and belts. It was a classic comedy situation. What was I supposed to do with my hands?

Two prisoners sprayed us from head to toe with an acid liquid. It burned my skin. We were sent, still naked, out into the cold to an icy shower. We rinsed off the burning liquid and were chased by whip-snapping guards through the snow and back to our barracks. It would have been better, perhaps, if we weren't so lucky. We would have been spared pain and torture.

We ran through the snow, naked and barefoot. Some men fell and barely moved. They froze stiff in minutes.

After what seemed like an eternity, they allowed us to enter our barracks. Another prisoner threw us bundles of clothing. "Get dressed."

We put the stuff on—thin, striped pants, striped jackets, torn underpants, shirts and thin coats—all the same blue-gray stripe, with matching caps. My pants were too short, the jacket too big, the cap hardly covered my head. All of it gave off a heavy, sick smell. We had no choice. I dressed.

It was six nights since we left Paderborn. We had no food or sleep for three days. The only water I had was what I managed to scoop up in a handful of snow. We stood in front of the bunks in the barracks, our teeth chattering in the frosty air. There was just enough room to walk between bunks. There was nothing else, not even a toilet.

We were so utterly exhausted that some of us collapsed onto lower bunks. I tried to guess how many of us there were. There were 4 rows of bunks and three levels. Three in a bed. There were almost 1,000 of us in the room. Suddenly, there was a commotion at the door.

"Who said you can lie down? Who gave permission?"

The voice came from a small, well-dressed prisoner who walked down the aisle while we got to our feet. I noticed that he spoke with a heavy Berlin accent. His head was shaven, just like ours. In his hand he held a rubber truncheon. The barracks fell silent.

"Are you out of your mind? Do you think this is a sanitarium? You are in a K.Z. In Auschwitz. This is Auschwitz-Monowitz. Or Buna. And you are lucky to be here."

He walked through the barracks. "Behave yourself and you may have a chance to live. Maybe. You understand?" We nodded. "Here are the ground rules. You listen. You don't ask questions. Keep your eyes open and your mouth shut. Anyone who can't do that, is dead. Understood?"

"Mister..."

"I am not a mister. I am the Blockaelteste (the barracks commander), responsible for this barrack (Block #10), and I want no trouble. What do you want?"

"My jacket is too small. Where can I change it for a larger one?"

The Blockaelteste laughed. "In Auschwitz everything fits. If it does not, I'll make it fit. One more piece of advice. Your bunks are to be made every morning. Tip top. Blankets lined up carefully. One exactly like the other. Anyone whose bunk is found messy, gets twenty-five."

"Twenty-five what?" someone asked.

"Twenty-five lashes. Listen carefully. You are to line up alphabetically, A through Z."

We lined up again and German bureaucracy took over. Name, name of parents, birth date, last residence, profession —everything had to be written down. The procedure took hours. We stood at attention the entire time.

Years later I was able to obtain my Auschwitz registration papers through the archives of what is now the Auschwitz Museum. Many of the records have been preserved.

Slowly, ever so slowly, the sun rose on our first morning in Auschwitz. A new day. When all procedures were completed we lined up for ersatz coffee and a piece of sawdust bread. It was bitter, but who cared. It was the first hot liquid we had in almost a week, the first food we ate in days. We drank from a tin bowl which we were to keep with us at all times.

There was nothing as tiring or demoralizing as roll call. We had to get used to it. Roll call twice daily. It was always the same.

"Move. Line up. Stand still. Close ranks. Attention. *Achtung!*"

We stood for hours through the count. It was bitter cold and my cap was too small. We had no gloves, and we weren't permitted to put our hands in our pockets. We tried, of course. Hell must be a 24 hour roll call.

Some men were weak, on the verge of keeling over. Many were feverish. It made no difference, roll call was mandatory. It was a ritual, and our lives depended on whether or not we lasted through it. After dismissal, we dragged the sick ones back to the barracks.

The Blockaelteste explained: "You are to sleep two or three in a bed. It will be warmer that way." Gerd and I shared an empty bunk and tried to sleep but before we could close our eyes, another command was issued.

"Out! Roll call! Line up the way you did before —alphabetically." I didn't think I could go on. It was too much. It was amazing what we could endure. We dragged ourselves out. The SS surrounded us again, their guns at the ready. It was evident we terrified them, or they wouldn't have needed all that firepower to control us.

"Roll up your left sleeve."

A number of prisoners were sitting at a row of tables laden with tattooing equipment. We were being tattooed! One by one, digits were quickly and permanently injected into my left forearm. I clamped my teeth so that I wouldn't scream with pain.

1 ... 0 ... 4 ... 9 ... 9 ... 5

Once upon a time, Ernst Michel was a human being, a kid in school who loved to play soccer and looked forward to growing up. Now I was Auschwitz prisoner #104995. That was me. My arm swelled as I looked at the ugly blue numbers which would forever be part of me. We held our aching arms and filed slowly back to the barracks. As we entered, two prisoners carried a body out the door. He still had his belt around his neck. Suicide. I remembered seeing him on the truck. I told myself he was better off and wondered what would happen to me. The SS man nearest the door laughed. "This one didn't last long."

When we got back, Ludwig gathered all the Paderborners together in a corner of the barrack. His face was still black and blue from the blow he received on arrival. He was one of the oldest in our group—quiet, serious, and full of inner strength. He was one of the few who was married, who had two small children with him in Paderborn. They were gone, just like Ruth and Lilo and the others who came with us. I couldn't imagine how he felt and yet, he tried to give us hope.

"Listen," he looked around to be sure that most of us could hear him in the tight space between the bunks. "We must try to help each other as much as possible. I know how you feel. Believe me, I feel the same way. But there is no point in letting go. Evidently we were sent here to work. Otherwise, the SS would not bother with all these details. The first few days are the worst. None of us expected this." He pointed to the surroundings.

"Men manage to live even here. You see them all around. It is important that we try to remain decent, just as we were in Paderborn, each helping the other. That is the only chance we have. Now, let's get some rest."

The Blockaelteste, a non-Jewish Communist who I later learned had been in the camps for ten years, made one more announcement. "I'll be brief. I tolerate only discipline. Those who steal a piece of bread will deal with me. Make your beds carefully. No shortcuts. The SS demands it. You will obey orders. Tomorrow is your first working day in Buna."

I didn't care anymore. Nothing mattered. As one of the youngest, I was assigned a top bunk. When Ludwig finished speaking to us, I climbed up, lay down, found someone next to me, was pushed by another and finally fell asleep.

Shots were fired outside, but before I could figure out what was happening, I was in an exhausted stupor. It was my first 24 hours in Auschwitz-Buna.

When daylight broke, we had to line up again. We were issued small yellow and red Jewish stars with our numbers stenciled on them. My arm was now swollen to twice its normal size.

We learned the significance of the different colored triangles which made up our stars. Jews: yellow. Red: political prisoners. Black: anti-socials. Lilac: religious prisoners, priests. Pink: homosexuals. Green: professional criminals and murderers. There were variations even in these categories. Sometimes the color was on the top; sometimes it was on the bottom. It was an ingenious way to immediately recognize why someone was in Auschwitz. Most of us wore yellow.

We also learned there were privileged ranks in Auschwitz. The greens had the cushiest jobs. Many of these criminals had been imprisoned for years and there seemed to be a clear rule that the green triangle gave you certain privileges, including immunity to the gas chambers.

We learned that Auschwitz was actually three separate camps, Auschwitz I, Auschwitz-Birkenau and Auschwitz-Monowitz or Buna. Auschwitz I was the main camp, where the Administration was located. The camp commandant was Rudolf Hoess of the SS. We were told he had a villa just outside the camp where he lived with his wife and five young children. Imagine bringing up kids here!

Auschwitz-Birkenau was where we arrived. It was by far the biggest of the three compounds. It had four gas chambers and four crematoria where the mass killings (up to 25,000 people per day) took place. Auschwitz-Monowitz was considered the best of the three (if you could call it that) and it was where the Buna factories were. Buna is artificial rubber. Since Germany had no access to natural rubber, I.G. Farben, the giant German industrial combine, needed slave labor to make synthetic rubber. Our job was to build the factory.

On the night of our arrival, the Nazis needed workers, but normally, once the daily "worker" quota was filled, those not chosen were immediately sent to be gassed. It was just the luck of the draw. On days when slaves weren't needed, all new arrivals "went up the chimney."

Auschwitz. We had to find the strength to survive. Our first meal was served. Soup. It came in great vats and each of us got half a bowl. That was it. Nothing else. I wolfed it down, and discovered a few potato peels in the bottom of my bowl.

Our chances for survival depended on where we stood in line and whether our portion of soup was taken from the top of the vat or the bottom. The top was water; the bottom contained potato dregs. If you were lucky, you'd find a piece of potato in your bowl. The prisoner in charge, usually one with a green triangle, had the power to distribute the soup evenly by mixing it, or to dish it out unstirred. Like everything else in Auschwitz, it was pot luck. Literally, pot luck.

Saved by Calligraphy

IT WAS PASSOVER, 1943. A few of us from Paderborn—Gerd, Onny (he had worked the sewers with Gerd and me) and Piese, who got to Buna a few months before we did, were discussing the implications of Passover. We had no matzoh, traditionally known as the bread of affliction. We had no wine, just watery potato soup. Elijah's cup was a battered tin bowl.

Passover, Pesach. The time of our liberation. We remembered traditional feasts and family gatherings. We also remembered the endemic Passover pogroms and false accusations called "blood libels." We were slaves in Egypt, led out of bondage to build a nation and way of life that would endure. We were slaves in Auschwitz and we, too, would endure. We dreamed and talked of freedom. We played a game of "What if?"

"What if the Americans came and liberated us?"

"What if we could have anything we wanted to eat?"

"We have no Seder, we should think about the service."

"Well, then, next year in Jerusalem."

"You're crazy," someone said.

"We'll never get out of here."

"If we do, we should get together. Why not?"

"Sometime, someplace."

"If we survive."

"If we live."

53

"If we don't go up the chimney."

Sometime that summer I caught a vicious blow to the head with the butt of a gun. The SS guard who hit me was biting into a meat sandwich. I was thinking about Buna soup and he must have caught me looking at him.

"You lazy Jew!" he yelled, just before the blow landed. "Get to work!"

He hit me so hard, I fell and lost consciousness. When I came to, I was bleeding profusely and had a splitting headache. A few days later the wound became infected and I developed a fever. It got so bad, I could hardly keep up at work and, although my friends tried to protect me, I knew that unless I did something, I wouldn't last. My physical condition was rapidly deteriorating. I didn't need a mirror or a scale to tell me I looked like a 'Muselman,' the label used for those ready to go up the chimney.

Under normal Auschwitz conditions, you could last four to six months. After that you were so weak, SS officers picked you for the short journey to the gas chamber. That was a fact of life. We were driven, to hang on another day, another week. We wouldn't give up. Something might happen. We'd finagle an extra piece of bread or soup from the bottom of the canister, and we'd last a bit longer.

Nobody wanted to go to the KB, the Krankenbau, the camp hospital, until they had no choice. Word got around. Regular or random selection at the KB increased your chances of being gassed. Many went. Few came back.

I could hardly walk. I couldn't eat. I was afraid the SS would pick me out at the gate. I told my friends I was going only to get the wound cleaned and bandaged. I wouldn't stay overnight and run the risk of a selection the next morning. I took the short, scary walk to the gate separating the regular camp from the KB.

A guard told me to go to the barracks where injuries were being treated by prisoner-doctors. I later learned some were world-famous specialists, transported to Auschwitz like everyone else. Dozens of prisoners had very serious injuries, mostly from beatings and work-related accidents. Compared to them, I was in good shape, but I wanted to get the wound cleaned up and return to my barracks.

I waited for more than an hour.

Abruptly, an apparently important prisoner wearing the KB armband strode into the room, carrying lists.

"Does anyone here have decent handwriting?" Nobody moved. It was probably a trick. You never knew what they were up to.

On impulse, just as he was turning around to leave the room, I raised my hand. What did I have to lose? Maybe I could earn an extra piece of bread.

"I do."

He stared at me for a moment. "I studied calligraphy at home."

"Follow me," he directed.

I got up and followed him into the next room. He handed me a pen and some paper.

"Here, write. Name, Auschwitz number. Then add: Koerperschwaeche, 'weak of body'. Go ahead."

I sat down, remembering how my father—it seemed a lifetime ago—persuaded me to learn calligraphy and how I protested. For a few moments, I forgot my pain and discomfort. I took the pen and started to write. I couldn't remember the last time I held a pen. Slowly it came back to me and I wrote "Koerperschwaeche" next to the prisoner's name and number.

I still didn't know who the KB official was or the meaning of the exercise. He stood behind me, watching. After a minute, he stopped me.

"Fine. You'll do."

I looked up, dizzy from the unaccustomed effort. "Can I get this taken care of?" I said, pointing to my infected head wound.

"Sure. Wait here."

A moment later, another prisoner in his forties, probably a doctor, entered the room. I showed him my injury.

"I'll take care of it." His accent was Eastern European. In a few minutes, my wound was cleaned and bandaged. I began to feel better, although I was still very weak.

I spent the next two hours writing the same words over and over again. It didn't take me long to figure out what I was doing. The list contained the names of those who were shipped to Birkenau and the gas chamber. The Nazis, with their usual efficiency and attention to detail, kept records of all inmates sent to be gassed. Only nobody died by being gassed to death. They all died by being "weak of body"—'Koerperschwaeche'—or from 'Herzanschlag'—heart attack.

Every once in a while, the prisoner who gave me the job came by to see how I was doing. Satisfied, he left me alone. I later learned his name was Stefan Heyman, Chief Registrar, or Schreiber, of the KB—a Communist and a long-time camp inmate.

After the war Heyman became the first Minister of the Interior for the East German government. He was one of the most decent inmates in Buna and saved many Jewish lives.

When I finished, he offered me two bowls of bottom-thick Buna soup as compensation. Never, in all my time at Buna, did I strike it lucky and get soup from the bottom of the canister. My joy lasted a moment—the first spoonful was so salty, it was inedible. Somehow the salt settled to the bottom, along with the potatoes. I gagged, unable to get it down. It was a low blow. The last straw. I was so fed up, I wouldn't have cared if I they took me to Birkenau right then and there.

When Heyman came back with more lists and learned why I didn't eat the soup, he made up for it by getting me two slices of bread with margarine. I had not eaten that well since... I couldn't remember when.

"Your handwriting is good," Heyman complimented me as I wolfed down the bread. "Stay here overnight and work on other lists tomorrow. You'll get some rest and something extra to eat." Looking me up and down, he added: "You can use it."

I hesitated. After all, I didn't know Heyman and I was afraid of a "selection," the picking out of prisoners for the gas chambers.

He sensed my concern and addressed it right away. "You don't have to worry. I'll protect you if there's a selection. You will be listed as a convalescent who will go back to work in a few days. In the meantime, you'll work on the lists."

Somehow, I trusted him and agreed to stay. It turned out to be the best decision I could have made. The job as the assistant registrar led to a permanent position as an orderly on the KB staff. Eventually, I learned to handle the injured and sick.

For the first few weeks, they listed me as a patient soon to be discharged. I learned the KB routine and continued writing lists. Tallies were kept of those headed for the gas chamber and regular prisoners who came to the KB. Some came for a short stay, many were sent to Birkenau. Most who came were in serious condition. Otherwise they wouldn't have risked visiting our compound.

For a few days, I worked for Dr. George Kovacz, a Jew from Slovakia. He offered me the job as a permanent orderly and I quickly accepted. There is no doubt in my mind that Stefan Heyman and Dr. Kovacz saved my life. I never could have made it without them.

The KB consisted of five barracks, each with its own staff of prisoners, from the Blockaelteste to the head doctor, his assistant and the orderlies. There were three or four of us in each barracks. The head of the SS was in charge of the entire operation. The Lageraelteste, the prisoner in charge, was a Pole named Dr. Bujaczek. The SS liaison officer was SS Sergeant Neubert and there were the ever present SS guards.

If you did your job (and there was plenty to do), they usually left you alone. We took the responsibility of caring for the sick seriously. We needed to get those on their way to recovery out of the KB as quickly as possible, for obvious reasons. We dreaded the regular selection process.

Every morning SS Oberscharfuehrer Neubert, accompanied by Dr. Bujaczek and a guard, entered the barracks. We, the orderlies, stood at the entrance.

"Muetzen auf!" "Hats off!" Heinz Lippman, the barracks leader (a Communist from Berlin) would yell. We took off our caps and stood at attention.

"At ease."

"Infection Barracks: 165 men, 22 corpses. All accounted for!" Lippman reported.

I was assigned to the barracks for infectious diseases. Under our minimal hygienic conditions, almost everyone had lice and lice led to outbreaks of typhus. Those suffering from that dreaded illness were immediately sent to the gas chambers.

Slowly Dr. Bujaczek, Lippman, Neubert and Dr. Kovacz made the "rounds." There was always an ominous silence. They hardly spoke as they went by the patients. Neubert, although not a doctor, knew who was sick just by looking at the men in their bunks. Every so often he would ask Dr. Kovacz for an explanation. Decisions were made very quickly. A brief nod, the number was noted on the pad, and we knew that one more man would be on the next truck to Birkenau. Many prisoners were so far gone they didn't react, but every once in a while someone would plead for mercy. Seldom was it granted. Dr. Kovacz was in a tough spot. He knew that if he protested Neubert's decisions too often, his own role would be jeopardized.

I met two young men who became my closest friends and comrades. They were Honzo Munk from Prague, Czechoslovakia, who was in Auschwitz since 1942, and Felix Schwartz from Poland. We became inseparable and depended on each other throughout the trials and tribulations of camp life. We shared everything. Together we worked to save what lives we could.

Honzo was 21, bright and energetic, and had inventive solutions to every problem; he taught me a lot. He also saved my life when I caught typhus in 1944. I had a high fever and was often delirious, but Honzo washed me several times a day, kept my temperature down and hid me from the daily selections. Felix was a year younger; tall, brash and camp-smart. If there was a short cut, Felix knew it and put it to good use.

The worst part of our work was the disposal of the bodies. In our barracks alone, dozens died daily. Hunger, disease, diarrhea and the results of heavy beatings took their toll. We took the corpses to a special storage room attached to the barracks. We carried thousands of bodies during my stay in the KB, first to storage, then, on the same afternoon, to the trucks which took them to the crematoria. Most of the adults were skin and bones on bodies weighing less than 80 pounds. There were also children ten and twelve years old.

One young boy was from France. Every night I would watch him search through the Buna soup for a piece of potato. He'd eat the liquid, saving the potato for last. He'd look at the potato for a while, examining it from all sides, and then would eat it, bite by tiny bite. For his birthday, we decided to give him a present. When our soup was distributed, we all looked for a piece of potato and held it aside. We put 40-50 pieces of potato into one tin cup and gave it to him. He didn't know what to say or do. He sat there looking at the bowl of potatoes and at us. Then he got up and with tears in his eyes, told us it was the most beautiful birthday present he ever received.

VII

Walter

A FEW WEEKS after my appointment as a regular KB orderly, I received permission to visit my old block. The wound had healed and I'd gained a few pounds. I carried with me a few slices of bread for my friends.

When I suddenly appeared, as if out of nowhere, my Paderborn comrades thought I was a ghost. I wanted to find Walter. I hadn't seen him since I left for the KB. He came to Buna a few days after I did, and I missed him. He was the only link to my life in Mannheim.

"Who's the stranger?" they wondered. "Who's this guy in a clean uniform? How come his ribs aren't showing?" their faces seemed to be saying. Slowly, they realized who it was.

"Ernst! Ernst Michel! What happened to you? We were sure you went up the chimney!" I calmed them down. "I'm all right... I'm an orderly in the KB Diarrhea Block."

Other inmates came over—familiar faces and new ones. The familiar ones looked at me in disbelief. "They told us you weren't in the barracks for the injured. We were sure you were gone for good. What happened?"

I reassured them all, watching the mixed feelings on their faces—relief, concern, maybe a little envy. I looked around.

There was one face missing. "Where's Walter?"

"He's in his bunk," they told me. "He was kicked hard by one of the SS. In the ribs, in the stomach. Over and over again. It happened a few days after you left. Since then he's not the same. Go, let him see you alive, it'll be good for him."

I walked the few steps to our old bunk and climbed up to the third tier. There he was, my old friend from Mannheim. The change in him was frightening. He'd lost weight. He was skin and bones. His eyes were closed. I shook him gently. "Walter, it's me." Slowly he opened his eyes, grabbed me.

"Ernst! You? Is it really you? I am not dreaming? You are not... They didn't send you to the...?"

"No, Walter. I'm real."

With effort, he raised himself on his elbow. His face had the look of a man about to give up the struggle. I told him how my fortunes changed at the hospital. I tried to make it exciting, to convince him there was hope. He didn't respond.

"Are you getting lazy?"

No answer. The look in his eyes was easy to read. It was clear that he wasn't fit to get up and go to work. He'd collapse. Unless he could get some medical help, he wouldn't survive the next 36 hours. He coughed and turned away. I could see he was hiding something from me.

Walter, who was always so open... withdrew into himself. Walter, who was always so strong, was so weak, he had reached the point of helplessness. Walter, who was always ready to laugh and bring smiles to others, was tight-lipped and grim as death.

I needed to help him. He had helped me, just a few short weeks ago, when I was in a bad way. Now our roles were reversed. I didn't have to do the heavy work, I didn't have to line up for roll call. But how could I help Walter?

"Walter, tomorrow morning, come to the KB. Be there early. I'll be at the gate to take you in. Don't worry about a thing, do you hear? Everything will be all right."

He tried his best to look relieved, to sound hopeful. "Are you sure you can do that?"

"Yes, I'm sure. Just leave it to me."

His face was still full of questions. I didn't give him a chance to say a word. I climbed off the bunk and told him I was going back to work. "If I'm late—who knows—maybe they'll fire me and throw me out of the camp!"

"Ernst, thanks."

"Oh, shut up. Don't thank me."

"I'll be there early tomorrow."

"Keep your spirits up, Walter. You're going to be just fine."

I put confidence in those words, but deep down I wasn't so sure I could help him. He seemed too far gone. I had to talk with Dr. Kovacs and Heinz, our Blockaelteste—the prisoner in charge of my barracks, the diarrhea block.

Dr. Kovacs was transferred to another block. His place was taken by a recent arrival from a Greek transport, Dr. Samuel Samuelides. He was a small, wiry, energetic and very efficient individual who encouraged us to keep up our spirits and held us together as a working team. He was an excellent doctor, a warm human being and an inspiration to many of us.

It took some doing, but we managed to get Walter assigned to fixing the lights in all the hospital barracks. He received a special pass and had time to rest during the day. I also got him extra soup and bread. The trouble was, he had no appetite.

The next day he told me the truth. "Ernst, I can't keep it to myself any longer. I'm spitting blood. I thought it would stop, but it's getting worse." I knew it. Tuberculosis.

Walter's job was temporary. If we kept him around much longer, Neubert would become suspicious and all of us would be in trouble. I met with Izzy and the remaining Paderborners. How could we help Walter?

Izzy, dependable Izzy, managed to get Walter transferred to the garbage Commando. He had more to eat, but found it harder and harder to keep food down. Things got worse. He developed severe diarrhea, and constantly had to go to the toilet. In the camp, that was not easy. More than once, he didn't make it in time. I managed to get some medicine to stop it. Izzy— I don't know how—got him some soft food.

Despite our efforts, Walter continued to weaken. Worse, his face had the telltale look of a Muselman; he gave up, lost the will to fight. How many times had I seen that look? Every time I saw it, death was near. Why couldn't I get used to it? This was Walter, and I would never get used to it.

There was only one option left, one we hesitated to use. We admitted Walter to the KB as a patient. If the SS Untersturmbannfuehrer, Dr. Koenig, saw Walter on his regular selection tour, he'd be the first passenger on the short truck ride to Birkenau. I arranged to have him admitted to my barracks, so I could keep an eye on him.

Walter didn't resist. He was more lethargic than ever. Not a trace of energy was left in that once robust, joyous body. He was a skeleton. The hell with regulations. I managed to get some of our friends to visit him. It was *streng verboten*, but they came for Walter.

I was able to obtain bread, even some margarine, but he made no effort to eat. I sat with him, fed him. There was some improvement. I changed his KB report to indicate that he was getting better. Dr. Koenig passed by, saw the report, left him alone.

After two weeks, we had to discharge him. We had taken too many chances. "Walter, how is the blood?"

"Much better. Really. I haven't seen any blood for several days. I feel better. Really."

Was he telling the truth? His face looked just as hopeless, his eyes just as resigned.

"Can you manage clean-up *Kommando*?"

"Sure I can." He knew, and I knew, that he was dying.

I saw him a few days later. He was carrying garbage, barely able to stay on his feet.

The next day, he collapsed at the feet of an SS officer.

"Get up!"

"I can't."

"You won't. You are another lousy, lazy Jew!" And he kicked him. Once. Twice. Walter tried to get up. It was obvious, even to the SS man, that he was in great pain. He turned away. Walter crawled all the way to the toilet. Izzy found him there, holding his stomach, and brought him to the KB.

When I saw him I knew it was over. His face had no color. Deep shadows were under his eyes.

"Ernst, it's no use. I can't go on. I'm finished." He lurched past me to the toilet. I found him there, tears streaming down his face.

"What have I done, that they beat me and torture me? I want to get away. Far, far away. I want to rest, to sleep. Help me." I couldn't do anything. What could I say?

I carried him to one of the cots and arranged to have him officially readmitted. I got him a bowl so he wouldn't have to keep running to the toilet.

One night, one of our barracks friends showed up with two small flowers for Walter. Flowers in Auschwitz! I wondered where they came from.

The next morning, as I cleaned him up, I saw blood. A lab report confirmed the diagnosis, "Advanced status of TB." If this appeared on his chart, it would be over. I threw out the card and started a new one every few days. If they caught me, they'd throw me out of the KB and take me for a truck ride. I didn't care. I wouldn't let Walter be sent to Birkenau.

He needed butter, milk, nourishment. He needed the sun, a sanitarium. Instead, he was in the stinking diarrhea barracks of Auschwitz with death all around him. He ate watery soup and sawdust bread. Once in a while, he'd have a piece of margarine. It was the best we could do.

It wasn't easy, but time and again we managed to get Walter past the Birkenau selections with help from Heinz, our Blockaelteste, who usually accompanied Dr. Koenig on his selection rounds. Without him, it wouldn't have worked.

The routine was always the same. Dr. Koenig entered the barracks. We stood at attention. Heinz reported.

"Attention! Block Twenty, Diarrhea, with two hundred twelve prisoner patients. Nineteen bodies. All accounted for."

Dr. Koenig nodded, always elegant in his long leather coat, hands folded behind him. Accompanied by the Polish prison doctor, Bujaczek, he walked slowly and deliberately through the barracks. Honzo, Felix and I stood at attention, not moving a muscle, our caps in our hands.

He stopped at some beds to look at the patients and the written reports, pointed quickly and went on. An hour later, the truck came by and we loaded it with those he pointed to. Most of them were silent and resigned, too weak to care. An SS man with a drawn machine gun stood next to the truck. When he was gone, I carefully noted the new count. It was down to 146. Walter was still with us.

Dr. Samuelides told me Walter wouldn't last much longer. I knew he was right. I'd seen enough men in his condition. Nobody had ever stayed in the KB as long as Walter. He just lay there. We moved him to a corner, out of sight of the endless stream of dead bodies going out the door, as many as twenty a day. Many were newcomers—Frenchmen, Dutchmen, Greeks, Hungarians—Jews from all over Europe.

One evening, as I was feeding him, he stopped me. "Ernst, do me a favor." He looked me straight in the eye.

"Ask all our friends who are still around if they would come to see me tomorrow."

He knew. I could see it in his eyes. "I will," was all I could answer.

He touched my hand with his gaunt and bony one. Izzy, Peter, Horst, Onny, Gerd, the remaining Paderborners, came to the barracks the following night. He tried to shake their hands and nodded to each of them. Their greetings sounded hollow. "You don't look so bad. How about coming to work again? We could use you. Lazy guy, look at him..."

He smiled wanly, then waved his hand. He looked from one to the other, lingering a moment on each face. "I know how much you have helped me. I want to thank you. Don't..."

He fell back, then struggled and tried again. "I know it's only a matter of time. If some of you survive—or only one of you—don't forget me." One after another, wordlessly, each man touched his hand and left.

Two days later, Friday morning, Walter lost consciousness and went into a coma. That night, after my tour of duty, I sat on his cot. Dr. Samuelides told me to stay as long as I had to. Just before midnight, I saw it was over. I sat there for hours, looking at my dead friend.

I closed his eyes, then slowly picked him up—he hardly weighed anything—and placed him in the adjacent hall with the other corpses. I swore that one day I would tell his story.

I've kept my promise, Walter.

VIII

Medical Experiments

NEXT TO THE ENTRANCE of the KB, in the first barracks, was a special room with a locked door. Days earlier, we saw a truck deliver equipment but nobody knew what it was for. There was an unusual amount of tension among the SS.

One morning, the door was open and I caught a glimpse of the inside of the room. There were electrical wires, a special high table, and some strange objects with all kinds of buttons and levers. The door was closed quickly and I went on my way. It wasn't healthy to see too much but the guessing game was on. What were they up to? The SS head doctor was often seen coming and going. One day a Red Cross truck drove up to the KB and stopped out front. It was different from the trucks used to pick up the bodies of those destined for Birkenau.

One of the aides accompanying the truck motioned to us. "Come over here. We need blankets, at least a dozen or so. On the double! Bring them here! Right away!"

As I listened to him, I saw first one, then another, then a third, and then more women climb out of the truck. I couldn't believe my eyes. They were assisted by a woman orderly wearing a KB armband. She was a prisoner like us. It couldn't be. In Buna? I hadn't seen a woman since our arrival. As far as I knew, no woman had ever come into Buna. Now they sent in a truckload. I couldn't figure out why they looked so strange.

69

"Get going! Stop staring! Get the blankets!"

I ran to my barracks, looking for Honzo. "Honzo!" I grabbed him coming out of the morgue. "There are women in the KB. A whole group of them. Maybe six. Maybe more. What's going on? They want us to bring blankets. Right away!"

He hesitated for a moment, but he knew from my voice that I wasn't joking. We took a dozen blankets—they were so thin anyway—and went back to the first barracks. The truck was still there.

"Here are the blankets," I told the officer guarding the entrance. "We're supposed to take them inside." When he saw our KB armbands, he let us in. The room was empty except for a row of cots. There were eight of them. We were spreading the blankets out when the door opened. An SS doctor unfamiliar to us stood there. He ordered, "Help her down from the table."

Honzo and I went inside. There were a number of SS doctors standing around, among them the notorious Dr. Joseph Mengele. I remembered him from the first day of our arrival, during the selection at the tracks. I went cold with fear. Mengele! The Chief Doctor of Auschwitz handled the selections and directed the medical experiments. Mengele, the Death Doctor himself, was right in front of me.

Experiments! That was it! They were conducting medical experiments on women! I put two and two together. It explained the look on those women's faces. They were mentally disturbed. Now I understood their strange looks and strange behavior. Just as quickly I realized what the machine was for—the wires, the box with buttons and the switches. Electricity!

A young girl lay on the high table. She couldn't have been more than sixteen. Her eyes were closed. Her chest was heaving. She was strapped down by her ankles and her arms. Her teeth were clenched around a roll of paper and sweat poured down her face. Mengele and the other doctors were standing in the corner and we could hear snatches of conversation.

"Expected more dead... considering the voltage... more the next..."

Honzo and I lifted the young girl from the table and placed her carefully on a stretcher. Her arms were rigid. Her breath was coming in short spurts; her eyes were still closed. We took the stretcher to the next room and put her on one of the cots.

Even in her agitated state I could see that she was beautiful. She had short black hair and clear skin. There were scratches on her arms. What had happened to her? Who was she? I thought of Ruth and the night we arrived in Auschwitz. I remembered holding her one last time as they ordered the women to the side, to the gas chambers.

I shook my head.

"Don't think of it. It's no use. Stay strong. Live for each day, then the next. Some of us will come out alive and tell the world what happened here."

Inside the next room I could hear the voices. "More... More..."

When I looked at the girl again, she relaxed a bit and looked around, obviously disoriented. Her big dark eyes looked at me and Honzo, helpless and totally confused. The roll of paper was still in her mouth and I sensed it bothered her. I gently removed it. "Hello, beautiful." I didn't know what else to say. What language did she speak? Where did she come from?

The door to the room where the experiments took place opened again. Two other orderlies brought out another woman. She didn't look well. Her face was frozen in a grimace and she wasn't moving. She was stone, cold, dead.

"Couldn't take it," one of the orderlies said, nodding at her. "They gave her too much." One of the doctors appeared, looked at her again to make sure. "One less. No problem. There are enough of them!"

Is that what happened to 'my' young girl? I dreaded to think about it. I went back to her. "How do you feel?" She looked at me uncomprehendingly.

Honzo tried to speak to her in Czech. There was no reply. On a hunch I pointed to her. "Budapest?"

The young girl suddenly clapped her hands together and began to laugh. "Budapest. Budapest."

Woman number three was older, in her thirties. Her skirt was torn, and it was pitiful to see what was left of a once attractive woman. It was difficult enough to watch men and boys waste away day after day. But women? Why were the Nazis treating us this way? What had we done to deserve such inhumane punishment?

I bit my teeth together so I wouldn't scream; I knew there were no answers. In the meantime, I was more determined than ever to hang on to life as long as possible.

Other doctors and SS men came through, quickly looking at the women lying on the cots. They did the experiments with eight women. Three were dead. The others were in various stages of stupor or agitation. One of them tried to move her upper body as if she were dancing. Anytime someone came near her, she screamed and wouldn't let anyone touch her.

Dr. Koenig and Dr. Mengele, having evidently completed the experiments, entered the room and exchanged observations. "On the next trip I think we should increase the voltage," one of them said as they left the room. They didn't give us so much as a glance. We didn't exist.

An SS guard ordered us to take the women to the truck and clean up the rooms. I quickly moved over to 'my' girl and, with Honzo's help, carried her carefully outside, to the truck.

"Goodbye, my friend from Budapest," I said quietly, although I'm sure she had no idea what I was saying. "Come back." And then I quickly corrected myself. "No, don't come back. Just get well." I felt she had no chance at all.

Honzo and I cleaned up without a word, each caught up in our own thoughts. I was despairing. It couldn't last forever.

A few days later, they brought the women back. We were put on alert by Heinz and told to be ready to help. My thoughts were focused on the young girl from Budapest. Was she with them? If so, what condition was she in?

Honzo and I rushed out, took the blankets and assisted the women. Most were ambulatory. Mengele and Company were already there.

I looked for her and I almost didn't recognize her as she stepped out of the truck. In a few days, she had aged years. She was sick. There was an empty expression in her eyes and she was obviously disturbed, walking as if she were in a trance. Her clothes were ripped and dirty.

This time the experiments were much more severe, and it showed. Those who survived never recovered consciousness. Among them was 'my' young girl. The female orderly from the Women's Camp who accompanied them told me the young Hungarian girl's story.

"Her name is Diana. She came to Auschwitz from Hungary two months ago, together with her whole family. It was one of those busy days when there were no selections. The gas chamber worked full blast. Her whole family was immediately taken away. One of the high SS officers, taken by the exquisite beauty of the girl, pulled her out and took her to his barracks. You can imagine what happened.

"When the SS officer was through with her, he assigned her to one of the most horrible jobs in the camp. Diana took little children away from their parents and brought them to the gas chamber. The children would follow her more easily and without a fuss. She had no choice. She brought them to the place with the sign 'Bath and Disinfection.'

"One day she recognized a cousin of hers, a four year old boy. It was the last straw. She attacked the SS officer running the operation with her bare hands and began to laugh with a horrible, angry expression on her face.

They brought her to the KB. We tried to help her but she didn't have a chance. She became more and more agitated and confused and Dr. Koenig selected her for the electric shock experiments. The rest you know. You've seen her. She'll never come back. On the outside, maybe. Not here."

I don't know how long I stood there, in shock. I could see her as she opened her eyes and hear her say: "Budapest."

"Hey you! Don't just stand there!" It was an SS man. "There are still some women inside—get them out!" I pulled myself together and went back into the barracks to help the other women.

I will never forget Diana.

A Foiled Escape from Auschwitz

WHENEVER SOMETHING needed fixing in Buna, the call would go out for the "Beton *Kommando*," Chaim, Jannek and Leo. They were old-timers, and everyone knew who they were and liked them for their resourcefulness and willingness to help. The three men exemplified camaraderie and friendship. I knew Leo because his brother, Freddy, was a friend of mine.

A few days ago they fixed the door to our barracks. Now they were in solitary confinement. In the "Bunker." Word spread through the camp like wildfire. "The Special *Kommando* is in Solitary."

No one could believe it and rumors immediately began to circulate. Everyone heard a different version. Sabotage? Talking back to an SS officer? Smuggling? They tried to escape. Escape from Auschwitz? Impossible! We were surrounded by barbed wire, guarded by the SS with machine guns. It couldn't be.

Eventually, the story emerged. Chaim, Jannek and Leo had indeed attempted the impossible. The true story was known only to a few, but I managed to piece together the information from those frightening days. We can only guess at some parts of the story.

The three, because of their extraordinary know-how and ability, were often asked to handle special jobs at the SS barracks.

They even did repairs on the electrically-charged barbed wire which fenced in the entire camp.

Their knowledge of the camp and its surroundings, the easy access they had both inside and outside, must have given them reason to believe they could.

They managed to steal civilian clothing and arranged for outside work on the day chosen for the actual escape. Their plan was to hide in one of the many sheds on the construction site until nightfall and then make their way into the countryside. Once away, they hoped to join up with Polish partisans. They knew they had time until the evening roll call before they'd be missed. By then the three would be gone.

It didn't work out that way. They forgot to factor in the German shepherds sometimes used by the SS. Somehow. On that particular day, the dogs were deployed, and even before all of the *Kommandos* returned to camp, Chaim, Jannek, and Leo were caught.

They were taken to the punishment hole, 3 feet by 3 feet, which wasn't big enough to stand up in or lie down in. They were charged with attempted escape and their sentence was death by hanging. Camp Commander SS Hauptsturmfuehrer Schwarz, his deputy, Oberstfuehrer Schoette and two other SS officers, Traute and Wiszorek, used the escape attempt to punish the entire camp.

We were called to the Appellplatz, the roll call assembly place, where the entire camp spent the night out in the open—standing at attention. Nobody was permitted to sit down. Those who could not stand, were taken out by the SS and shot. In the morning, just as the sun was rising, Schwarz, accompanied by his entourage of SS officers, made an announcement.

"The three camp inmates," and he read out the numbers of Chaim, Jannek and Leo, "are sentenced to death by hanging as punishment for their escape attempt. The sentence will be carried out tomorrow in front of the entire camp. Let this be a warning to all of you. As further punishment, all rations will be cut in half for the rest of the week. Dismissed for work!"

My parents on their
wedding day, 1921.

With my first grandchild,
Noga, in Jerusalem, 1988.
(Photo by Richard Lobell)

Class picture taken in 1932. I am third from the right. Also in this picture are my friends Heinz Manz (front row, seventh from right) and Kurt Hess (second row, third from left, arms folded).

Above: Lotte and me as youngsters.

Left: My father with Lotte and me.

I took this picture of my parents and my sister Lotte the last evening we were together, May, 1938. The next day Lotte took the train to France.

This is our bombed-out house in Mannheim in 1945. We had lived on the ground floor.

The main synagogue in Mannheim before and after Kristallnacht, 1938.

The yellow star which all Jews were forced to wear on the left side of the outer garment.

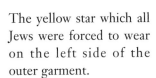

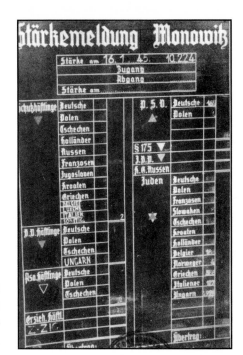

Roster of inmates of Auschwitz-Buna (Monowitz) concentration camp. This photo was taken January 16, 1945—two days before the evacuation of all inmates.

A copy of my official admission paper to Auschwitz.

Above: Lotte and me at our first meeting in Israel, 1955.

Below: The Michels and the Reins (Lotte's family) gathered together at
Lauren and Chaim's wedding in Jerusalem, 1987.

Scenes from my retirement dinner, May, 1989.

Top: With Honzo Munk (he now calls himself John Marek), with whom I escaped from Auschwitz.

Right: My daughter Karen, addressing the crowd.

Bottom: My son Joel and me.

Al and Lee Hutler, with my daughter Lauren and her 2 children, Noga and Yair. Jerusalem, 1992.

Here I am addressing the National UJA Young Leadership Mission at Auschwitz-Birkenau, 1990. *(Photo by Richard Lobell)*

With my beautiful wife, Amy Goldberg. *(Photo by Robert A. Cumins)*

We found out later that our friends were tortured until they confessed, then were thrown back in the punishment cell, where they stayed without food or drink.

The mood was tense. The SS guards knew it. Guards at all posts were doubled and the dogs were always in view. One wrong move and the situation could lead to a massacre.

Although all of us lived with death every minute of the day and although we witnessed cold-blooded murder every day, this was the first time the entire camp would be forced to witness a hanging. It was especially repugnant because the three were popular.

It was a bleak Saturday morning in October. We gathered at the Appellplatz. There were three gallows at the spot where the camp commander was customarily given the result of the roll call. The orchestra, comprised of prisoners, some of the best musicians in Europe, was playing, "Do not cry, yes, do not cry..."

We'd never seen so many guards, and their machine guns were pointed directly at us. The place was beginning to fill, as *Kommando* after *Kommando* reported to the SS officer on duty. "*Kommando* 12 with 42 prisoners. All accounted for. Hats off!"

It took more than an hour for the entire camp to assemble. Hardly a word was spoken. The tension grew.

Even we, the orderlies from the Krankenbau, were ordered to line up. Heinz, our Blockaelteste, told us that because our barracks was where all the corpses were gathered before being shipped to the crematoria, after the hanging, we were going to take down the bodies of Chaim, Jannek and Leo and move them to the morgue. There was nothing we could do. Somebody had to do it. Honzo and I were given the job.

From where we stood, we could see them being brought in, one by one, their hands tied behind their backs. They were surrounded by SS men in uniform, and marched to the front of the entire camp. There were between 12,000-15,000 people present.

The entire SS hierarchy was assembled from Schwarz down. I recognized Koenig and Mengele among the officers. It was deadly quiet. No one spoke a word. Only the voices of the SS broke the silence. The three stood in front of the gallows. They wore their regular prison uniforms. Their faces were blank. Three comrades. Three of us.

Chaim was on the left. Jannek was in the middle. Leo was on the right. Wiszorek, in his dark gray long leather coat and officer's cap, came forward and read the official death sentence.

"In the name of the Fuehrer and Chief of the SS, it is my duty to inform you..." and then he read out the details. The tension grew stronger. Fingers on hair-triggers made us nervous. One wrong move by an inmate and there would be a blood bath unlike anything we had known. Fight them? With what? Bare hands?

We stood at attention, some of us with tears in our eyes, as we watched the ghastly proceedings. Wiszorek finished reading the sentence. Two SS officers took Chaim up the few steps to the gallows. One of them threw the rope around his neck. His hands were tied. Just before the SS officer kicked the stool out from under him, he yelled as loud as he could: "Farewell, comrades!" And then his body swung and Chaim was no more.

As Jannek reached the gallows, his voice reverberated over the entire assembly. "We are the last!"

It was now Leo's turn. Before they fastened the rope around his neck he, too, raised his voice. "Long live Freedom! Don't Forget us!" It sounded like an echo, bouncing off the barracks. "We are the last!"

We stood, taking it all in, never to forget the moment three of our best were killed. Killed for what? Because they wanted to live as free men. The orchestra resumed playing as, one after the other, the *Kommandos* dispersed.

Honzo and I moved forward to cut down the bodies. We placed them carefully in a cart and wheeled them to the morgue next to our barracks.

Silently, almost reverently, we carried their still warm bodies into the cold room where many bodies were lying in a heap. The day's toll. There those who died of malnutrition, disease or murder by the SS. We placed our friends side by side, away from the others, and then stood with our heads bowed.

Chaim, Jannek and Leo. Three of our best.

The Russians Are Coming

"IT CAN'T LAST much longer. The Americans have penetrated the German border. From there to Cologne isn't very far. Once they cross the Rhine they'll break through. It's only a matter of time."

As 1944 came to a close, this was the main theme, the only theme, in Auschwitz. You could feel it. It wasn't going to last much longer. The important thing was to stay alive. If the rumors were true, Germany, sooner or later, would have to capitulate. It would be suicidal for the Germans to keep fighting. We had to hold out.

The news from the Eastern Front was that the Russians had reached Warsaw, then Tarnow. One rumor was that the Red army had captured Lublin and was moving West. How long would it be before they reached Krakow and then Oswiecim-Auschwitz? How long before they get here?

Here we were, the remnants of the millions who had come in on the trains to Birkenau. We were the survivors, 40,000-50,000 of us, in the three camps called Auschwitz.

What would the SS do with us? Would they let the Russians march in without a fight? What would happen? Would they let the Russians see the murder factory, the gas chambers, the crematoria, the emaciated corpses?

None of us, even the most optimistic, believed that the SS leadership would simply give up and turn us over to the Russians. So what would they do? Kill us all? forty to fifty thousand of us? Why not? They'd done it before.

Come on, you Russians. Come fast, while there is still some hope. Free us! Liberate us! Can't you hear our silent prayers? Come! Soon!

Those were our thoughts, hopes, and prayers during those cold, bitter winter days and nights. December turned to January. It was 1945. It was five years and four months since my arrest in Mannheim.

One of the men who frequently went to Birkenau said the gassing had stopped. We heard that the gas chambers and crematoria were dynamited by the Germans. That made sense. The selections, too, came to a halt. The flow of bodies stopped. The transports from the KB to Birkenau stopped. The trains also, finally stopped coming.

More new rumors.

"The SS plans to move us to Germany before the Russians get here!"

"Impossible!"

"How can they ship forty to fifty thousand prisoners on trains to the West? There aren't enough cattle cars. Even if they shove eighty of us into each car, they'd need over six hundred cars!"

That's how it went. The rumor mill was going full blast. Every day, every hour. We worked halfheartedly. Even the SS men became less vicious. There were fewer beatings, and the killings stopped.

Someone claimed to have seen a German newspaper. It confirmed what we already knew. The Germans were retreating, en masse. Cologne was taken by the Americans... Goering's been shot... Hitler fled... Gas war... What was true? What was rumor? The only thing we knew for sure was that one way or the other, something was going to happen—soon.

The thermometer hovered between 30 to 40 below zero at night. The patients were restless. We tried to allay their fears as much as we could and assured them that the transfers to Birkenau were over. There were no new admissions. The sick and injured avoided the KB for as long as they could.

On January 15, a new rumor swept the camp. The Russians had broken through and were on their way to liberate Auschwitz. Later that night, the rumor was confirmed.

Gerd, who had special privileges as a kapo, came to see me at the hospital.

"Ernst, it's true. They broke through. In a week we'll either be dead or free. The chief engineer at the plant told me he heard it on the radio."

He grabbed me by the shoulder. "We'll make it. We will!"

I was skeptical. I knew all about false hope.

"Gerd. Be sensible. Do you believe the SS will surrender without a fight? Do you think they'll turn us over to the Russians just like that? After everything we know about this place?"

Were we to be liberated or murdered?

We continued to follow the daily routine. The *Kommandos* went to the factory and work on enlarging the camp went on. The orders were always the same. "Move! Move!"

At noon one day, all the barracks commanders were ordered to meet at the Appellplatz. For a change, even the Blockaelteste of the hospital barracks was included. "Something big is happening," Heinz Lipman, our Blockaelteste told us. He put on his cap and buttoned up his jacket. "It also means our worst fears won't come true. They won't kill us. Otherwise, why would they assemble the barracks heads?" He walked off.

In less than half an hour he was back. We met him in the hallway, desperate to hear what he had to say.

"We're all being evacuated. We leave tomorrow or the day after."

"How?"

"On foot."

"On foot?!" We looked at each other with disbelief.

"That's the order."

"Where to?"

"They won't say."

"How about the patients who can't walk or are too weak? What will happen to them?"

Heinz's eyes hardened. "Orders from the SS. Those who can walk, walk. The others will remain."

I looked at Heinz.

"What does that mean?"

He looked me in the eye. "I don't know. We asked that question. They ignored it. My feeling is they don't care. They have other problems. They can't worry about a few hundred sick prisoners."

Now we knew. Evacuation on foot. The waiting was over. The uncertainty gone.

"Listen carefully." Heinz said after we had a few minutes to let the news sink in. "All patients must be carefully evaluated. No one is to say a word about evacuation. Anyone who can walk will be discharged as quickly as possible. Those who can't, will be fed before we go. Try to leave enough food and water so that they can help themselves when we're gone."

We went to work, immediately. "Are you well enough to get out of the hospital? Yes or no? Can you walk?"

There was no other way. We had to let those who had a chance know the options. We all knew what it meant to march in the dead of winter, with no socks, in wooden shoes, without coats or sweaters, in snow and ice. No one could know how long we would last and where we were being taken.

"What will happen to me if I stay?" was the question most often asked. I told the truth. "Honestly, I don't know."

We left the decision to each individual. Most of those who could, decided to get out. There were some heartbreaking scenes as brothers, fathers, and sons faced the most agonizing decision. Stay or go? Was there a right answer? It would be a hard for a healthy man to march in 30 to 40 below zero weather. How could a sick person possibly manage? What chance did he have? How long could he last?

Come on, you Russkies! Hurry up! Save those who stay behind!

In the middle of the night, our last in Auschwitz, a tremendous blast woke us from fitful sleep. A second followed. Then a third. In the distance we could hear the noise from airplanes. Russians? Germans?

One explosion after another shook the camp. All the lights went out. Even the guard towers were blanked out. The sound of the plane engines soon faded.

In the morning we discovered that Russian bombers had destroyed the railroad tracks leading to Auschwitz and that Russian troops captured Krakow, 30 miles away. The hope spread that they would arrive before we were marched away. No such luck.

Immediately after roll call, the order was given. "Prepare for the march! All barracks march as one. Hospital barracks last. Anyone who tries to flee will be executed on the spot!"

One hour later, SS Obersturmbannfuehrer Dr. Koenig arrived at the KB. "We are leaving. Anyone who can walk, walks." That made it official.

At 1:00 p.m., the first of the inmates of Auschwitz-Buna shuffled through the gate. We each were given two pounds of bread. That was all. We were told it had to last for five days. No other food would be distributed. With the SS guards gone, chaos reigned. Anyone who could, stormed the kitchen to take whatever food was there. Others raced to the clothing storage to grab coats, caps, shoes—anything they could get their hands on. We needed to keep warm for the march.

The camp had become a place of anarchy. Prisoners ran from one block to the next. They came to the hospital to search for friends and relatives. There was no one to stop them. They entered the quarantine area, where those suffering from infectious diseases were housed.

Honzo, Felix and I prepared for the worst. We had two jackets each. Even better, we had heavy paper to stuff under our clothes. Paper gave good protection from the cold.

Dr. Samuelides, our barracks doctor, worked until the end to ease the suffering of those most seriously ill. He left medicine behind, hoping it would last until the Russians came. He hoped at least some of the inmates would live long enough to be liberated and cared for.

The departure took longer than the Nazis anticipated. All three camps were being evacuated at once. This meant 40,000 to 50,000 inmates began the march that day. Barracks group after barracks group, marched out the gate. We were among the last.

I took a final walk through 'my' barracks and tried to comfort those who had to stay behind.

"It won't be long till the Russians come. They're close. You're better off than those of us who have to march." I shook hands with some of my patients, wondering who would survive to greet the Russians.

"Krankenbau—March!"

That was us. We left the hospital compound for the last time. I remembered the first time I came through those gates and how lucky I was to survive for the last 22 months. Without my father's calligraphy course, I would have died a few weeks after the SS officer slammed me in the head with the butt of his gun. That was July, 1943. Now it was January, 1945.

How many bodies did I carry during those months? Thousands. Among them were Walter and some of my closest friends from Paderborn. Ludwig, Guenther, and all the others, all those nameless ones. They came from all the corners of Europe and spoke different languages. They were individuals, each one once part of a family and having a future. Then they became numbers, tattoo marks on an arm. Who would remember their names?

Of the 100 Paderborners who arrived almost two years ago, eleven were left. Of the 3,000 who arrived on our transport, fewer than 150 survived. Our endurance quotient was higher than some of the others. We passed the Appellplatz and Barracks 10, where I spent my first night of horror an eternity ago.

Late in the afternoon of Thursday, January 18, 1945, I marched through that gate for the last time.

I had lived through 674 days in a man-made hell.

Six hundred seventy-four endless days and nights.

Six hundred seventy-four nights in the abyss.

And so the march began.

Auschwitz to Buchenwald

"**KEEP GOING!** Pull yourself together!"

"It can't be much farther to the rest stop."

"If you give up now, you're dead!"

Tired and weak, we encouraged each other to keep going. Honzo, Felix and I stuck together. We were a team with one goal—survival.

We marched for 15 hours straight, without rest. Those who couldn't keep up littered the roadside—living corpses. Earlier, the Nazis shot stragglers. Now, even they were too weary to care. They simply left them to fall onto the ground where they would certainly freeze to death in the snow. Some prisoners feigned exhaustion and dropped. They probably hoped to meet up with Polish partisans in the area.

When the SS guards showed signs of fatigue, they climbed onto carts drawn by inmates. We dragged ourselves through villages and along main roads. We made a ghoulish panorama—tens of thousands of prisoners in striped prison suits, guarded by the SS, dragging themselves trailing through snow and ice. It took hours for our columns to pass. The Polish men and women along the way stared at the spectacle, but rarely said a word. They looked at us without pity and just shook their heads.

Prisoners began collapsing in droves. They lay helpless in the snow, unable to continue. Thousands were dying from exposure.

At first we tried to help them up and get them going, but we weren't effective. We realized we needed to preserve our own energy reserves, now badly depleted. The cold was numbing, despite the heavy paper and our extra jackets. For three snowy and icy days, we shuffled and staggered over Polish roads. It was death by attrition.

We spent the first night in a huge brick factory, crowding together to keep warm. The second night we were in Gleiwitz, where, rumors had it, we would be boarding trains to Germany. By day three, we were out of bread.

We reached the train station just outside the city and we were crammed into open cattle cars. The last time I was herded into one was almost two years before, when we left Paderborn for Auschwitz.

The train ride took five days and nights. On the second day some bread was thrown into the car. Lack of water was a major problem, but the snow saved us. Our ranks shrank as dead bodies were tossed out of the car. We'd lost half of those who began the march, almost 20,000 people.

The SS had a very simple disposal system. They ordered us to stack the corpses in the first car. Then they filled the second car. Those still able to move were transferred to boxcars with those of us who were still alive. The Nazis obviously didn't want to discard the bodies in the villages, so we all rode together, the living and the dead.

Something amazing happened on the way. It happened near Prague. As the open train and its skeletal passengers passed by a factory, we were recognized by the workers, undoubtedly because of our striped prison clothing. Within moments, they bombarded us with anything useful they could get their hands on. Sandwiches, sausages, shirts, hats— whatever they could find was thrown into the open cars and quickly grabbed by those of us who were lucky. It was a rare outbreak of spontaneous compassion from people who didn't have much and reached out to those who had nothing. Thank you, Czechs. We've never forgotten you.

It was a bitter, glittering day. Eight days had passed since Auschwitz. We marched into KZ Buchenwald, through the gate inscribed, "Right or Wrong—My Country." Directly underneath were the words, "To Each His Own."

The camp was jammed beyond capacity, and new transports arrived continuously.

Buchenwald was in the heart of Germany, located near Weimar, the city of Goethe. It was being used as the dumping ground for prisoners from camps in danger of being overrun by the Allies.

That night, we were put in Barracks 58, in the so-called "small camp." A thousand of us were trying to find a place to sleep in a barracks designed to hold no more than 300. I don't know which was worse, the hunger, the dirt, the fatigue or the lice. It was quite a combination. There were no blankets, no mattresses, not even straw. All we had were barren wood planks. The three of us decided to take turns so we could all get some sleep.

There were major differences between Auschwitz and Buchenwald. First of all, there was absolutely nothing to do. We stood around all day, waiting for one of two meals: a breakfast of sawdust bread in the morning and thin soup at night. The death *Kommando* made rounds through the barracks each morning to collect the bodies. There were no washing facilities. Toilets were filthy and disease-laden. Many who survived the march died.

The second major difference was the way we were treated by those in charge of the barracks. Most were old-time prisoners. There were no beatings, no unnecessary harassment. Their attitude was to maintain the status quo and not increase the distress factor.

There was one more thing. Twice each day, loudspeakers in the barracks would broadcast the latest official German news. And despite the fact that they continued to claim victory as they reported the heroic battles of the German armies, the cities they named made it clear that the Allied armies were slowly, but surely, advancing on all fronts.

We could hardly wait for the newscasts. They gave us the incentive to hang on. Without them, Felix, Honzo and I would not have had the courage to fight to stay alive. I later learned what happened to those we left behind in Buna. Auschwitz was liberated by the Russian army on January 23. The inmates who survived the five days between when we left and the Russians arrived, were cared for by Russian doctors. I met some of the survivors after the war.

Meanwhile I continued to wonder what would happen to us.

My friends' faces had changed. We were all skin and bones. Felix looked like a walking skeleton. Honzo didn't look any better. Did I look like them? How long could we go on?

One day, I witnessed cannibalism. Some of the barely alive prisoners were eating the flesh of those newly dead. It was a horror and is still etched in my mind.

Escape

XII

MARCH, 1945.

For days, the sound of artillery fire could be heard in the distance. Although we'd heard news of the German retreat, we waited for something to happen. The SS were hardly visible. Food was scarce and there was nothing to do. So we waited and hoped.

There was a roll call every morning and every night. Then word of transfers trickled through the ranks. Fear and tension increased and our optimism soured. One morning, the Blockaelteste read names off his transport list. Honzo and I were to be sent to another camp, two hours away. Felix wasn't listed, so we begged the kapo to allow Felix to join us and he agreed. The three of us, with 40 other prisoners, were loaded into a truck and transported to the sub-camp Berga, which held 1,500 prisoners. Here, for the first time, we encountered American POWs.

We were put to work digging tunnels for underground munitions factories. The Americans were working right next to us, forced to do the same hard work. We observed their leather shoes and their wrist watches. We had seen neither in years.

When I tried to speak to them in German, some, to my total surprise, replied in Yiddish. They were Jews—American Jews! American Jewish prisoners of war!

During our meager lunch break, we learned that they had been captured and taken to a POW camp where the commandant tried to separate the Jews from non-Jews. The non-Jewish POWs wouldn't let him do it, and ordered their comrades not to move. Some, afraid of being singled out, threw away their dog tags, which bore a tell-tale 'H' for 'Hebrew.'

When no one stepped forward, the camp commandant announced that they had twenty-four hours to change their minds. The prisoners were told that unless the Jews would identify them-selves voluntarily, they would be found out and killed. In addition, those who had agreed to hide them would be executed, as well.

The next morning, Jewish POWs, unwilling to let their com-rades die in retribution, stepped forward. They were separated from the rest and wound up in a POW camp near Berga, where they lived under miserable conditions, received the same bad food and bad treatment we did.

Unable to withstand the conditions—sickness, starvation, and lice infestation—many American-Jewish POWs succumbed. Between early March and the liberation of the camp in the spring, 70 out of 200 died. The rest were reduced to skeletons and were saved only when the camp was finally liberated in April, 1945. One of the soldiers was so far gone, he offered to trade his gold watch for a few potatoes. I don't know if he lived to be liberated.

The SS guards were nervous. They knew that it was only a matter of time until the war was over. Their demeanor showed it. They were less brutal, perhaps because they hoped to buy some "protection insurance" by behaving almost civilly towards us. The sound of the battles raging west of us seemed to come ever closer, and they heard the guns as clearly as we did.

"Any day now. Let's hold out. Let's not do anything to provoke the guards," we kept repeating to each other.

Once again, our hopes for liberation were shattered. The SS announced it would evacuate the entire camp. The date was April 11. We were told to take along one blanket and our tin bowls. We assembled early in the morning and began another march.

"Where do you think we're going now?" I really didn't expect an answer. Felix and Honzo knew as much as I did. Nothing.

"Rows of five. Line up! Quick!" the officer barked. Within minutes, Berga was behind us. Each of us had one piece of bread in our pockets. That was all. The SS guards, with their weapons ready, were marching at our side. We trekked along small country roads, avoiding farms and villages. The pace was leisurely. The sounds of battle faded. We didn't talk much, and tried to conserve our energy. There was little yelling and no hitting. The guards, too, were obviously aware the end was near. And for them, as for us, the future was unknown.

In the evening we stopped at an old factory, ate part of our chunk of bread and drank some cold *ersatz* coffee. Dead tired, using our blankets together, we huddled close and tried to get some sleep.

Early next morning, we were hit with a surprise announcement when we lined up.

"Achtung! I have important news." The SS officer, using his mega-phone, stood on a large rock at the edge of the forest. "The American warmonger, President Roosevelt, is dead!"

It was another one of those moments that remain with me, etched in space and time. I remember Honzo's expression, the dazed look in his eyes, his mouth open, his hand reaching out to me. "It can't be! Not Roosevelt!"

Ever since I could remember, in my early days at school, the American President, Franklin D. Roosevelt in a wheelchair, was a symbol of everything we hoped for and did not have—freedom, stability, democracy, and full acceptance as Jews. We knew Roosevelt opposed Hitler and choreographed America's entrance into the war, the creation of the Allied Forces and, finally, the landing in Europe on 'D' Day in June, 1944. The only other person whose name mattered as much to us was that of General Dwight D. Eisenhower, the commander of the Allied Forces.

The survivors stirred restlessly.

"Listen!" the officer shouted. "This is the turning point of the war! Germany will throw the Allies back! The Fuehrer will succeed. And now, form your rows. March!"

In shock, we regrouped and the march continued. The march to nowhere. On the third night, after watching a random incident, the three of us decided to try to escape.

Several men were pulled from the transport, taken to a clearing and, in full view of all of us, were summarily executed. The pretext, according to the SS officer's warning, was that they had tried to steal some food from a farm during the night.

"Let this be a warning to all of you!" he yelled after the men had been shot. "We will not permit this. You are still camp inmates. My responsibility is to deliver all of you, and I mean all of you, to our destination. We expect to be there in a few days."

I don't remember which of the three of us first uttered the word escape. We tried to weigh our chances carefully. How could we do it? When could we do it? Should we organize a mass escape and take the chance of a large number of us being killed?

Should we try to overwhelm the SS men? We quickly discarded that idea. The SS were positioned so that there was always a backup with machine gun at the ready. Any attempt to overpower them would result in a blood bath with few survivors.

Honzo closed the discussion, whispering quietly as we curled up in our thin blankets out in the woods. "Look, I didn't survive three years of concentration camps, hunger, murder, dirt, and lice to get shot within the sound of the Allied armies. They'll be here in a matter of weeks, maybe days. Mass escape is out of the question."

He was right. "We must think of a better way. Think about it and give me some ideas." It took a long time to fall asleep. Escape. How?

Our chance came on the sixth day. The SS chose a young forest for us to spend the night in. They positioned themselves around us, and took turns on the watch. At night, a smaller force was on the alert. They were either sitting down or slowly making their rounds.

Felix came up with a plan. "The only time we'd have is at night. No daylight attempt would work. The transport consists of fifteen hundred men. We march in rows of five. That makes three hundred rows, stretching out over a total length of one thousand meters, or three thousand feet. It's a long column. The SS has several hundred men with machine guns. Each SS man, walking on the outside, keeps his eyes on a few rows."

"So?"

Felix spoke with intensity. "Instead of marching in the same row, we position ourselves on the outside, a few rows apart, just behind an SS officer with his gun. Once we reach a spot, in the evening, near dusk, just before we usually camp down, when we go through a few bends in the road, I'll give a signal. Each of us, positioned behind an SS man, kicks him in the back and we immediately run zigzag into the woods. But, we need a young forest, thick with trees. Otherwise, we'll be shot."

Honzo and I listened attentively. "Not bad." I said. "What are our chances?"

Honzo said, "Not great. But what are they if we don't try something?"

The more I thought about it, the better I liked it. With one exception. We were concerned about what would happen to all the others. They would have no idea what was happening and we couldn't afford to share our plans with too many of them. They were at a disadvantage and many of them could get shot. It was a major flaw. There had to be another way.

They both looked at me. Nobody said a word. I tried to pick Felix's plan apart. Would it work? Would the guards recover quickly and take aim at us before we reached the safety of the woods? What about all the others? What would happen to them? Would there be reprisals? Would some of them get away? Without advance notice, their chances might be less than ours. If we weren't careful, we would assure the massacre we all feared.

Honzo was right. We had to get away. Otherwise, death was almost certain.

Late in the afternoon of April 18, just as it was getting dark, the three of us slowly walked a few steps into the woods, and pulled down our pants as if we were following a call of nature. We weren't the only ones. Others were doing the same thing. The difference was that we kept going, slowly sneaking deeper and deeper into the woods.

My heart pounded so loudly, I thought I could hear it. I was scarcely able to breathe. Honzo was 30 feet to my left; Felix was ahead of me, about the same distance to my right. We moved further into the woods, putting a considerable distance between ourselves and the group. Faintly, we heard the Nazis order the columns to march. We ran through the trees. I looked around and couldn't see anyone but Honzo and Felix.

Totally out of breath, I fell in the middle of the forest, tears streaming down my cheeks.

I was free. Free! Free!

For the first time, in many years, I wasn't surrounded by guards, dogs, wire fences, or machine guns. There was no one to order me around, no one to tell us what to do. There was nothing but utter silence. I was overwhelmed, and a feeling of exhilaration, a kind I never experienced before or since, swept over me. I was alive!

We moved through the forest, westward towards the Allied troops. We walked at night, sleeping in the daytime. We avoided roads and listened for anything unusual. Felix found a few rotten potatoes and we devoured them. We took water from a pond. Our only other food was grass, tree bark from young trees and corn left in a field.

On the second night, while crossing a road, we heard voices.

"Down! Quiet!" Honzo pushed me behind a bush. Felix, a few feet away, pressed his face to the ground. Twenty yards away, a group of German soldiers walked by. We stopped breathing. If one of them glanced in our direction, we were done for. Hour-long minutes passed and then they were gone. We lay on the ground, catching our breaths. We pulled ourselves together and moved on, more carefully than ever.

On the third day, we saw a barn that seemed deserted. We decided to spend the day under its roof and try to find something to eat. We were climbing through an opening when we heard faint whispers from the other end of the barn. Were they women's voices?

We called out to them and discovered we'd come upon a small group of Jewish women from another transport. Like us, they'd escaped and found shelter in the barn.

"Where are you from?" Felix whispered in Yiddish. Someone replied, in a whisper, "Wilna."

"What camp were you in?"

They named several camps and ghettos in Poland. We wished each other good luck. Exhausted, the three of us slept.

When daylight came, we were ready to move on, they were gone. Hunger gnawed at our guts. Somehow we had to get some food.

We decided to look for an isolated farm, where we'd pretend to be foreign laborers and offer to work for food and lodging. It was April, time for spring planting, and farmers could use all the help they could get. We found one in a valley. After watching it for hours, we approached the farmhouse. Since I spoke German, I was appointed spokesman. Dogs barked as we neared the farm yard, and a heavy-set woman came out to meet us.

"Hello," I said, as she looked us over suspiciously, "we are three forced laborers. We were separated from our transport after an air attack and are looking for work. We will do anything in exchange for food and lodging."

She didn't say a word. She just stared. I realized that I was speaking to a German woman for the first time in a long time. "We are hungry. We need some food. Any kind of food. We'll work for it."

"Stay here! I'll ask my husband." She spoke with a heavy Saxonian dialect which I found difficult to understand.

I nodded. "Yes, ma'am. We'll wait. But, please, if we could get a piece of bread, we would be grateful. We haven't had any food for days."

Wordlessly, she walked into her house and came back a few minutes later, laden with a pitcher of milk, a loaf of bread and some butter.

"Wait here!"

Milk, bread and butter! No food ever tasted that good. We devoured it.

"Let me warn you." Honzo said after we wolfed down everything. "Our stomachs aren't used to this kind of food. As much as we need and want it, we have to get used to it slowly."

Honzo's warning was on the mark. After the liberation, I heard stories about former camp inmates who were fed bars of chocolate by well-meaning G.I.s. Their stomachs couldn't digest the fats and sugar and they died shortly thereafter.

The farmer came from the barn, looked us over and told us that we could work only if we received permission from the local authorities.

"Who's that?" I asked.

"The Buergermeister."

"Where do we find him?"

"It's about half an hour from here. He's there now."

"If we get the permit, will you give us work?"

"If he gives you the papers, yes. At least one of you. The others can go to another farm."

It didn't take us long to find the little office of the Buergermeister. If he was a Nazi, we were in trouble, but we had to take the chance. We used the same story we told the farmer and it seemed to work.

We kept our jackets on to hide our Auschwitz numbers.

The Buergermeister was 'our' farmer's cousin. He accepted our story and didn't ask questions, since the farmers needed help in the fields as much as we needed food and shelter. He wrote our names on a piece of Nazi stationery, and stamped it. These were our working papers. He made one request, which, after a silent conversation with our eyes, we had to accept. We had to separate, to work on different farms in the little village.

We started our new lives working, but apart. We were fed and, in a few days, became regular members of our respective households. My farmer and his family didn't ask questions. They seemed satisfied to have an extra hand around for the planting season.

Honzo, Felix and I met every other evening. We knew how lucky we were. In this small hamlet time seemed to have stopped somewhere in the 19th century. There was no evidence of war, no soldiers.

Remembering Honzo's warning about eating, I ate slowly and felt some of my strength coming back. The work was hard, but the food made all the difference.

We'd been farmhands for just over two weeks. I was helping the farmer repair a fence in the field when we saw his wife hurrying towards us. I assumed she was bringing our lunch. I can still see her in her formless green dress, a kerchief covering her head, coming to us in her heavy boots.

"The war is over. It's on the radio. Germany has surrendered!"

I stood there with a 2 x 4 in my hand. I didn't know whether to cry, laugh, scream, or run. Against all odds, I had survived. It was over.

The farmer acted as though the news didn't concern him. He went on with his work. His wife went back to the house. I stood transfixed, allowing reality to sink in, until the farmer gave me a shove, "Come. Work must go on."

The moment I had been praying for since 1933 finally arrived. The Nazis were vanquished. The killing was over. The war was over. As a Jew, I wanted to celebrate. I reached for my 2 x 4 and went back to work.

When Felix, Honzo and I got together that night, we were exuberant but still not totally able to shed our disbelief.

"What do we do now?" Felix asked.

"You know what?" I said as much to myself as to my two friends, "I never really thought about what life would be like afterwards. We concentrated on survival. Now we're free, and we really have to decide what to do and where to go. The future we never though we'd have is ours."

"I know what I'm going to do." Honzo declared. "I'm leaving tomorrow morning to go to Prague. I doubt any of my family survived, but at least I know Prague."

Felix was less sure. "I can't see myself going back to Poland. But I can't see staying here, that's for sure."

Honzo and Felix left the next day. Our farewells were difficult. We'd been inseparable for almost two years. We shared food, helped each other through very tough times, some perilous moments and often depended on each other for our lives. Would we ever see each other again? Where? When? I didn't have an address. I had no home. Where would I be next week? Next month? How does one say goodbye under such conditions?

For a few minutes we sat quietly, each absorbed in his own thoughts. Then we embraced, trying, unsuccessfully, to hold back our tears.

Honzo's hair was beginning to grow back. His farmer had given him some work pants and an old jacket. Felix and I wore the same outfits in which we had escaped. Just before he left, Honzo gave me his old address in Prague. I gave him mine in Mannheim, not knowing if I would ever get there, and, if I did, what I would find. We hugged one last time, and then they were gone. I was alone.

I went back to my farmer. I was all alone, really alone, for the first time in my life. It was a strange feeling.

Lindenau, the little hamlet where we had found refuge, was in the only part of Germany never occupied or overrun by either the Russian Army or the Allies. Nobody bothered, the place was just too unimportant. Its future was uncertain. And so was mine.

Work went on as before. My farmer asked if I would remain. With the war over, he offered to pay me. I told him I'd stay until I made up my mind about what to do. 'Why not stay?' I asked myself.

I even toyed with the idea of changing my identity, using a new name, pretending to be a non-Jew, and making a new life for myself. Ever since I was a kid, I had been persecuted for being a Jew. I lost my youth, my family, everything but my life. Why not change everything and let go of the past?

Mutti's voice on that morning in Mannheim whispered in my head. "Be a good Jewish boy" were her last words to me.

Did I survive the horror of the camps, the endless years of disease, death and hunger to live the simple life of a farmer? What about the promises I made to bear witness, to tell the world what I'd seen and experienced?

We now had Allied broadcasts that spoke of dramatic changes. Germany was under total Allied occupation. Hitler's "New Germany" was in ruins.

All German newspapers were shut down. Radio was run by the occupation forces.

And here I was, wracked with indecision. I performed my daily farm chores. I gained weight and puzzled about what to do next.

Coming "Home"

IN EARLY JUNE, nearly one month after the war ended, I made my decision. I would return to Mannheim, to learn what I could about my family. I was 22 years old. I had no job, no education, no possessions. Nothing. The only thing I knew was how to survive in concentration and labor camps. I had no idea how far this would get me in the real world.

My farmer's wife, trying to persuade me to change my mind, packed what seemed to be a month's supply of food and bade me farewell. The family had been good to me. Although I was still much below my normal weight, I felt better with my strength coming back.

On a beautiful summer morning, I left the farm, heading west, towards what I assumed would be the Americans. I walked through small villages. I met refugees coming the other way. At night I slept in barns. Nobody bothered me.

On the third day, coming around a bend in the road, I was stopped by a black American, a black soldier. I had never seen a black person before in my life. He was carrying a rifle and ordered me to stop. He didn't speak German and my English obviously made little sense to him. He motioned me to the side of the road where I joined a group of other men, about 20 or so, most of them German soldiers. I thought it best not to say very much and to keep to myself.

A few hours later, a truck showed up and we were told to get into it. I wound up in yet another camp. This one was a German prisoner of war camp. So, after weeks of freedom, I was once again behind barbed wire. My attempts to speak to the Americans brought the reply, "You'll have your turn! Wait."

Indeed, my turn did come. One by one we were interrogated by a German-speaking American soldier who sat at a small table and took down all pertinent information. He hardly looked up from his papers.

"Name?"

"Michel."

"First name?"

"Ernst."

"Age?"

"Twenty-two."

"Place of birth?"

"Mannheim."

"Were you ever a member of the SS?"

I couldn't help but laugh.

"No."

"What army outfit did you serve in?"

"None!"

"Come! I haven't time for games. What was your Army unit?"

"I wasn't in the Army. I was in camps."

He looked up for the first time. An American soldier wearing glasses, clean shaven, speaking German without an accent, obviously born in Germany.

"What do you mean, you were in camps?" I looked at him, wondering how to say it, how to answer.

"I've been in camps since 1939. The last one was Buchenwald. Before that I was in Auschwitz."

He stared at me. "You were in Auschwitz?"

"Yes."

"You have a number?"

"Yes—104995." I showed him the tattoo.

"What are you doing here? This is a prisoner of war camp."

"I've been trying to get someone's attention but I was told to wait."

Then: "Are you Jewish?"

"Yes."

The young American got up from his chair and grabbed me by the arm. "Come with me!" he urged. Turning to the others standing in line waiting their turn, he said, "Wait. I'll be back."

He led me to what seemed to be the officers' barracks. "Sit here." He left and came back minutes later with two officers. They stared at me as if I were a visitor from another planet.

For the next hour I had to tell the story of what happened to me in the camps, beginning with *Kristallnacht*, 1938 until the escape. My words were interpreted by the young soldier, who, he told me later, was born in Berlin and emigrated with his family to the States in 1936.

The trio listened attentively. I was the first camp survivor they'd met. That night I was fed a scrumptious dinner. I slept in a real bed in the officers' barracks.

After a great night's sleep, the young soldier who separated me from the German POWs, asked me about my plans. I told him I wanted to get back to Mannheim. "I don't know where else to go."

"How will you get there?"

"I'll walk."

"Do you know how far it is?"

"Well, all I've got is time. Nobody's waiting for me."

He thought for a moment. "Have you ever ridden a motorcycle?"

"No. Why?"

"You can't walk to Mannheim. Too difficult. Too dangerous. You're alone. There's a curfew in effect and no way for you to get there."

"So how do I get a motorcycle? I have no money."

He laughed. "That's not a problem. We've confiscated hundreds from the German Army. All kinds. Big and small."

The next day I was the owner of a motorcycle. It took me another day to get the hang of it.

My new American friend provided an official document for me, stating that I was a concentration camp survivor, that the vehicle was given to me by the U.S. Army, that I was on my way to Mannheim and finally, most important, that I was to be given all possible assistance by all U.S. Army personnel.

The letter worked like a charm.

After thanking my benefactor, I began my journey to my hometown, a city I had last seen in September, 1939. When I needed gasoline or food, I stopped at an Army installation, showed my papers and, bingo, I was taken care of.

The destruction I saw on the way is difficult to describe. Whole cities were destroyed and the main roads were often impassable. Only the countryside was peaceful and serene. I saw trains and trucks full of refugees being transported by the U.S. Army to different destinations. Every city was under Allied control. There was no German government.

I remember one particular stopover. Since there was a 9 p.m. curfew, I needed to find an Army post before that hour. I was in a small village outside of Frankfurt when I had a mechanical problem with my motorcycle. I was unable to find a place to stay. As time ran out, I knocked at a house and asked if I could stay for the night.

It turned out to be a family where one of the parents was of Jewish descent. They were able to hide and survived intact. The family consisted of parents and two daughters in their early twenties. I told them a little bit about myself and spent a very warm, pleasant evening with them. It was the first time I found myself in a private home since the last night I spent with my parents. The girls entertained me and taught me how to dance to the latest American hits. I heard "You are my sunshine, my only sunshine..." It's still one of my favorite songs.

Two days later, I reached Mannheim. By coincidence, it was my twenty-second birthday, July 1, 1945.

What a homecoming. The city was in total ruin, with hardly a building left standing. I rode through streets I remembered from my childhood, but was often unable to recognize the neighborhood. The place where the synagogue had stood, the school I went to, the center of town—were all rubble. The few people walking around seemed to be in a trance-like state. All the shops were closed. Finally, with some trepidation, I drove to what used to be our apartment building, 26 Richard-Wagnerstrasse.

Only the lower floor, where our family had lived, was left standing. The street number, 26, could still be seen. I stopped, turned off the motor and walked to the door. Nobody lived there. Nobody lived on the street. Everything was rubble.

I stood there, transfixed by my thoughts, when a jeep with the markings 'Military Police' braked to a halt. The MP officer called me over. He spoke broken German.

"Don't you know it's curfew? You have to be off the street."

"I have no place to go. This used to be my home," I said, pointing to the destruction behind me.

"I'm sorry. You can't be on the street. You have to find a place to stay overnight."

I tried to explain to the MP that I'd been in a camp. I showed him my Army paper which he studied carefully, then turned and whispered to the other soldiers. "Follow us."

I got on my motorcycle and followed them. I had no idea where they were taking me. It turned out to be the Mannheim jail. It was, ironically, one of the few buildings in the city that was somewhat habitable. An American officer, speaking German, motioned me to sit down.

"You were in a concentration camp?"

"Yes. Several of them."

"You were born in this city?"

"Yes. We lived here till I was deported. My parents were deported a year later."

"What happened to them?"

"I don't know. I came back to find out."

"Where did you think you would stay?"

"I don't know. I didn't plan."

The American shook his head. "I really don't know what to do with you. You can't stay on the street." He ran his fingers through his hair. "I'm afraid you'll have to spend the night here. There are Military rules and I can't let you run around town. Tomorrow go to the Military Government Headquarters, DP section. They'll take care of you."

"What is DP section?"

"Displaced Persons. People who were deported and have no place to go."

I spent the night of my 22nd birthday in jail. It was indeed a strange homecoming. I hadn't known what to expect, but I certainly hadn't anticipated that I'd spend time in the Mannheim jail.

In the morning, I rode over to the Military Government Headquarters, parked the motorcycle, locked it and walked in. The building used to be a school. It was now occupied by the U.S. Military Government. There were officers with various insignias on their lapels. As I looked closer, I noticed one particular officer with an unusual patch. It looked to me like the tablets of the Ten Commandments. The man was talking to another officer, but rudely, I kept staring at him because I couldn't figure out what the strange patch on his uniform meant. After a while, he noticed me and came over.

"Why are you staring at me?"

He was clean shaven, wore glasses, was rather short and looked at me with a friendly smile. He spoke broken German.

"Your uniform has tablets on the collar. I've never seen that before."

"Do you know what it means?"

"No, but I know what it stands for."

"Are you Jewish?"

"Yes. Are you?"

"I am a Jewish chaplain with the United States Army. I am a Rabbi."

I kept staring at him. "You are a Rabbi?"

"Yes. I am Chaplain Abraham Haeselkorn, attached to the U.S. Third Army. Who are you?"

Briefly, I told the Chaplain who I was and how I got there.

He shook his head. "I can't believe it. I've been looking for Jewish people in this town and have only found some half-Jews." And then he asked me to go with him.

"I want you to meet the DP officer. He'll be surprised!"

I went with him to another building, and we climbed up to the second floor. On the door was a sign, 'Albert A. Hutler, Lt. U.S. Army Displaced Persons Section.'

"Wait here a moment."

He walked into what was evidently the office of the Displaced Persons officer. A sergeant and another G.I. were busy interrogating a German. They hardly looked at me. I just stood there, waiting. After a few minutes, the chaplain came back.

"Come in. Lt. Hutler wants to talk to you."

I followed him into the small, spartan office. I had no idea how profoundly this meeting would affect the rest of my life. Lt. Hutler was in his thirties, with dark hair. He wasn't tall, but was solidly built, with warm, friendly eyes. Chaplain Haeselkorn did the translations. The lieutenant shook my hand and asked me to sit down.

"I understand from Chaplain Haeselkorn that you were born in Mannheim."

"Yes. In 1923."

"You are Jewish?"

"Yes."

"And you spent the war years in Nazi concentration camps?"

"Yes. Auschwitz, Birkenau, Buchenwald."

"You have a number?"

"Yes." I rolled up my left sleeve and showed him my tattoo.

He looked at it, as did the Chaplain, shaking their heads.

For the next hour or so I told Lt. Hutler and the Chaplain what happened to me since the deportation. I told them about my family, the forced labor camps, Auschwitz, the selection process, life in the camps, the escape and my arrival in Mannheim yesterday. Both men hardly interrupted me as I told them my story.

"And so you came back to where you were born and spent the first night in jail?"

I nodded.

"Do you know that you are the first Jew from Mannheim who has come back?" Lt. Hutler asked.

"No. I didn't know, but I'm not surprised."

The two men talked to each other. I couldn't understand what they were saying. "What are your plans now?" Lt. Hutler asked.

"I really don't know. I thought I might get some idea here. I would like to find out about my parents and my sister."

"You don't have a place to stay, do you?" he asked almost rhetorically.

"No."

Taking his military cap, he motioned the Chaplain and me to follow him. He turned to the GIs in the outer room who had obviously been waiting for him.

"Take care of the store. We're going for a ride."

"But, Lieutenant, you have to meet with the Colonel in half an hour!" one of them protested.

"Make an excuse. I'm busy. See you later."

With that, the Chaplain and I followed him to the parking lot and his jeep. In less than half an hour we were on the outskirts of Mannheim in an area which was surprisingly undamaged.

He turned to me, "Which house do you like?"

I didn't understand.

"Just tell me which of these houses you would like to live in." I was puzzled by what he had in mind.

"I don't know. All of them look fine to me."

He stopped the jeep in front of a pleasant house with a small garden, jumped out and knocked on the door. A man answered, well dressed, tall, a German.

"By order of the Military Government in Mannheim this house is being taken over. You have ten minutes to vacate."

When the man protested, Lt. Hutler answered, "You have nine minutes. This is an order!"

He attached an official looking document to the front door, stating that this house was now occupied by the U.S. Military Government for an unspecified period.

That's how I found my first place to live. Later, Lt. Hutler sent some other DPs to live in the house with me. It certainly was a lot more comfortable than jail.

So began my new life in Mannheim. The next day, Lt. Hutler asked me to work for him as interpreter and personal aide. I got to know the rest of his staff, Sergeant Harold Weiss, PFC Andrew

Sikora and Paul Vennekor, a Dutch DP, who had been a forced laborer in a factory near Mannheim.

The Displaced Persons Section, under Lt. Hutler's command, was responsible for the lives of literally hundreds of thousands of DPs of all nationalities in the area. During the months I worked with him, we repatriated Russian, French, Polish, Dutch and others who'd been forced to work in German industry who were now ready to go home.

Shortly after beginning my job at Military Government, I had an extraordinary experience. An American GI came to our Displaced Persons section. He was Heinz Kuhn, my childhood friend who lived around the corner, one of the boys I played soccer with. I don't know who was more shocked, he or I, as we stared at each other. "Ernst, what are you doing here? What happened to you?" He could not get over seeing me in the office.

Heinz, now Staff Sergeant Henry Kuhn, had come to Mannheim to look for any friends or relatives who might have survived. He was told to come to the Displaced Persons section and I was the first person he met. It took a while for both of us to get over the shock. We spent the evening together catching up on what happened to us. Henry got out of Germany in 1938 and was now living in Chicago. He gave me his address and I promised to get in touch with him if I ever came to America.

During that initial period of adjustment to normal life, I first learned about the Joint Distribution Committee, an American-Jewish organization primarily concerned with the thousands of Jewish survivors from all over Europe. They helped us find housing, family members and work and offered medical care and financial assistance to those like me, who found themselves stranded in Germany, waiting for an opportunity to pick up their lives.

We were the remnants, the lucky ones. But the question loomed large. What now? I knew that my work with Lt. Hutler could not last forever and that eventually I would have to decide what to do with my life. All efforts to learn the fate of my parents or my sister were unsuccessful. Wherever I turned, I ran into a stone wall.

I assumed they were all dead, that I was the only surviving member of my family.

A Reporter at the First
Nuremberg War Crimes Trial

SOME TIME DURING the early fall of 1945, Lt. Hutler received his orders to return to civilian life. I was sad to see him go but I realized that my work with the Displaced Persons Section of Military Government would come to an end sooner or later.

Watching him work on a daily basis, and being part of the small team of Americans responsible for the orderly repatriation of the thousands of DPs, taught me to respect him greatly. He seldom lost his temper under pressure. He made life and death decisions, always keeping in mind the welfare of those whose future was in his hands, and he had a special feeling for 'his' Jews.

I suppose I symbolized the survivors for him since I was the first Jew from Mannheim to come back. There were other survivors who found themselves under Hutler's wing, most of them Polish, Hungarian, or Rumanian. A few of them shared 'my' house, but none of them wanted to return to the countries of their birth— most of them wanted to go to Palestine to help create the Jewish State.

There were rumors of an underground group, organized by American servicemen and members of the Jewish Brigade. It was said they smuggled people from country to country and then onto ships bound for Palestine. It was a risky trip. Many survivors were caught and arrested as illegal immigrants. I often thought about making the trip, but somehow took no action.

111

One afternoon, Lt. Hutler asked me to come to his office. Standing near his desk were two young officers with a Mogen David insignia and the letters 'Palestine Brigade' on their jacket sleeves. I heard they existed, but it was the first time I had seen a 'Jewish' soldier.

"Lt. Hutler, you wanted to see me?"

"Yes, indeed." He turned to one of the members of the Brigade, he introduced me.

"This is Ernst Michel."

I wondered what was happening. What did the Palestine Brigade want of me? The officer approached me slowly.

"You are Ernst Michel?"

"Yes." He took something out of his pocket.

"You are born in Mannheim?"

"Yes."

"I have a letter for you."

A letter? I couldn't believe it! Who would write to me from Palestine? Who knew I came back? The envelope was addressed to "Ernst Michel, Mannheim." I didn't recognize the handwriting.

"You'd better sit down. This may shock you."

I wasn't hearing him, I was oblivious to everything but the letter. I looked at the bottom of the page, at the signature.

Lotte! My sister Lotte! How could that be? Was this a trick to test me somehow? I raced through the contents of the letter, and I still remember how it began.

"My dear, beloved brother Ernst. I don't know if you are alive or if this letter will reach you. But I want to do everything to find out if you survived."

I sobbed and then I began to cry. The letter really was from Lotte. She was in Palestine. She'd made it! She'd gotten out! The letter wasn't very long.

"Lt. Hutler," I cried, "Lieutenant. It's from my sister! From Lotte! She's alive!" Tears streamed down my face, blurring everything. The men in the office, Lt. Hutler, they were all crying, too. I sobbed, I laughed. I didn't know what to do first. Lotte was alive!

She skipped details. She heard that a few Jews came back to Mannheim from the camps, so she wrote, hoping I was one of them. She had nothing to lose. She'd been through difficult times; she was hidden by Catholic nuns and eventually arrived in Palestine on a Youth-Aliyah transport in 1944. She wrote about our parents, who were deported from Gurs in 1942. Lotte wasn't sure, but she believed their final destination was Auschwitz.

I felt like I was reconnected to the past.

Lt. Hutler hugged me. "Ernst, we're happy for you. We're privileged to share this moment with you."

After I calmed down, the officer from the Palestine Brigade told me that he was carrying letters from people in Palestine who heard that some of their relatives survived and were living in various DP camps. He described himself as a delivery boy who hoped he could reunite lost family members. As he wiped his eyes, he told me that no one could ever repay him for the joy he felt when families were brought back together. He offered to arrange for my response to be delivered to Lotte, who would have it in a month's time.

Before Lt. Hutler left Mannheim, he thanked me for being so helpful and handed me a slip of paper. "This is my address in Chicago. Let me know what you'll do. I'm sure you'll find your way. You're an unusual young man and I'm honored to know you. If you ever come to the United States, my family and I would be happy to see you."

I was touched and told him how much I was in his debt. I had no idea what an important role he was going to play in my life.

Around then, I received an interesting offer from another American Military Government officer, Captain Picard. I met him during his visits to Mannheim to meet with Lt. Hutler. He worked on German rehabilitation, a subject of much concern to the American occupying forces. How do you deal with a country of 60,000,000 people that, for all practical purposes, had no government?

"How would you like to work on the first new German newspaper?" Captain Picard asked me. He explained how the Military Government intended to let proven non-Nazis publish daily papers in a few German cities. At that moment, only one newspaper existed for all Germany, and that was published by the Military Occupation Force.

"One of the first papers will be published in Heidelberg. The editor will be Theodor Heuss. He was ostracized by the Nazis and lived in seclusion during the war. I told him about you and he would like to meet you."

With my job with the DPs coming to an end, I thought about what to do next. It was late summer. I had discarded my dirty camp clothing weeks earlier and felt ready to move on. I climbed onto my motorcycle and rode to Heidelberg. It was only a short distance from Mannheim but, oddly, had not been touched by the war at all.

Dr. Heuss welcomed me graciously. A conservative, soft-spoken, gray haired man, he introduced me to his associate editor, Dr. Rudolf Agricola, and told me how pleased he was that I was joining his small staff.

A few days later, I began my career as a newspaperman. I always enjoyed writing and despite my lack of formal education, I had no problems covering some local stories for the 'Rhein-Neckar-Zeitung.'

Gradually, as other newspapers received permission to publish, the Allies created a news agency, DANA, to distribute international, national and local news.

One of the major breaking news stories at that time was the approaching Nuremberg War Crimes Trial, where top Nazis, Goering, Keitel, Ribbentrop, Von Papen, Kaltenbrunner and others, were to be tried by an Allied Military Tribunal. Twenty-two Nazi leaders were scheduled to go on trial in late November.

I wanted that assignment.

I spoke with Dr. Heuss about it and he agreed to recommend me. With his support I got the job. After several days of briefings, I received press credentials as a special correspondent to the trials. Bill Stricker, a German-born American, was in charge of the news team and our Nuremberg stories were dispatched by DANA to all the newly licensed German papers. There were now approximately 50 of them, and more joined the syndicate daily.

My colleagues were all young Germans carefully chosen by the Military Government. I was the only Jew among them. They regarded me with something close to awe when they learned of my background. I was Jewish, though I didn't parade that before them, because I didn't want it to get in the way of our working together.

I couldn't have concealed it long, because in addition to my regular assignments, Bill Stricker asked me to write some personal stories under the byline "Special correspondent and Auschwitz survivor, #104995, Ernst Michel."

I wrote some personal reflections which were published in all the German papers. It threw me back into the twilight zone. Less than six months ago, I was an inmate in a Nazi concentration camp and now I sat in the courtroom at the Nuremberg Hall of Justice. The scum who were responsible for the greatest crimes against humanity sat less than 25 feet away from me, on trial for their lives.

I had an assigned regular seat in the press section and I followed the proceedings via the simultaneous interpretation system, which was used for the first time at the trials. (It is now the standard at the United Nations and all multi-lingual conferences.) To my right were the eight judges, two each from the U.S., the Soviet Union, France and England. On the left were two rows with the 22 defendants, including Goering. Their defense counsel sat in front of them and MPs guarded them from the rear.

I was the only Holocaust survivor to serve as a reporter at the trials and many American and British newsmen wanted my reactions. One interview with an American reporter appeared in papers throughout the U.S. and found its way to Israel where my sister saw it. If that member of the Palestine Brigade wouldn't have found me, Lotte would have learned about my survival from the interview.

I pinched myself every morning as I entered the courtroom, to make sure I wasn't dreaming. There sat Julius Streicher, editor of the anti-Semitic hate sheet "Der Stürmer," who had incited the German people against Jews with his lurid propaganda and imaginary atrocities.

There sat Ernst Kaltenbrunner who was among the higher echelon who ran the death camps. He, with Himmler, was responsible for the systematic slaughter of our people in the concentration camps. His attitude was one of disdain.

There sat Von Papen, the patrician, elegant head of the Reichsbank, which became the depository for the billions of dollars worth of Jewish property confiscated by the Nazis.

There sat Rudolf Hoess, the Deputy Fuehrer, who flew to England during the war in an abortive effort to end it. He seemed the strangest of all the defendants, and behaved as if he didn't belong there.

I stared at the lot. I couldn't keep my eyes off them. These were the men who were determined to wipe out the Jews of Europe. If they had won the war, they had plans to murder all the Jews in the rest of the world. They were responsible too for the suffering and deaths of millions of others including people of conscience, Jehovah's Witnesses, homosexuals, Gypsies and Communists.

Sometimes I wanted to jump from the press gallery to shake them by their shoulders and yell in their faces. "Why did you do this to us? Why did you kill my friend Walter? Why did you hang Leo, Jannek and Chaim? Why? Why?"

The trial proceedings were conducted in an almost antiseptic atmosphere. Documents were presented. "Is this your signature, sir?" 'Objection, Your honor!' 'May it please the court?' It was all very civil. It wasn't easy to keep my personal feelings separated from my job as a reporter, but fortunately, in addition to my regular assignments, I was given the opportunity to write a few feature stories, where I could vent some of my emotion.

After a particularly harrowing day in the courtroom, when evidence about the death camps was presented to the court, I wrote the following story, in English, for *Stars and Stripes*.

AUSCHWITZ PICTURES TELL A STORY
By Ernst Michel, DANA Staff Correspondent
(Formerly prisoner No. 104995 at Auschwitz concentration camp)

NUREMBERG, February 20 (GNS)—I have a book in front of me. A picture book. But not a picture book for children. A book which in Russian carries the title "International Military Tribunal, Nuremberg" and on the middle of the bindings says "Auschwitz Camp." The last two words are underlined.

The book has no preface at all and very little text. As I said it is a picture book, but a picture book of reality. And it is simply "exhibit No. such and such." Nothing more. And the Russian prosecutor who introduced it in court doesn't say much about it.

In fact, that isn't necessary at all, for these pictures speak for themselves. They speak of the life—or rather the death—of the prisoners at the Auschwitz concentration camp, which was the largest of all German concentration camps.

Three miles from Auschwitz there was Birkenau. A nice name, giving the impression of a birch wood, an opening in it and a small, quiet village. But that was not the Birkenau that I am speaking of. The Birkenau near Auschwitz was something different. It was a camp where about 100,000 prisoners were quartered—one can't say "were living."

And behind this Birkenau camp there were five large smokestacks, which were smoking steadily. These were the five giant crematoria and the four giant gas chambers of Birkenau, which were working day and night, where not tens of thousands, not hundreds of thousands, but millions of human beings were gassed to death. That was our Birkenau.

And my glance rests again on the little picture book with the title "Auschwitz Camp."

There is the electrified double-barbed wire fence with the sign "danger" and the death's head, the wire into which 20 of my co-prisoners were driven in one night.

I am leafing through the book and see another picture showing a large blackboard. This blackboard used to hang in the staff headquarters at Auschwitz and listed the daily changes in the numbers of prisoners. The board in the picture is dated Jan. 16, 1945, the last day it was used. The number of prisoners that day was 10,224. And the next day 9,000 of us began to march along the icy roads of Upper Silesia, "fleeing" from the advancing columns of the Red Army. The remainder was left behind—they couldn't march any longer.

And when we arrived at Buchenwald after three days of marching and five days of travel in open freight cars in blizzard weather, there were but less than 4,000 of us left.

The book is finished. It is again in front of me. I pick it up. It doesn't weigh much. But it is the history of millions of my co-prisoners, and today, here at the Nuremberg trial, where the bill is to be paid, it weighs much, very much.

Shortly after this article appeared in the press, I was asked to meet General Rudenko, the Chief Russian prosecutor. By agreement, the Russians presented the evidence of the atrocities committed in the concentration camps. They had lost the largest numbers during the war, and it was felt they had that right. I met with General Rudenko in his office at the Palace of Justice with an interpreter present. He heard through the grapevine that I was an eyewitness to the medical experiments Dr. Mengele conducted in Auschwitz. He wanted details.

"When did these experiments take place?" he asked.

"In Auschwitz-Buna in 1944."

"Was Dr. Mengele present when these experiments were conducted?"

"Yes."

"Did you see him?"

"Yes, I did."

"Did he conduct the experiments?"

"Yes."

General Rudenko was the first person I could tell about the electric shock experiments Honzo and I witnessed. I thought of Diana.

The General scribbled as I talked and then asked me if I'd be willing to appear as a witness for the Russian prosecution on the subject of medical experiments. Of course, I would. I'd be keeping the promise I made in Auschwitz, to Walter and the others, the promise to bear witness. I also thought about the story angle, the reporter in me always at work. "Reporter is Witness at Nuremberg Trials."

Nothing came of it. I waited in vain for the date of my court appearance, and as the prosecution prepared to rest its case, I contacted the General and asked for an explanation. His staff was very evasive. Finally a junior staff member took me aside and told me the truth.

"It's because you're German," he told me.

"Me? German? Yes, I was born in Germany, but I'm Jewish and that's why I spent almost six years in the camps!"

"Our government's policy is not to call on any German witnesses, regardless of their religion. The one exception is Field Marshall von Paulus, who was the General in charge of the German Army at Stalingrad. There is nothing we can do to change this."

As a goodwill gesture, he handed me a copy of the official document presented by the prosecution, which unrelentingly gave the graphic details of the atrocities and horrors of Auschwitz, including the medical experiments.

One of the photos was taken by a Russian Army photographer in Auschwitz-Buna a few days after the Russians moved in. The photo showed the official count of our camp on January 18, the day we evacuated, which accurately listed the categories of prisoners, Jews, criminals, gypsies, political prisoners, homosexuals, and so forth. I had the picture enlarged and framed with my other memorabilia from the camp. Eventually, it will all become part of the permanent exhibit at the New York Holocaust Museum.

As part of my journalistic assignment, I was to interview some of the defense lawyers, to get comments and reactions to the proceedings. Dr. Stahmer, Goering's chief defense counsel, followed the reports in the German press with special interest, as did the other defense lawyers.

His assistant was a young, attractive woman in her early twenties, and I asked her to arrange an interview. Before Goering's first court appearance together, we spent the evening together working on source material for the article. It was getting late, and she asked me to walk her home. Then she invited me in to continue our conversation in her apartment, and promptly proceeded to seduce me.

I was 23 years old and a virgin. From the day I arrived in Auschwitz—the day Ruth was sent to the gas chamber—I had encountered two women. The first was poor Diana from Budapest, the beautiful victim of Mengele's brutal and vicious curiosity. The other was my farmer's wife. Sex was not something that preoccupied me. For six years, I was focussed on finding food and the need to survive.

My lady friend didn't let me down. She arranged several interviews with Dr. Stahmer. I found him to be a very able defense attorney who was fighting a lost cause. He used every legal means at his disposal to defend his client.

One afternoon, at the end of the proceedings, he took me to the sparse prison cell where Herman Goering passed his time. There was a bed, a small table which held a photo of his wife, and a chair. That was all. It was a far cry from the opulent palace where the high living Reichsmarshall threw his famous parties.

The meeting was arranged with the condition that it remain off the record. This is the first time in almost fifty years that I feel free to write about it.

I was nervous. What should I say? Should I shake hands? Ask questions? Since I couldn't write about it, why did I want to go through such a painful experience?

Goering stood up when Dr. Stahmer and I entered his cell, which was constantly under guard. "This is the young reporter," Dr. Stahmer said, motioning to me, "you asked me about."

Goering looked at me, started to reach out to shake hands and, sensing my reaction, turned away for a moment. I stood frozen.

What the hell am I doing here? How can I possibly be in the same room with this monster and carry on a conversation? How could I talk logically, unemotionally?

Mr. Goering, how does it feel to be here? What do you think of the proceedings? Are they treating you well? Should I shout at him, tell him that he was responsible for my six years in the camps? Should I blame him for my lost childhood? For the death of my parents?

I did nothing of the sort. I stood there and stared while Dr. Stahmer discussed the next day's proceedings.

Then, on an impulse, I bolted for the door and asked the MP to let me out. I couldn't take it. I couldn't remain. I had to get away. There was no discussion, not a word was exchanged, no comments or statements were made. I was there, and then I was gone. Period.

I regret the incident to this day. I regret agreeing to meet him and I regret standing there silently and then running out. It was irrational. But, as I look back at that period of adjustment in my life, I realized that I was overwhelmed by the experiences crashing in on me, by my survival and my role as eyewitness. Standing with Goering in his cell was more than I could handle.

Towards the end of the trial, on April 11, 1946, I had the opportunity to witness, and then report on, the incredible appearance of Ernst Kaltenbrunner, the former chief of internal Nazi security and one of the leading architects of "the Final Solution." He had agreed to appear in his own defense and my fellow reporters, as well as the judges and the prosecution, were eager to hear from the one individual who knew more details about the Nazi killing machine than any of the other defendants.

We were in for a surprise. Kaltenbrunner, 6'6", entered the witness stand at 10:45 in the morning, dressed in a dark blue suit, and repeated the oath in his broad Austrian dialect. He swore "to tell the truth, to hide nothing and to add nothing."

His testimony was incredible. He denied any complicity in or knowledge of the activities in the concentration camps, and went so far to say that he had been responsible for the rescue of Jewish camp inmates. He recounted how, in 1944, at the behest of Himmler, he arranged for the transfer of 1200 Jews from Theresienstadt to Switzerland.

"What was your reason for this act?" his defense counsel asked.

"To obtain favorable headlines in the American press for Himmler."

What Kaltenbrunner didn't mention was brought out in cross-examination. An American Jewish organization paid one million dollars for this "humanitarian" gesture. The prosecutor, Dr. Kaufmann, then elicited astonishing replies from the defendant.

"How many concentration camps were there?"

"To the best of my recollection, I knew of three camps. At the end of the war there were a total of twelve. In addition, there was a camp for the SS. That was all. I never created a concentration camp. That was done by Himmler."

From the trial records, the transcripts quote his words: "I never saw a gas chamber and did not even know they existed. "

"The meaning of the Auschwitz camps was not known to me. "

"I am convinced that it was only due to my intervention that the persecution of the Jews came to an end in October, 1944."

"I never knew that atrocities were committed in the concentration camps. "

"Only a handful of men, Himmler, Glueck, Pohl, etcetera, dealt with the camps. I never heard about deaths in the extermination camps."

These replies came from the man responsible for running the camps. Then, under cross-examination by Col. Amen of the American staff, Kaltenbrunner was shown a damaging document carrying his own signature. "This is not my signature!" Kaltenbrunner yelled at the unbelieving prosecutor. Even the judges showed astonishment.

It was, to me, a remarkable coincidence that Kaltenbrunner's appearance on the witness stand took place on the exact day when, one year before, we began the forced march from Berga which led to my escape.

America the Beautiful

THE NUREMBERG TRIALS ended in April, 1946. By then, I was a bona fide journalist with a solid reputation based on my work at the trials. I had a lucrative offer to run one of DANA's regional offices.

Perhaps because I was one of the few Jewish survivors who was becoming widely-known in Germany, I met people who would later play key roles in the emergence of a democratic German government. Dr. Heuss, the newspaper publisher in Heidelberg, was being mentioned as a possible future president. I also met Konrad Adenauer, who'd read my articles on the Nuremberg Trials. He told me he was pleased that someone with my background was writing for a German news agency.

Despite my satisfaction with my growing career and the acceptance I experienced in a totally new German environment, I couldn't escape feelings of discomfort and even revulsion, from living in the country of my birth. Every time I met a German, I couldn't stop asking myself where were they when I was in Auschwitz. Were they SS? Did they kill Jews? What did they do on *Kristallnacht*?

I was twenty-two years old, it was less than a year after my escape, and I often had to pinch myself to make sure the life I was living was real, that I wasn't dreaming. My world was certainly changing.

I spent a great deal of my time working with Abe Laskove, director of the Joint Distribution Committee in Germany. I knew about the "Joint," as we called it, because they helped rescue Lotte in France. I learned even more while I was working with Lt. Hutler at the DP section in Mannheim. I saw how much the Joint was doing to rehabilitate and relocate the survivors.

There were tens of thousands of survivors living in DP camps all over Germany and Austria, hoping to go to Palestine. The illegal immigration, which was later depicted in *Exodus* by Leon Uris, was in full swing. Although I had a job and didn't live in a DP camp, Abe Laskove told me that thousands of DPs would be permitted to emigrate to the United States under a special DP quota.

I had three choices. I could remain in Germany, with the almost certain assurance of a promising career in journalism. I could join the thousands of former camp inmates on their way to Palestine, who hoped to create a Jewish state—or I could go to America.

The only person I was able to talk to about my dilemma was Abe Laskove, who became my friend. I respected his opinions and valued his judgment. He filled me in on his organization's history, and that's when I first heard of the United Jewish Appeal.

Although Abe in no way influenced my eventual decision to come to the United States, he planted the seed that was to flower into my involvement in the Jewish community and eventual full-time career with UJA. The other person who steered me in that direction was Al Hutler, but I'm getting ahead of myself.

It was an agonizing decision for me to make because I was on my own. I asked for advice, but deep down I realized I couldn't really depend on anyone but myself. I eliminated the first option very quickly. A promising future and being comfortable in my mother-tongue weren't enough. I simply couldn't stay in the country that caused me so much agony and was soaked with the blood of all those dear to me.

The final decision then, was between Palestine and America.

I always admired and envied the way people lived in the United States. It was *the* power in the post-war world and I was more and more convinced it would provide greater opportunities for me. And so, in June of 1946, I was among the first Jewish DPs who boarded the U.S.S. Marine Flasher in Bremerhaven for the voyage to the United States.

I carried a small suitcase with a few personal belongings, including one item I kept from the camps—the belt I wore in Paderborn, Auschwitz and Buchenwald. It didn't fit anymore, but I kept it as a memento. Today it hangs in my office, behind my desk. Eventually it, and other items I kept from the camps and the post-war era, will be part of the exhibit in the New York Holocaust Museum.

I remember the food best. We were served delicacies I hadn't tasted since I was a child. Though the ocean tossed us around a bit, it didn't stop me from eating. There was Spam, jams, jellies, eggs and more.

Halfway across the Atlantic, JDC representatives gave us permission to send a cable to the States. I decided to send mine to Lt. Hutler in Chicago, certain he would remember me. I remember the cable.

"Lt. Albert A. Hutler
4721 Greenwood Avenue
Chicago, Illinois
*   Just wanted you to know that I am coming to America with the U.S.S. Marine Flasher. Hope to see you someday. Best regards to you and your family."*

All of us assembled on deck as the ship approached New York. We heard so much about the Statue of Liberty and were eager to see her, but our first sighting of the New World was a place called Brooklyn. Our disappointment was forgotten as soon as we saw the majestic Lady standing in the harbor with the New York skyline behind her. We fell silent, each of us wrapped in our own thoughts. What would the future bring in this strange, powerful country? Although the streets were rumored to be paved with gold, I had few illusions. I knew it wouldn't be easy to adjust to a new and strange environment, where I didn't speak the language.

The voice from the loudspeaker scattered my thoughts. "Please have your papers and identification cards ready as you proceed through immigration."

And then: "Would Ernst Michel please identify himself? You have someone waiting for you at the gate."

I was bewildered. Who knew I was arriving? I hadn't informed my relatives because I preferred to contact them after I arrived. So who was waiting for me? The mystery was solved when I reported to the official from the Joint.

"I'm Ernst Michel."

He looked at my papers.

"Okay, there are two ladies looking for you."

"Two ladies? Who are they?"

"I don't know. They asked for you."

I was escorted to two well-dressed ladies in their sixties. One asked if I was Ernst Michel.

"Yes. Are you sure you are looking for me?"

"My son told me to expect a young boy. I'm Al Hutler's mother, and this is my cousin. Al called me from Chicago and asked me to meet a young Jewish refugee who was arriving on the Marine Flasher. He also asked me to bring you to my apartment."

I stood there with my mouth open. Lt. Hutler got the cable I sent from the ship! That's what happened! How did he find out where and when I was arriving? I would never have sent the telegram if I thought he would go to the trouble of having someone greet me at the pier. I was embarrassed.

Al Hutler's mom was non-plussed, too. She was as embarrassed as I. The little boy she came to meet was a grown man. A representative of the National Refugee Service who brought me to these wonderful women stood nearby. He suggested I join the other DPs. We were being bused to one of several hotels for processing, consultation, and counseling. I wound up at the Hotel Marseille, just off Broadway.

As I was settling in for the night, there was a phone call for me. It was Lt. Hutler in Chicago, and he was welcoming me to the United States. He'd just come back from San Diego, where he was being interviewed for the top position at the Jewish Federation.

When I called him Lieutenant, he told me to call him Al. When I began to apologize for imposing on his family, he cut me off and insisted I come to Chicago and stay with his family. They had a room for me. How should I respond to this generous offer? What would I do after a few days? And where was Chicago?

In the morning I met with the social worker from the NRS. I told him about Lt. Hutler and his invitation to Chicago.

"What will happen if I stay here?" I asked.

"Well, you rest at the hotel for a few days. Then we'll help you find a job and a room. We'll help you with some financial support for a reasonable amount of time, until you can take care of yourself."

"And if I go to Chicago?"

"In that case you will be pretty much on your own. We'll give you a train ticket to Chicago and a few dollars pocket money. When you get to Chicago, contact the Jewish Federation office. They'll help you."

I phoned Al the next day to accept his invitation. I searched out my relatives in New York, an uncle and cousins who were very nice. They had left Germany just before America entered the war. They were all struggling to make a living, and there was no way I would impose on them. When I told them I was going to Chicago, I'm sure they were relieved.

My first days in New York were unforgettable. Photos and movies were one thing. Manhattan was fantastic. The traffic, the skyscrapers, the different ethnic faces from all over the world—it was almost too much. But more than all of that, the one impression that overrode the others was the one left by supermarkets. I had never seen so many shelves filled with fruit, vegetables, meat, cakes, ice cream, whatever your heart desired. Just looking made my mouth water. Could Americans understand what it meant to subsist on a piece of bread and a bowl of soup? I promised myself that I would never, ever, take anything for granted.

I carefully counted the money the social worker gave me and headed for the first restaurant I could find. It had linen tablecloths, and the tables were set with fine china. I sat down and ordered 25 cents worth of whipped cream. I had dreamed about whipped cream in the camps. To me, whipped cream was the ultimate dining experience.

"That's all you want?" The waiter looked at me incredulously.

"Yes. That's all. I've had dreams about whipped cream for years. When I was in one of those camps in Europe, all I could think about was whipped cream."

He stared at me for a moment. "You were in a concentration camp?"

"Yes."

A few minutes later, he came back with three pieces of cake, each topped with generous portions of whipped cream.

"I read about what happened to you people," he told me. "I'm Irish. My people were also persecuted, a long time ago. I know how you feel. Enjoy. No charge. It's on the house."

It was the first time I was in a restaurant since I was a child, when my parents took Lotte and me for a treat. All I could think of as I gobbled down the cake and whipped cream was that rotten potato Honzo, Felix and I had shared in the woods after our escape. It was a highlight of my brief stay in New York.

Two days later, I was in Chicago, and the Hutlers were at the train station to greet me. Al looked different in civilian clothes, but he had the same open smile and warmth I remembered from Mannheim.

I met Lee, his wife, and their two daughters, Suzie, and Frankee. They quickly made me feel at home and welcomed me as a member of their family. I felt awkward calling the Lieutenant Al and his wife by her first name, but I got used to it. The girls called me Ernie, and that's the way it's been ever since.

The Hutlers lived on Chicago's South Side. Al was an executive with the Jewish Federation in Chicago, and just before I arrived, he accepted a position as the Executive Director of the Jewish Federation in San Diego. The whole family was looking forward to the move to California and were making exciting plans about buying a house and preparing for the change in their lives. We all spent evenings talking about the future.

"Well, Ernie, now that you're beginning to get a feel for America, what do you want to do?"

Al began what I knew would be an important discussion.

"Before you answer, there are a few things you should consider. Ever since Rabbi Haeselkorn brought you to my office in

Mannheim, I've looked at you like a younger brother. We've accepted you fully and we know that you, too, feel at home with us. You're an unusual young man who's come through a horrible experience. I could never have lived through what you went through. Despite all that, you're healthy, you've got a great attitude and I have no doubt you'll be a success in America."

Lee nodded her head every once in a while and I listened carefully.

"The way I see it, these are your options. You can stay with us as long as you want. You can take a night job and go to school and we'll pay the tuition. Consider it a loan. Your English isn't bad, it's lots better than my German. After a while, we'll help you find a place to live. I can even help you find a job through the Federation. Your other option is to come with us to San Diego and we'll help get you started there. But first, decide what you would like to do."

I was overwhelmed by their warmth and generosity. They had taken me in as if it was the most natural thing to do. I visited Al in his office at the Federation and learned something about his work. I discovered he knew Abe Laskove through their common work with the DPs in Germany. Al earned his law degree and decided to go into social work in the Jewish community, and his army assignment in Germany turned out to be a natural.

Through Al I learned how funds were raised in the Jewish community, how they were spent to help the Holocaust survivors, and how they were used for the maintenance and development of Jewish institutions at home. More than once Al would say, "With your background you could make a valuable contribution to the Jewish community. But first you have to finish your education and improve your English."

During these discussions, which continued on and off for several days, I'm sure the seeds were sown for my eventual professional career in UJA-Federation. I've often felt, subconsciously, I suppose, that there must have been a reason for my survival. It would be natural for me to go into Jewish community service and contribute in some way towards Jewish continuity and survival. It would be one approach to guarantee that what happened to us in Europe would never happen again.

But first I needed a job, any job. And I needed to improve my English.

There was one bizarre encounter I will never forget. Remember my childhood buddy, Henry (Heinz) Kuhn, who found me in Al Hutler's office in Mannheim in July, 1945? He lived in Chicago, too, and I called him after I moved in with the Hutlers. He took me to his home and when I admired his brand new car, he asked me if I knew how to drive.

"Of course I know how to drive. What a question!" I retorted, despite the fact that I'd never driven an automobile in my life. I didn't think it was going to be tough.

"Do you want to take it for a ride?" he asked.

A few minutes later I was sitting in the driver's seat trying to find the starter button. Henry sat next to me. When the car started, I shifted gears. Instantly, the car careened backwards across the street, knocked over a fence, uprooted few bushes, and was suddenly intercepted by neighbor's stoop, where it stalled. The whole adventure lasted less than thirty seconds. Henry was as shocked as I was.

"I thought you knew how to drive," he glared at me.

I was too scared to say anything.

Within moments, the police hauled us into the paddy wagon and we were on our way to the local precinct house. I was so stunned and upset, I could hardly talk. Here I was, less than a week in the United States, with no driver's license and no papers, on my way to jail. I had visions of being deported.

Henry was engrossed in conversation with one of the officers and I saw him reach into his pocket and take out some bills. The driver pulled over and we were ordered out of the vehicle with a warning.

Henry and I walked back to the house, and I stood there while he apologized to his neighbor and promised to pay for all the damages.

Despite the expensive driving lesson, Henry is still one of my closest friends and has never allowed me to repay him.

The First Year of My Second Life

"A TICKET TO Port Huron, Michigan, please."

"One way or round trip?" the teller at the Greyhound station in Chicago asked.

"One way."

"You'll have an hour to change in Detroit," he said, handing me the ticket.

Three days ago, I'd never heard of the place. Now I was setting out on my own, taking responsibility for myself.

When I arrived in Port Huron earlier in the evening, I immediately looked for the *Times Herald* building. The place was practically deserted. The publisher was gone for the day, but he would be back in the morning, and there was nothing for me to do but find a place to sleep.

It was a warm August night in 1946, and I spent it sleeping on a bench at the bus station in Port Huron. I had ten dollars in my pocket, the change left from the purchase of my ticket to this little Midwestern town, population 30,000. It was located on the shores of Lake Huron, 60 miles northeast of Detroit.

I was job hunting, and so far, I'd struck out—and had been rejected by every newspaper in Chicago. I finally stood my ground at United Press, and forced my way into the Midwest Regional Bureau Chief's office. I told him I wouldn't leave until I got work. He stared at me as if I had fallen from Mars. In fractured English, I asked Mims Thomason for a job. He was the first person who took the time to listen to my story. Then, after a half hour of discussion, he suggested I apply for a job at a small town newspaper, where I could improve my English as I learned about America.

The next morning, my bones aching from a few hours of fitful napping on a bench, I washed up in the station's washroom. I looked at myself in the grimy mirror in the dim light and wondered if it really was such a good idea to show up in a strange town on the basis of a conversation with a man I barely knew. The scrap of paper in my pocket was my only security—it was a letter of reference from Thomason to Mr. Louis A. Weil, publisher of the *Port Huron Times Herald*.

I presented myself at the receptionist's desk and told her Mims Thomason had sent me to see Mr. Weil. In a few minutes, I was ushered into his office.

"What can I do for you?" Mr. Weil was a tall, distinguished man in his seventies with white hair and friendly blue eyes.

"Mims Thomason of the UP in Chicago told me I might find a job here. He gave me this letter for you," I said as I handed it to him.

Weil looked at me with some surprise, but he took it, opened the envelope and read it. I stood waiting.

"How long have you been in this country?"

"Five weeks, sir. I arrived in New York at the end of June."

"And you want to get a job on our paper?"

"Yes, sir. I want to become a reporter."

"Sit down, young man," he said in a friendly voice. "Tell me about yourself."

And so I told him my story. I told him about Germany, my life in the camps, the escape, my work at the Nuremberg Trials, and my arrival in the United States. When I was finished, he asked me questions about Germany, the war, and my family.

His reaction was quite different from that of most people I had met. I did not sense that he felt sorry for me. I tried several times to lead the conversation back to the purpose of my visit but he refused to be hurried along. An hour went by.

"Well, Ernest, that's quite a story. We read about these events, but you lived through them." He paused for a moment. "Now, about the job."

My hands were shaking and I tried to keep them under control.

"Your English isn't bad, considering the fact that you've only been here a few weeks, but it's clearly not good enough for me to hire you as a reporter."

I was waiting for the ax to fall. No job.

"And we can't afford a specialist on German affairs. But..."

I held my breath.

"... we can use a copyboy. That way you can improve your English and learn how a small town newspaper works. We'll pay you twenty-five dollars a week. It's not much, but it's a start."

I had to restrain myself from jumping out of the chair and throwing my arms around him.

"You mean I've got a job?" I couldn't believe it.

"Yes. You have a job."

I danced, more than walked out of the office. Twenty-five dollars a week. My first job in America and on a newspaper!

It didn't take long to find a place to live. Mrs. Low, the tall, white haired widow of a World War I veteran, had an upstairs room for rent for $5 a week. It included use of the refrigerator in her kitchen. She was a bit standoffish, but checked with the paper and then accepted my $3 deposit. Now I had my own place, my own bed, my own job, for the first time since 1939. I was on my way, and I was thrilled.

That evening, I strolled down Main Street, past the movie theater, the bank, the five and dime store, the corner drugstore. I was part of America.

At eight o'clock the following morning, I presented myself to the city editor. He told me my duties and introduced me to the other members of the staff. Nobody asked me any questions, and if my accent surprised them, they did not comment.

My job was easy and in time, I became familiar with the reporters, the editors, and the men in the printshop. I started out by being formal, calling people by their last names. It didn't take long, though, before we were all on a first name basis and they called me Ernie, a nickname that has become part of my very being.

For the first time since coming to the States, I was forced to speak English all day. In New York, and even in Chicago, I could always lapse into German when I found myself looking for words. Now that safety net was gone. If I couldn't think of the right word I had to find a substitute or make myself understood in some other way. It forced me to learn fast—faster than if I had stayed in New York or Chicago.

Lunchtime was my nightmare. I dreaded the moment when the reporters who had completed their morning assignments would unwrap their sandwiches and discuss some of their activities. These sessions were fascinating and stimulating to me, but I felt awkward for not eating. I couldn't afford to buy a sandwich. I needed to stretch my $5-a-week food budget, which allowed me only breakfast and a skimpy dinner. When the men invited me to join them for lunch, I decided to skip breakfast and eat lunch instead.

Those hours were an informal seminar on American life. I learned about the New York Yankees and the Detroit Tigers, about local primaries, the news from the police beat and the City Council, the Junior Chamber of Commerce. I learned about Li'l Abner, Dick Tracy and Orphan Annie. Whenever something came up that was new to me, I would ask questions, but mostly I listened. Some of the staff were veterans who had seen action in Germany, and so we had something to talk about.

They couldn't believe I chose Port Huron as my first home in America. I didn't know anyone there. I took a risk looking for a job. Mostly, they couldn't believe that I survived eleven camps. When one of them accidentally noticed the tattoo on my arm, he looked at me as if I had come from a different world.

The nicest thing about my co-workers was that they were eager for me to feel at home and went out of their way to help me in every way they could.

On the sixth day, my money ran out. The next day was payday and I received my first pay envelope. My first salary in America! It was an exhilarating moment and no compensation I received since, regardless of the amount, has ever meant quite as much to me. My net pay, after my first donation to the Internal Revenue Service, was $19.75. That evening I splurged on a steak and treated myself to a movie. I was really living!

I read each issue of the newspaper from cover to cover. In my second week, Ed Snover, the city editor, took me aside.

"Ernie, I've got an assignment for you. We have a daily feature on the paper," he continued, "called 'Events of Yesteryear.' It recalls major events of general interest—ten, twenty-five and fifty years ago, locally, nationally and internationally. So take a look at that column for the last few days, then read the papers in the morgue and let me see what you come up with."

And so I was given a chance to learn about America and its past. I always loved reading old newspapers, and I read contemporaneous accounts of the Prohibition, the Teapot Dome scandal, the fight over United States membership in the League of Nations. I read about Presidents Wilson, Hoover and the assassination of President McKinley. I read about Babe Ruth and the Four Horsemen of Notre Dame.

Local and regional events became familiar to me. I learned about the Rotary Club and who spoke there, the proposed changes in the City Charter and the local High School referendum. I became acquainted with the bond issue to build a new sewer system and many issues concerning life in Port Huron. I was enjoying myself, loving my every day.

But there were sad and very lonely moments, too. I spent most of my evenings at the library, or I went to the movies. When I came back to my little room, I'd sit there and listen to the radio.

As time went by, I made a few friends. Sometimes a reporter would invite me for dinner with his family. I accepted eagerly, not just to avoid an evening alone, but because I enjoyed the discussions with my colleagues and, realized more and more how vastly different their lives were from mine.

I specifically remember the utter bewilderment of one of the reporters when I tried to explain— I'm sure unsuccessfully—that Hitler's only reason for the extermination of 6,000,000 Jews in

Europe, including my parents, was that we were Jews. It seemed so far fetched, so beyond belief, that I knew he accepted it with some skepticism.

The fall of 1946 saw the beginning of the Cold War. With the fighting over, friction began to develop between the United States and the Soviet Union. British Prime Minister Winston Churchill delivered his famous speech about the "Iron Curtain" descending on Eastern Europe.

I knew and lived with many Russian POWs in the camps, and they were often treated as badly as the Jews. I found it difficult to understand why—only a year after Hitler's defeat by the Allied Forces and great sacrifice on the part of the Russians—there would now be a serious rift between the former Allies.

After giving it some thought, I sat down and wrote about the Russians I had known, about their suffering during the war. I must admit, today, that I was a bit naive, but I felt strongly about the subject and wanted to express my point of view.

On the spur of the moment, convinced that I had written a masterpiece, I sent it with a brief note to Mr. Weil. When I didn't receive an acknowledgment, I assumed it had found its way into the waste basket.

When I opened the Sunday paper, I was stunned. Mr. Weil ran a weekly column entitled, 'Between You and Me.' That week he described how a young man came to Port Huron a few weeks ago, looking for a job on the paper.

It gave some of my background and then—I couldn't believe my eyes—he quoted my Russian piece word for word, even to the point of leaving in all the mistakes I had made.

My friends congratulated me when I came to work on Monday, and I was proud of my first published piece.

The next day, a student from the local junior college called.

"Mr. Michel, I'm president of the Foreign Relations Club at Port Huron Junior College. My friends and I read about you in the *Times Herald*. We had no idea that someone with your background lived in Port Huron."

We chatted a bit and then he asked me if I would speak about some of my experiences at the next meeting of the Foreign Relations Club.

I protested. "But, my English isn't good enough to speak at a college."

"We only have about a dozen members," he told me. "It's no big deal. Just tell us a bit about yourself, your experiences during the war and the Nuremberg Trials. Then we'll ask questions. It's all very informal."

I let him talk me into it and for days I prepared notes, rehearsing for the meeting.

If I was stunned when the paper published my article, you can imagine how shocked I was when I was greeted by an auditorium full of people, standing room only. The young student who invited me apologized. In addition to the brief announcement in the *Times Herald*, the campus newspaper ran announcements which advertised the talk as: 'From the gas chambers in Auschwitz to the Nuremberg Trials—An Eyewitness Report!'

"The demand was so great, we needed to change the venue." He did not seem at all unhappy.

I was petrified. I didn't know what to say or to do. My first inclination was to run like hell for the exit. I hoped for an earthquake, but they never happened in Port Huron. There was not much hope for that. As I literally shook in my boots, I followed the young student into the packed auditorium.

I don't remember how I got to the microphone.

I was facing hundreds of young Americans. Youth was the only thing we had in common. They grew up in normal surroundings, protected by their parents, free to enjoy their lives, their freedom and their education. At 14, I'd been thrown out of school, subjected to hatred and discrimination. While those guys worried about making the cut on the football team and who they would date at the prom, I was taking care of Walter in Buna, watching Ruth shuffling down the line toward the gas chamber, seeing Diana's torment. While they hung out at the soda shoppe, I was scrounging for potatoes and sharing one thin blanket with two inmates who never made it. While they studied biology, I witnessed Mengele's murderous experiments.

True, many of these students were war veterans, had experienced hardships and faced death, but at least they had weapons to fight back with and knew how to defend themselves. All we could do was stand by helplessly, surrounded by electrically charged barbed wire and SS guards with machine guns, watching the systematic slaughter of people all around us.

Undoubtedly, these thoughts spilled over in my remarks. I discarded my notes and talked about what happened to me as a young boy growing up in Germany, what it felt like being kicked out of school because I was Jewish. I talked of the slow, methodical enslavement of millions of people in Europe, of life in the camps, of the constant hope of survival which died a thousand times, and how liberation finally came to the few who managed somehow to stay alive.

My words tumbled in an uncontrollable stream. Even in my poor English, it became a catharsis. I lost all track of time. In the middle of a sentence, I stopped. My throat was dry. I couldn't go on.

There were no questions, no applause. The students filed out quietly. I was totally spent. The student who had invited me came over to shake my hand, looked at me, didn't say a word and left.

I was sure I laid an egg.

The next afternoon Mr. Weil asked me to come to his office. It was the first time I was in his office since the day he gave me the job. I wondered if he was going to fire me.

"I heard you gave quite a speech last night," he greeted me.

I stood there silently.

"Well, Ernie. It must have been quite a talk because I had a number of calls from parents of students who heard you.

"Now, what do you know about the Rotary Club?"

What did I know? After reading through old newspapers for days, I knew about the Rotary Club and also about the Lions, the Exchange and a number of other clubs, as well.

"I want to invite you to come as my guest and talk to our members. I want you to tell them about some of your experiences. But I have one request, Ernie—no more than 25 minutes. Not like last night." He smiled.

"How long did I speak?"

"More than an hour and a half!"

When Mr. Weil introduced me at the following week's Rotary Club meeting, I was as proud as I had ever been in my life. He described me as "the newest member of the *Port Huron Times Herald* staff who, despite his young age, has seen more of life than most of us do in a lifetime."

Little did I realize then that I was rehearsing for an even more important job—a job that would fulfill all the promises I made to those who perished in the camps.

XVII
Learning America

BEFORE VERY LONG, my reputation as a guest speaker in Port Huron began to spread. Pretty soon, I was receiving a steady stream of invitations to speak.

One request rather baffled me. A lady phoned and introduced herself as a member of the Daughters of the American Revolution. She invited me to address their monthly tea, but I had never heard of them and was reluctant to accept. After all, I had been in the country only a short time and wanted nothing to do with revolutionaries. Later, the full significance of the request hit me. I accepted.

A few months later, Mr. Weil spoke to me about my work, my new life, and about the progress I made since I first arrived. Then he came to the point.

"Ernie, how would you like to write a daily column for the paper?"

I floated out of Weil's office on Cloud Nine. My daily column was called "My New Home." I wrote about anything that struck me as unusual about America in general, and Port Huron in particular. I also received a raise. I was more thrilled with the recognition I was getting. Now I was a legitimate newspaperman.

And so began another new phase in my life. I wrote about all the things that happened to me as a newcomer. Some incidents were humorous, others serious, but all pointed to the vast differences between life in a free country and my life in Europe. Fan mail arrived at the paper, most of it sympathetic and encouraging, but there was also a sprinkling of poison pen letters—all of them unsigned.

I was introduced to that strange phenomenon of American life, the blind date. The reporter on the paper who initiated me into this experience explained, in reply to my startled inquiry, that the young lady in question was perfectly able to see. He gave me some pointers as to what to do and what not to do, but omitted one vital factor which to him was so obvious, he never mentioned it to me. I'd never dated anyone before...and I knew nothing about dating etiquette.

I picked her up at the appointed hour, and we decided to see a movie. At the box office I bought a ticket for myself and waited for her to do the same. She just stood there, until I finally realized something wasn't quite right, much to the amusement of the cashier and doorman. It took me a while to get it. I was supposed to pay for both of us! Embarrassment is a good teacher. I chalked it up as another lesson in the customs and mores of America.

It took a few weeks, but soon, anyone who needed a speaker knew where to find me. After my column appeared for a few weeks, a minister from one of the largest churches in town invited me to address his congregation at the Sunday morning service. I asked him whether he really wanted me, a Jew, to speak in his church. He assured me that he and his parishioners were eager to hear what I had to say. He reminded me that others, in addition to the Jews, also suffered in the camps.

That's how, one Sunday morning, I found myself standing in the pulpit of the First Methodist Church in Port Huron, speaking to the congregation about the true meaning of religious freedom. I told the listeners how miserable I was as a child because I was born a Jew and was persecuted for it. I tried to describe a world that accepted hatred for and discrimination against Jews.

I explained that as Jews we were prohibited from carrying on normal relationships with persons of different faiths, that we had experienced savage hatred directed against us by non-Jews, and how that, in turn, isolated us. I tried to explain how drastically and dramatically my attitude had changed in the few months since I came to Port Huron.

I stressed that I was Jewish, but it seemed not to matter to anyone, except me. Being Jewish validated my experiences, and people wanted to hear about them. I never understood the meaning of religious tolerance and the real meaning of American democracy—its goal of equality for all people—as forcefully as I did in those moments I spent standing in the pulpit of that church.

The most indelible memory I have of my stay in Port Huron took place that summer. Once again, I was summoned to Mr. Weil's office, this time to meet the principal of the Port Huron High School. After complimenting me on my column, he looked me in the eye and said: "Mr. Michel, on behalf of the faculty and members of the student body of Port Huron High School, I have the pleasure to invite you to deliver the commencement address at the graduation exercises of the senior class of 1946."

I didn't know what to say and looked from the principal to Mr. Weil. He just stood there and smiled. I was very moved and delighted to accept.

On graduation day, I put on my new suit and went to the high school auditorium. I saw many of my colleagues and friends at the *Times Herald*—some were parents of graduating children—but others came to hear me speak. It was the first ceremony of this kind that I had ever witnessed. I was tremendously impressed with the pomp and circumstance, the choir, the procession, the dignity of the occasion, the presentation of the scholarships, the valedictorian address—everything that makes this such a meaningful event.

I sat on the platform between the high school principal and a city official and watched the students slowly march down the aisle to receive their diplomas. And as I sat there, I thought about my own parents who were denied the happiness of seeing their children grow up.

The points I made during my address were designed to impress the students with the blessings of freedom they were privileged to enjoy. I tried to explain how the denial of these freedoms meant denial of life itself. I explained that millions of people in many parts of the world live under repressive and totalitarian regimes and do not know what it means to live in a democracy.

"Don't ever take these freedoms for granted," I told them. "Be aware what these freedoms mean. Enjoy them, but at the same time cherish them and work for them as part of the responsibility you carry as Americans and as free men and women."

I was accepted and made to feel completely at home in a community where only a few short months before I arrived as a stranger, unknown and unfamiliar with the fabric of American society. Port Huron had, in the real sense of the word, become my hometown. I firmly believe that the luckiest break of my new life was the privilege of spending my first year in this small and friendly mid-western city. I learned the meaning of living as a free man.

As time passed, I joined the Junior Chamber of Commerce. My social life was active and I made a number of friends. My financial situation, too, was improved. My salary was substantially higher than when I had started as a copy boy. Although I never asked for any compensation for my speaking engagements, many clubs and organizations added an honorarium to the customary letter of thanks. I owned three suits, moved to my own small apartment and contemplated buying a car. My English had vastly improved and I had begun to think in English, not in German.

I was an avid radio fan, and one day, in response to a promotion by a shaving cream company, I decided to enter a contest called "My Closest Shave." I wrote about my escape, and mailed it in. I realized that there must have been thousands of entries, and my story had a small chance of winning. After a few weeks, the advertising agency sent me a notice suggesting I listen to the radio at a certain hour, on a certain evening, when the winners would be announced.

That evening, I was glued the radio as the announcer read the winning entry. I don't remember the story, but I remember the first prize was a trip for two to Hawaii.

Then they announced the second prize winner. I could hardly believe my ears when the announcer said, "Second prize in the contest goes to Ernest W. Michel of Port Huron, Michigan" and read my story on the air. I had won a new car. It was better than Hawaii, because I would have had no one to take with me. A few weeks later, I received the sponsor's official letter, telling me to pick up my car at the local dealer, that I could choose the color but that I had to pay for all the extras and would be liable for any taxes. I ordered a tan 4-door Ford V8.

Following one of my speeches in one of the Michigan communities, a man came to talk to me and introduced himself as the chairman of the local United Jewish Appeal campaign.

"Mr. Michel," he said, "our annual United Jewish Appeal drive is being held this evening. It would be a privilege if you would stay over and speak to us about some of the things you talked about during your address this noon. I know it would have a profound effect on all those coming to our meeting."

I accepted. After the meeting the professional representative of the organization asked me whether I'd be willing to address some other functions of the organization in the area and maybe even in other parts of the United States. He felt that, with my background, I would make an excellent addition to their roster of speakers.

I was willing, but I told him that it would depend on whether or not Mr. Weil would allow me leave of absence. The next day Mr. Weil and I discussed the offer. He readily agreed, but added one condition.

"I have no problem with your accepting these invitations as long as you continue to write your daily column. You will have some interesting experiences traveling around this country, experiences our readers will want to hear about. They enjoy your column and look forward to reading it."

The national office of the United Jewish Appeal in New York called to tell me "We'd like you to come to New York to discuss it. Could you be here next Monday?"

Thus began my new career. One invitation followed another. I went to Texas, to Louisiana, to the northwest and eventually to California.

I wired my column to the newsroom from wherever I was, and it was printed the following day. I described my travels and my experiences. One day I even sent in a column from jail—I had car trouble, no motels were available, and the local sheriff allowed me to spend the night in his hoosegow as a gesture of his hospitality.

I was in Port Huron for more than a year and I felt the time had come to move on. It was a difficult decision to make and I wrestled with it long and hard. I was dating a young Irish girl. Her family was very nice to me. However, I knew my religion was an issue. It was another reason I felt it was time to move on.

My car was ready, and I took it as a sign from Providence. Mr. Weil, one of the finest and most understanding bosses anyone could ever wish to work for, wholeheartedly approved of my decision. He regretted my departure, but he understood and encouraged me to get on with my life. The time had come for me to say goodbye to "my hometown."

The last week was a difficult one. As I wrote my final column, I felt sadness and a genuine sense of gratitude towards the people of Port Huron. They made me feel as if I belonged. I wrote:

> "This will be the last column of 'My New Home.'
>
> I wanted you—the American people—to see through the eyes of a newcomer, what a great place this country is and how everyone should appreciate that he can live in this country. I did not just want to tell you some stories or to entertain you—my boss would not have allowed the space for that anyway—but I wanted to show to you in little examples how other people in other parts of the world used to live and still do. I wanted to tell you how I hoped for a chance to live again and how I found it.
>
> And more than all, I wanted to show to you how much I appreciate that I was given the opportunity to start life all over again in this country.
>
> Fourteen months of life in America have made a new human being out of me. I have been given a new lease on life. The horrible experiences of six years in concentration camps in Europe are fading away. Sometimes I don't believe that they were true. It seems like a terrible dream to me.

In three years and ten months I will be an American.
I will wait and work for that day when I really can call
it MY HOME."

It wasn't easy to say good-bye to my colleagues at the *Times
Herald*, and to the friends I made in Port Huron. At the farewell
luncheon, I read genuine regret in their eyes about my decision to
leave, and I felt like I was leaving home. Mr. Weil gave me a
farewell gift, a token of respect and friendship from him and my
colleagues, which I have always treasured. Then, slowly, with tears
in my eyes, I walked down the stairs of the newspaper for the last
time.

A year before I had ascended these steps with fear and trepidation wondering if my decision to look for a job in an unknown
town was foolish. I knew I couldn't have had a finer welcome to
America.

I left Port Huron in my new car, with all of my belongings
packed in the trunk. I knew that the decision had been the right
one. As I passed down Main Street for the last time, I remembered
distinctly the fear and the anxiety with which I looked at it from
the Greyhound bus the evening I arrived. The buildings and stores
were familiar to me now and so were many of the people.

It was at that moment that I fully recognized how much I had
changed during that first year. I was no longer isolated. I shed the
feelings of insecurity that haunted from my childhood, whenever I
found myself in a non-Jewish society. The people of Port Huron
offered me a home in the truest sense of the word. I will always be
indebted to that town.

XVIII

The Wild West

I FOUND ONE OF my childhood friends in America. Her name was Alice, and she was married and lived in Detroit. She was amazed I had survived. When I lived in Port Huron, I visited her and her husband often, and when I left Port Huron, I moved in with her parents and spent six months in a mundane job for a department store.

I was attracted to the wild, wild west. I spent the summer of 1946 hitchhiking to Colorado, where I spent a few weeks in the German Student's program at Colorado College. I didn't feel comfortable in Detroit, so I thought about going west, about following the pioneers. I packed up the Ford, and cruised Route 66 to California.

I was doing a lot of public speaking for UJA all over America, and I derived a great deal of satisfaction from it. I easily identified with the organization's major objectives, having been a recipient of its help when I first arrived in America. I remembered my talks with Al Hutler. Out of these talks I developed my eventual decision to serve the Jewish community in a professional capacity. I attended the UJA's national conferences, which were held in Atlantic City, and met many of the leaders and supporters.

Times were changing. The DP camps were closing and the survivors were being resettled in different countries around the world. Many were being smuggled into Palestine, where they and others who came before them were attempting to found a homeland. It was a critical time in Jewish history, and I felt a part of it.

The national UJA Chairman was Henry Morgenthau Jr., President Roosevelt's former Secretary of the Treasury. He was the only one of FDR's inner circle who, during the war, tried to call attention to the plight of the Jews of Europe.

I was there when UJA launched its first $100,000,000 campaign. No one believed the goal would be reached. I met William Rosenwald, one of the giants of American Jewry, whose family was the first to contribute the unheard of sum of one million dollars. I didn't know that one day I would work closely with him. When I attended these conferences, I saw an outpouring of love, devotion and determination: to help the survivors and send them on their way to Palestine, to the United States or to wherever they could emigrate.

We listened to the words of Ben Gurion, Golda Meir, Eliezer Kaplan, and Chaim Weizmann, and they inspired us to continue in our work. I met some of them personally. They became the architects of the first Jewish state to exist in 2,000 years. I was there when they assumed the mantle of power.

My friend, Al Hutler, had settled into his job as Executive Director of the San Diego Jewish Federation. I spoke with him about my plans. I expressed my belief that my lack of formal education would stand in my way. All the UJA professionals I met were born in America and had college degrees.

"Nonsense, Ernie." Al countered, "you have something to contribute that nobody else in this field has—you lived it. You symbolize the work in which we're involved. People respect and listen to you."

On November 29, 1947, I was alone in a hotel room in Colorado Springs when the vote to partition was called at the U.N. I listened to the historic roll call of nations which comprised the UN membership. They began with Australia's 'Yes' and concluded with Yemen's 'No'. The final vote was 33 for, 13 against, 10 abstentions and 1 absent. Ben Gurion's voice, strong with emotion was transmitted by shortwave radio from Jerusalem: "The name of the State shall be Israel!"

It was only two years after Auschwitz was liberated. What a miracle! Jews had created an independent state, but I also realized that my friends who survived the camps and settled in Palestine, people like Piese, Onny and Lotte were about to be caught in another war and might be killed. It was incomprehensible.

Israel was going to need all the financial help it could get. On May 13, the day the U.N. resolution took effect, the Arab nations invaded the new state and Israel fought for its life.

That was just about the time I received a call from UJA. At the suggestion of Al Hutler, I was offered a temporary job. I accepted and was assigned to their West Coast office.

I drove my trusty Ford to Los Angeles, taking with me the few thousand dollars I'd saved from my Port Huron job and the honoraria I received for my speeches.

Before I started at the UJA, I wanted to invest my money and answered an ad in the local paper. Soon I was a co-editor of a publishing company that supposedly had a book and film deal with James Cagney. Two short weeks later I was out of a job and out of money. Hooray for Hollywood. That's when the UJA asked me to take on a 3-month temporary job.

My first assignment was canvassing the Western states: Utah, Idaho, Montana, and Oregon. My salary was $90 a week, plus expenses: $8 a night for lodging; $1.25 for breakfast, $1.75 for lunch, and $2.50 for dinner. They gave me a plane ticket, a list of cities which were now my responsibility, and the names of the key contacts in each town. I was also handed a batch of report forms which I had to submit after every visit. That was just about all the training I received.

My first stop was Ogden, Utah, a small town, about an hour by bus from Salt Lake City. My first contact was Ralph Benowitz of Benowitz's Men's Store. After checking into the small local hotel, I went to see him.

"Hello, I am Ernest Michel," I introduced myself, "the field representative of the UJA."

That was the beginning of my 42 years with the UJA.

Ralph Benowitz was a most responsive and caring individual. He invited me to his home for dinner, and I told him a bit about my background. He and his family couldn't hear enough. I was the first Holocaust survivor they'd met. Together, we made plans for the UJA campaign in Ogden, and set a date for a meeting to which all the Jewish families in town would be invited. I prepared a letter of invitation and Ralph agreed to follow it up with phone calls or personal contacts.

I told him that in view of the urgent need to raise funds for the new Israel and the refugees, it was necessary for him to personally lead off the meeting with a generous contribution of his own.

And so it went. From town to town. Ogden, Utah. Pocatello, Idaho, Idaho Falls, and then Butte, Montana, Billings, Bozeman. I headed for Wyoming next. When I was a kid in Germany I voraciously read all the adventure stories of Karl May, stories that were set in the Wild American West. But what I saw was so different. There were no cowboys and Indians. The small towns I visited were community-oriented, and the Jewish people I met were retailers who lived in the town centers. Their grandfathers had settled down in the days when the pioneers were heading for California and the Gold Rush. They stayed and became merchants. They opened small synagogues and raised their families. Now their children were hungry for Jewish news.

I loved my job. It fit me like a glove. I met some of the nicest people, and they responded generously to my requests. Evenings, I was usually invited to the home of one of the community leaders. Al Hutler was right. My lack of education didn't affect my work at all.

The people I met were anxious to hear about Israel. Because I attended the conferences, I could talk first hand about Ben Gurion and the other Israeli leaders I had met. I could tell them about the historic developments in Israel, and the progress of the War of Independence. And I could tell them about how other Jewish communities in America responded to our plea. It was an exciting time to be Jewish.

Most of the people I met had spent their lives in these small western towns. They maintained their Jewish identity and knew everyone worth knowing. They owned the local dry goods store, the haberdasher, the jewelry shop. They knew the local, county and state politicians. They knew how to make things happen.

In 1949, I decided to organize a statewide UJA conference in Butte, Montana, with the Governor and Lieutenant Governor participating. They were most agreeable, and they gave the whole campaign impetus and enthusiasm. The results showed it. I proudly filed my regular report, and received a commendation and congratulations from my boss. It felt great!

I fell in love with the space and grandeur of the west—Yellowstone Park, Old Faithful, the wide open spaces of Montana. Sometimes I pinched myself to make sure all those things were really happening. I walked down the street and enjoyed the simple feeling of being free. I was proud of being Jewish and I was no longer afraid. There was nobody with a whip or a gun behind me. I wasn't hungry. I could go into any store and buy what I wanted. I was free, free, free and I was doing something of importance. My major theme, the one I often spoke of, was the difference between my past and present. I sensed that those listening understood what I was trying to say, and it gave me a real sense of security.

By bus, by train, and by plane, I covered one town after another.

In one of the smaller towns, after the fundraising meeting was over, the chairman took me aside. "I want to ask you something," he said in a confidential tone. "We've approached just about every Jewish family in town—except one."

"Which one? I thought we had everyone at the meeting?"

"No. One wasn't here. She wasn't invited."

"Not invited? Why not?"

In confidential tones, he informed me that a Jewish woman in town owned a "pardon me—house of ill repute!"

"A whorehouse? A Jewish madam?"

"Yes. For obvious reasons, none of us in town can be seen going into her place. I thought you might give it a try."

He looked at me expectantly. Good thing I was young and single.

"Sure. Why not? What have I got to lose?"

Bright and early the following morning, I sauntered over to the establishment and rang the bell. It was located in the center of Main Street. It appeared to be a nicely-kept conventional-looking home. Someone peered through a peephole, and I announced that I had business with the lady of the house, using her legitimate name. Murmured whispers ssh'd behind the door. Then it opened and I was allowed to enter.

I found myself in a big living room with overstuffed furniture and lots of clocks. After a few minutes, the lady walked in. She was in her fifties, well-dressed, and spoke with a slight accent I recognized as Eastern European. She eyed me suspiciously.

"Why do you want to see me?"

"I'm here because, like me, you are a Jew. And, like you, I too have come from Europe."

Her mouth dropped, and so did her tough demeanor.

"You came to see me because I'm Jewish? How did you know that?"

I told her that the local UJA chairman gave me her name, and that I was in town to organize the local campaign. Then I told her about myself.

"So, you're here to ask me for money for UJA?"

"Yes. In view of what is happening in Israel, every Jew should have an opportunity to play a part in our history."

She smiled.

"I can't believe it! This is the first time this has ever happened to me. Me, being asked to give to the UJA!"

She asked me to wait. In a few minutes she returned with an envelope stuffed with five, ten and twenty dollar bills. When I counted it, I realized it was as much as the rest of the town had raised together.

As I left, she called after me, "Any time you come back, it's on the house!"

It's a pity they eventually outlawed prostitution in that county. UJA lost a generous contributor.

A Voice Sings for its Life

XIX

UJA KEPT ME BUSY with speaking engagements on the West Coast, but I'd never given up my dream of being a journalist, so I often spent time between trips at the UJA Federation office in Los Angeles. There I volunteered my services as a 'newspaperman' to the Federation monthly. It gave me a chance to meet other people my age and develop a sense of community.

"Here's a story made for you" my editor said, pointing to an article from the *Los Angeles Times* on his paper-strewn desk. It announced the appearance of a young tenor by the name of Miklos Gafni, who was making his Los Angeles debut at the Philharmonic Auditorium.

"What makes you think this is a story for me?" I asked him.

"Good question, Ernie." He turned towards me and looked me straight in the eye.

"It could be a great story but I'll let you decide. You might not want to do it."

I was intrigued.

"Come on, give. What's the story about?"

"Did you read the whole story in the *Times*?" He emphasized the whole.

I admitted I hadn't, although I had glanced at it—barely.

"Well, listen to this!" and he read me a paragraph. "'What makes Mr. Gafni's meteoric rise so astonishing is the fact that he barely survived the war, having spent time in a German concentration camp!'

"It could make an interesting feature, one camp survivor interviewing another survivor who has become an internationally acclaimed tenor. Take it from a personal angle, his background, how he survived—you know what I mean, human interest!"

I quickly found out where Gafni was staying, then I telephoned him for an appointment. He was receptive and we arranged to meet the following morning in his suite at the Biltmore Hotel. He spoke English well, but with a heavy Hungarian accent.

I spent the rest of the afternoon doing research on him. There wasn't much. He was discovered in Europe by an American impresario, and had come to America just a few weeks ago. At his Carnegie Hall debut, he was critically acclaimed as 'a great find' and "the Hungarian Caruso." *Life* magazine devoted three pages to the young singer and mentioned that he had been an inmate in a Nazi concentration camp.

My curiosity was piqued. If he was as good as the critics said he was, Miklos Gafni was on the verge of a great career.

The next morning, promptly at the appointed hour, I knocked on his door. I recognized Gafni from the pictures in *Life* magazine, but he was even heavier than he seemed in the photos. He weighed at least 250 pounds.

"Come in," he said pleasantly as we shook hands. He seemed hesitant for a moment, looked at me with a quizzical expression and asked, "Haven't we met before? You look vaguely familiar."

"I don't think so." Nothing about him seemed familiar.

He smiled, "Well, I must have made a mistake. You probably look like someone I know."

I began by asking him about his background. He told me he was born in Hungary and lost his family during the Holocaust. He spent the war years in German concentration camps, and returned to Hungary after his liberation.

"Just a moment, Mr. Gafni, not so fast." I interrupted him. "This is one part of your story that will be of particular interest to our readers. I am referring to the time you spent in a German concentration camp. Incidentally," I added, "I too, was in a concentration camp."

"How is that possible? You are American!"

"Now yes, almost, anyway, but not then. I was born in Germany and was sent to the camps by the Nazis shortly after the beginning of the war," I replied.

"You were! But you have almost no accent!" he exclaimed and added: "Which camps were you in?"

It was a strange interview. He was asking me the questions, instead of the other way 'round. I named a few of the camps I was in. Then, in an effort to get the ball back, I put the same question to him.

"Auschwitz, Mauthausen," he replied.

"What year did you get to Auschwitz?" I continued.

"Nineteen forty-four."

"Nineteen forty-four! I was there the same year. I knew many Hungarians in Auschwitz-Buna, one of whom I remember particularly. His name was Miklos and he was..."

What followed then happened so fast that I don't remember the details. He probably recognized me a split second before I recognized him.

He jumped from his chair, and grabbed me by the shoulders:

"I knew I'd seen you some place before! Auschwitz-Buna! The hospital!"

I stared at him, incredulous, my mouth wide open.

This wasn't possible.

"Miklos! Miklos Weinstock! Buna! The soup!"

Too excited for words, tears running down our faces, we fell into each others arms.

We couldn't speak. We just held each other, and shook our heads in disbelief.

Miklos Gafni was Miklos Weinstock, the young, emaciated camp inmate I met in Auschwitz-Buna in 1944. At the time he was one of the Muselman, a young man at the end of his rope, ready to run into the electrically charged barbed wire and end it all.

No wonder we didn't immediately recognize each other. When I first met Miklos, our heads were shaved, we were garbed in threadbare and faded prison uniforms and he didn't weigh more than 90 pounds.

I remembered him well.

He first came to my attention when he was admitted to the KB, the prisoner hospital, for a slight foot injury. After only three months in the camp, the hunger, brutality and the generally harsh treatment were already beginning to show. He had arrived with a Hungarian transport and was the only one left of his family. His parents, sister and younger brother were gassed immediately upon arrival. He was all alone.

He was my age and I liked him, so I helped him with some extra food and a few days rest to give him a chance to regain some of his strength.

He left the hospital in a much better state, and with the determination to hold on. He asked if he could see me once in awhile, even if it was from the other side of the wire fence which separated the main camp from the KB. Of course he could.

He regularly came to the gate and I often smuggled over a piece of bread or an extra bowl of soup. We became friends, and I got to know him fairly well. We'd fantasize about life after the camp and of a future we hardly believed in. He told me he wanted to be a singer but realized the chances were very slim.

"I know it doesn't make sense," he said, "but I won't let them kill my dream."

A few months went by. I hadn't seen Miklos for a while when he finally appeared at the gate one night.

He looked awful and sounded worse. The left side of his face was swollen.

"An SS man hit me with a rifle," he said matter of factly. "I can't take it much longer. In my bunk, two men are dying. I'm hungry all the time and I know I can't last much longer."

I looked at him and I knew he was right. He had lost weight again. His cheekbones were sticking out and he had the dull look of a Muselman.

I always remembered our last conversation. We were two young men, both of us just 20 years old, and we were debating the right of a human being to take his own life. We were two young men without youth, with no knowledge of what youth could be like. We hadn't really lived, and we were talking about suicide.

I tried to convince Miklos not to give in but I couldn't do it convincingly. I saw he was at the breaking point.

"Come back tomorrow," I told him as he was ready to go back to his barracks. "I'll have something for you. Don't give up!"

He nodded. "I'll be here."

He didn't come the next night or the one after that. I felt I would not see him again.

"They were all shipped to Birkenau," I was told when I asked about Miklos' whereabouts.

That was that. It happened every day. There was only one destination for a transfer to Birkenau—the chimneys.

I slowly walked back to my barracks, thinking of Miklos, a young man who dreamed of singing and would never get the chance.

Now it all came back to me as I looked into Miklos Weinstock-Gafni's sparkling eyes. He was a man who was obviously enjoying life and was on the verge of a great future.

"So what happened? How did you survive? I looked for you and was told that you were shipped to Birkenau."

He shook his head and sat down.

"It's a strange story. Sometimes I still don't believe it really happened. You remember that evening when I saw you at the fence at the hospital, when I was so low I wanted to kill myself?"

I nodded, remembering only too well.

"When I returned to my barracks that evening," he continued, "I felt that I had reached the end. Nothing mattered anymore. When our *Kommando* lined up for work the next morning, an SS officer pulled us aside; while the others went to work in the factory we remained standing.

"After a while, the SS announced that we would be transferred. We knew what that meant. Transfer! The end! The furnaces.

"Through the gate we went to what all of us knew would be our final destination. I was resigned. Better now than later.

"After a few minutes of marching, we were ordered to sing. 'Come on! Sing! You know how!' I was dumbfounded. Here we were, on our way to the gas, and he wanted us to sing. Most of us were so weak, we had trouble walking. And they expected us to break out in song!

"The German officer raised his gun, 'Sing, I said.'

"I don't know what made me do it, probably that instinct for survival. I started to sing an old Hungarian folk song my mother taught me when I was a little boy. The scene was incredible. The SS officer walking on our left with his gun cocked and pointed at us, ready to shoot. Guards were all around us. The group, dirty, hungry, resigned to their fate, marched in silence, heads bent. And there I was, belting out a song as loudly as I could."

Miklos rose from his chair and stood near the window, looking out into the clear California sky, as if he could see the group marching down that lonely road in Poland, just four years ago.

"I didn't think I had that much strength left," he continued after a moment. "But for the last time, I wanted to hear my own voice. In the meantime, the *Kommando* came to a halt. I don't know whether the SS ordered us to stop or if it was spontaneous. I remember the SS officer as he stood before me with a perplexed expression on his face as he stared at me. At last, I finished the song. The silence was overwhelming. Nobody said a word. We just stood there.

"'Another one!' the Nazi ordered.

"'What do you want me to sing?' I asked.

"'Anything!'

"So I sang a popular hit I remembered. Then another. The officer pulled me out of the line and, with the others grouped around me like a choir, I sang for my life. After the third song, I told him that I could not go on. I had no strength left. He stared at me again, as if speculating what to do. Then he turned and whispered something to the other guards.

"'You stay here!' he said to me. 'The rest of you, fall back in formation. About face! Forward. March!'

"There was no chance for me to say anything to them. They fell back in formation, dragging their tired feet along the dirty road, and I watched them disappear in the distance on their way to death."

We both fell silent, caught in our memories of a time not so long ago.

"What happened then?" I asked. Miklos shook himself like coming out of a bad dream and continued the story.

"The officer ordered me to follow him. We must have been quite a sight, the elegant SS officer leading the way and me dragging myself a few feet behind him. We took a side road to the SS barracks. Not a word was spoken. Then: 'Stay here! This may be the luckiest day of your life!' And he left.

"He returned accompanied by a high-ranking SS officer, who took one look at me, turned to the SS underling and shouted as he pointed at me with disdain: 'You tell me that thing has a voice?' The junior officer ordered me to sing.

"It may well have been the strangest audition in history. I was a Jewish prisoner, weighing some 90 pounds, half-starved, dirty, weakened beyond endurance, facing two immaculately dressed Nazi officers and singing a lullaby.

"With the last ounce of my energy I sang one more song. Strange lights danced before my eyes. My throat was parched and I shook all over. I must have collapsed, because the next thing I remember was coming to consciousness lying on a cot.

"I looked around. On a table beside me was the loveliest sight imaginable—two large sandwiches and a large glass of milk. I closed my eyes and opened them again, to make sure I wasn't hallucinating. Then I wolfed down the food. It was my first solid food since I arrived in Auschwitz. Nothing before or since has ever tasted so good.

"I spent the rest of the day in the room, with the exception of a brief walk to the washroom, where I was told to shower and change my dirty ill-fitting prison uniform for a new one. In the evening I was given another delicious meal and told to get ready to sing.

"I was taken into the SS mess hall where the guards were having their meal. While they ate, I sang.

"That's how I saved my life. Evenings, at noon, even in the middle of the night, whenever it struck the fancy of one of the guards to hear some music, I had to perform. Songs, arias, bal-

lads—anything I remembered. The SS treated me well. I received
ample food to slowly gain back some strength. I also did odd jobs
around the barracks, but mostly they wanted me to sing. As far as I
know I was the only prisoner in the SS barracks.

"This lasted until Auschwitz was evacuated in January, 1945. In
the confusion of that day, when everyone was packing to leave, I
managed to slip out and join the prisoner transport. Nobody asked
questions. After three days and nights of marching in the bitter
cold winter of 1945, we reached a railway station where we
boarded open cattle cars and, after a grueling ride, we arrived at
Mauthausen. We all knew that the war would soon be over. It was
simply a matter of holding on a while longer. A few weeks later, in
May, 1945, our camp was liberated by American troops.

"I made my way back to Hungary, determined to become a
singer. Having survived because of my voice, I knew I wanted to
make this my life's work. Shortly before my first concert, my manager suggested changing my name from Weinstock to Gafni, and
that's how I began my career. At one concert in Hungary, an
American impresario came to the dressing room and offered me a
tour of the United States. The rest you know."

Later that evening, I sat in the first row orchestra in the Los
Angeles Philharmonic Auditorium, and as I listened to the great
voice of Miklos Gafni, I understood why even a German SS officer
would be moved to spare his life.

Miki and I became good friends. I followed his career, which
took him to concert halls and auditoriums all over the planet. His
voice delighted audiences in Hong Kong, Sydney, New Delhi,
Jerusalem, and the United States. He gave a concert for President
Truman at the annual Jefferson Jackson Day Dinner, sang before
the Queen of England at a Royal Command Performance, and
entertained the Prime Minister of India. His records were enjoyed
by music lovers all over the world, and one of his movies won an
Academy Award for short subjects. Miklos Gafni went a long way
since the day he thought he was hearing voice for the last time.

Miki auditioned for the famous movie about Enrico Caruso,
but the role went to Mario Lanza. For one reason or another, Miki
never realized his full potential. He drifted into the record business

and continued to make some recordings. He married and had a daughter who was born with a severe handicap and is confined to a wheelchair.

In the 1970's, as he was hurrying to a business meeting, my friend Miki suffered a massive heart attack and died.

I miss him, and the recordings of his music comfort me to this day.

Hollywood

I MET MY FUTURE wife, Suzanne Stein, in 1949 at a Jewish Federation singles dance. She was pert and petit, a striking brunette I noticed from across the room. I had very little experience with women, but I was thrilled that she shared my aspirations. We were both interested in politics and world affairs. She was a history major at UCLA, and I was a lonely guy with a history who lived in a local boarding house between traveling assignments for the UJA. It was time to settle down.

Suzanne and I fell in love. Six months later, in the summer of 1950, we were married in a traditional ceremony by Rabbi Abraham Haeselkorn, the army chaplain I met on my first day back in Mannheim in 1945. Al and Lee Hutler, my adopted American family, stood in place of my parents.

We outgrew our tiny studio apartment when Lauren Freda was born in 1953. My beautiful baby daughter was named after my strong and loving mother. My son Joel was born in 1955 (J for Jacob, my grandfather, O for Otto, my father, E for Ernst and L for Lotte), and Karen was born in 1956. Then I was transferred to the UJA office in Los Angeles.

The chairman of the Los Angeles campaign at that time was Joe Shane, an investment banker in his early 40s. He was an avid tennis player, a game I was just beginning to learn, and he invited me to play with him. He was a down to earth kind of guy who applied the successful technique he used in business to the fundraising campaign.

I was having a tough time with a chairman in one of the larger California cities who rejected advice from the professionals. As a result, that campaign was failing dismally.

I called Joe and asked if he'd try to salvage the situation. He agreed, and when we arrived at the airport, we were greeted by two members of the committee.

They immediately began to tell us what we could and couldn't say to their august leader, and warned us not to ask for money. They wanted us to just make nice. Joe didn't say a word. When we were alone at the hotel, I asked him how he was going to handle it.

"Leave it to me. No problem."

The meeting was held in the local chairman's beautiful home, and we were graciously welcomed. I was very nervous. Then the chairman introduced Joe.

"We are very glad to welcome a distinguished lay leader from Los Angeles who's here to help us with our campaign. His name is Joe Shane, a business man who chairs the Los Angeles campaign." And he turned to Joe.

Everyone looked at Joe. The two men who met us at the airport were more nervous than I was.

Joe stood up. "Thanks for inviting me. I enjoyed meeting you." And he sat down.

There was total silence. Everyone was astonished.

"But Mr. Shane," protested the chairman. "We want to hear what you have to say."

Joe was silent for a moment. Then he stood up again.

"Well, I've got to tell you," Joe finally responded, "I was prepared to share some of my recent experiences in Israel, but I was told I couldn't say this, and I couldn't say that. And I was forbidden to talk about money. So I decided not to say anything."

His unorthodox approach worked like a charm. They asked him to tell them everything, and he did, with his usual flair. The campaign got underway and was a success.

He was the best teacher I ever had. He taught me the strategies of effective fundraising and how to deal with the details of administration. After every meeting, he insisted I keep a journal and write down everything that happened, including minute details like how the chairs were placed, whether or not the microphone worked, how long each person spoke, and so forth. He taught me to list the pluses and the minuses and to follow the same procedure for individual appointments. It was the best way to analyze and learn.

His methods were most effective and later I tried to pass them on to members of my staff. The man was in the right place at the right time because I needed all the help I could get with the people with whom I was dealing.

* * *

Movie stars. I was assigned to contact movie stars and persuade them to become personally involved in raising funds by making personal appearances at UJA functions. With some notable exceptions, they were egotistical, self-centered, and not at all interested in raising or giving funds to the new Jewish State. Very few made contributions.

I used a direct approach. "We would like to ask you," I said, whenever I was lucky enough to break through the barrier of secretaries, agents, maids, or personal representatives, "to appear at a luncheon or dinner on behalf of UJA, and say a few words. We will arrange transportation back and forth. We will, if you need us to, prepare your remarks. We'll pay all your expenses." Most of the time I could not get through the protective walls they had erected around them. When I did, I often found the non-Jewish stars more willing to appear than the Jewish ones.

The two exceptions were Jack Benny and Harpo Marx.

Jack Benny had a non-Jewish agent who handled all of his appearances. He was affable, interested in what I asked for, and promised to take it up with Mr. Benny. I'm not sure if it was generally known that Jack Benny was probably the most generous contributor among all the Hollywood stars. While his radio program and later his TV show, cast him as a stingy, cheap miser, he was always willing to reach deep into his pockets to help build the Jewish homeland.

He made more personal appearances than anyone else in Hollywood, paid for his own transportation, and never accepted a penny for expenses. His appearance at UJA events always guaranteed a big turnout and substantial contributions for our cause.

He always used the same technique. After a glowing introduction, he would enter from stage right and stand at the microphone without saying a word. He'd look straight at the audience. This created laughter. He was an unequaled master of timing and, as familiar as I was with his routine, I always laughed.

After he milked the moment of his silence as long as he could (it sometimes went a full minute), he'd do his trademark "Well...," and that would bring down the house.

He was, without doubt, one of the most popular entertainers of his era. But there was also a serious side to him. After his opening lines he would speak about his concerns and love for the new State of Israel. He was especially moved during the years when tens of thousands of survivors poured into the country. He talked about growing up as a young Jew in a small town in Wisconsin and his early struggle to achieve recognition in his field. He was proud to be a Jew. He was a real humanitarian, a man for whom I developed a great deal of respect and admiration.

Whenever we had a chance to spend time together, he allowed me to see the private persona, which was totally different from the image so familiar to the public. He was well read, concerned about the role of America in the post-war era, and committed to the survival of Israel. My relationship with him lasted well into the 70's, long after I left California for UJA New York. Shortly before his death, he graced us with his presence at our opening UJA dinner in New York.

He wanted it to be a very special evening and offered to play his violin, something he hadn't done for us before. We convinced Pinchas Zuckerman, the American-Israeli violinist, to appear with him. They played a duet which was so beautiful and so memorable, I've never forgotten it. The audience loved every moment. I regret that no tapes were made.

Jack Benny, I salute your memory.

The other Hollywood star who freely gave of his heart and head and pocket to the UJA was Harpo Marx. Harpo, the mute, zany, curly-haired lunatic, the thieving, harp-playing sex maniac was the oldest Marx Brother and, when I met him, was retired. I wrote and made the usual request. He called me back and we met at his Beverly Hills home.

"Well..." to quote Benny, the real Harpo Marx was a lot different than his insane image. Born as Arthur, one of five brothers, he was already in his seventies when we met. Without the wig, dressed in slacks and a sport shirt, I would never have recognized him in another setting. He looked like a retired Jewish tailor. The only thing that gave him away was the devilish twinkle in his blue eyes.

He married Suzie late in life, adopted four children and divided the family's time between Beverly Hills and their beautiful home in Palm Springs, where Suzie served on the town council. Harpo had no formal education but was self-taught, intelligent, and truly generous. We hit it off from the beginning.

When I asked him to appear for UJA at a major West Coast function, he wanted to know what I expected him to do. I hadn't given this much thought, assuming he would simply appear and make some appropriate remarks. I forgot that Harpo had never uttered a word on the screen and that the public was under the impression that he could not speak.

"Why don't I do part of my act?" he asked me.

This was more than I had the nerve to ask him for. But he did it. For more than five years, Harpo was a star performer for UJA. He appeared at major functions up and down the Pacific Coast. When he realized how much pleasure he was bringing to outlying communities, he accepted most of our invitations. We traveled together and nobody ever recognized him. At least not until he'd put on his wig, which left stewardesses and fellow passengers in stitches.

Usually after the serious part of our meetings, after the speeches and the fund raising were over, Harpo would make his appearance—dressed in his shabby mystery coat (you never knew what would fall out of his sleeves or pockets), and his frizzy blond wig. He'd begin his usual antics and was amply rewarded with a standing ovation from the audience.

"Speak, Harpo, speak!" they'd cry.

Harpo would stand on the stage, shaking his head, using his famous horn.

"Speak, Harpo, speak!" the chant continued.

After a minute or so, with the audience wondering "Will he or won't he?" he would finally relent and would capture those present when he described how much satisfaction he derived from participating in things which were the responsibility of all Jews.

I developed a tremendous affection for him. His face and personality were known throughout the world, but he often explained how grateful he was for the opportunity, so late in his life, to make an important contribution to the rebirth of the Jewish people.

One day he invited my whole family to spend an afternoon at his family home in Palm Springs. My kids will always cherish the photos they took of Harpo and his famous harp. My friendship with this fine and simple individual is one I, too, shall always cherish.

Most celebrities behaved like one of the Hollywood superstars who agreed to attend a major dinner on behalf of UJA. The star, who shall be nameless, came with a full entourage which included the secretary, the producer, and other staff. All flew first class. Limousines were on standby around the clock. Room service, flowers, long distance telephone calls, secretarial services—they charged everything to the hotel. During the following weeks, the bills began to pour in and eventually totaled thousands of dollars. I refused to pay all but the most essential and legitimate expenses, and wrote a letter to the star's office, explaining why I could not justify paying the other bills from charitable funds. In turn I received a nasty letter from the producer threatening to sue the organization. "Go ahead. Sue." I wired back, and I never heard from him again.

There were other superstars who have been supporters of UJA through the years. They are Dustin Hoffman, Steven Spielberg, Barbara Walters, Barbara Streisand, Paul Simon, and Alan King. Miss Walters and Alan King have often appeared at UJA-

Federation events in New York. Non-Jew superstars also contribute to the organization. Most prominent among them are Chevy Chase, Liza Minnelli, Rita Moreno, and the Chairman of the Board, ol' blue eyes himself, Frank Sinatra.

Hollywood brass is also well-known for contributing to the cause. Among them are the late Steve Ross and Marty Payson of Time Warner, the late Lee Guber, who was one of the most active Jewish leaders in the industry, Lou Weiss of William Morris, the late Nat Lefkovitz and Sumner Redstone. Marvin Josephson of ICM and Sy Malamud were also involved.

There are others who, over the years, have refused to make any contribution at all. Most prominent among them are Woody Allen and Neil Simon.

Some time in 1985, Lee Guber called our office to inform us that Neil Simon had agreed to be the guest of honor at the UJA entertainment division dinner. At first we were excited about the possibilities and we anticipated a turnout of at least 1,000 people, plus, we hoped, a major contribution from Neil Simon himself.

Ten days before the dinner, we had 70 reservations. We became frantic and decided to move the site to a smaller hotel. When we called some of our friends in the theater, we were told "If you'd asked us earlier, we'd have warned you. Neil Simon doesn't support any charity and so people don't want to support him, no matter how good the cause."

Our committee went to work to call in all markers. One hundred eighty-five people showed up for dinner, the smallest turnout ever in our entire history for this group.

Neil Simon asked us to reserve a table of 10 for him and his party. When only seven showed, he refused to pay for the other three. Not only that, but he also refused to make a contribution to the campaign. His manager, Manny Aizenberg, through whom we wanted to contact Mr. Simon, claimed that we had "used" Neil Simon to raise money and "how dare we" expect him to make a personal contribution.

I'm only citing the facts, Ma'am!

Lotte's Story

XXI

IT WAS 1955 AND I was finally taking my first trip to Israel. As we left LaGuardia Airport in New York, word came that an El Al airliner was shot down for violating Bulgarian airspace. The spiritual leader of the German-Jewish congregation of Essen, Rabbi Hugo Hahn, was one of the passengers who died in the attack. I knew of him because my aunt's family belonged to his congregation before the war. It made us all very nervous, but I was determined to focus on the positive.

I was anxious to see Lotte again. I hadn't seen her since that cold spring night in 1938, when Papi saw her off on the dangerous train ride to the German-French border. I wondered if I would recognize her, now that she was 26 years old and a mother of two little girls.

Our first fuel stop was Gander, and then we stopped in the Azores. It was going to take 24 hours to get to Tel Aviv and the ride seemed endless.

Finally, we crossed the Mediterranean and I looked out at the coastline below me, my heart bursting with pride. My thoughts went back to the Hachsharah camps I spent time at in 1941, when we believed we would be sent to Palestine. After Hachsharah, Paderborn, Auschwitz, Buna, Buchenwald and Berga, I would finally be setting my feet on Jewish soil. I thought of Mutti and

Papi, of Oma and Lotte, of Walter and Ruth, of Diana, and all those I had carried in my arms.

The war had ended ten years ago and only now was I able to weep. I cried like a baby when I saw the Jewish star, the Mogen David, on the tails of the airplanes at Lod, which at the time, was a ramshackle hut. I cried because we had a Jewish homeland, with Jewish soldiers. If we'd had a Jewish state in the 30's, perhaps six million Jews would not have died.

The first few days in Israel passed in a haze. I remember the road to Jerusalem was a narrow two lane road. And we could not get to the Kotel (the Western Wall), because the Jordanian border was right behind the King David Hotel.

I traveled north to Haifa, full of joyful anticipation, to meet Lotte. I paced nervously in my room at the Zion Hotel as I waited for a knock on the door. Lotte, Sami, her husband, and I had arranged to meet at the hotel between 3 and 4 p.m. They were taking the bus from Beit Shean. It was now later than that. The minutes ticked slowly by. I looked at my watch again. Only two minutes had passed.

My image of Lotte was one of a little girl standing on the station platform with her suitcase and her knapsack, wearing her best coat, excited, afraid, saying good-bye to Mutti, who was trying to hide her tears.

There was a quick knock at the door and then I held my little sister in my arms. Wordlessly, we cried for our parents, for Oma, for our childhoods and our friends. The little girl wasn't so little anymore.

"I never knew you had such blue eyes," were her first words to me.

"You're pregnant!" I crowed, as I looked at her bulging stomach.

"Number Three! Maybe a boy this time!" We smiled through our tears.

We almost forgot my new found brother-in-law, Sami. I liked him right away. He had an open face, a big grin, a firm handshake and an embrace, and I felt I was finally reunited with my family.

We talked until the early hours of the morning, trying to catch up on two lifetimes of experience. Over and over we repeated the refrain, "If only our parents could know we survived... if they only could have died with that knowledge. Then we made arrangements to spend Shabbat together on the kibbutz where they lived, Ein Hanaziv near the Jordanian border.

We settled down after dinner and Lotte told me her story.

"After Papi left me I was very scared," she began.

"I had only my German identity card. Papi told me over and over again what I should say at the border but I had forgotten it. What if they did not let me get across? How would I get back?"

We were sitting in Lotte's and Sami's single, primitive but clean room at their kibbutz located near the ancient city of Beit Shean. The girls had long since gone to bed with the other children.

It was a hot night in the Jordan Valley but I didn't feel it. I was too wrapped up in the excitement of being with my sister and tasting her delicious cake.

"All my worries were for nothing," Lotte continued. "A German policeman winked at me as if he knew, then walked to the next car. Fifteen minutes later the train arrived at Strasbourg. I took my suitcase and my knapsack and waited on the platform.

"Our cousin Erna Fey came to fetch me, and laughing and crying, took me into her arms. She was in constant touch with the French Jewish relief organization and learned I was coming. Papi's letter had never reached her. So she waited at the train station day after day, hoping to find me."

After a few days with our cousin, the relief organization farmed out the refugee children to various homes in Strasbourg. Lotte stayed with an Orthodox Jewish family, the Halfs. And she became Orthodox, because it gave her strength, even in the most difficult times.

The Halfs were Swiss, but lived in France until the Jews of Alsace-Lorraine were deported to the interior in the spring of 1940.

I sat there in bewilderment. My Lotte was a ten year old with short brown hair, full of mischief and a pain in the neck. It did not feel real to be sitting in her kibbutz, in the Promised Land, in Israel. It didn't seem real to see Lotte as an attractive wife, the mother of two with another one on the way.

Lotte continued her story. "When the order came for deportation in the spring of 1940, the Halfs decided to return to Switzerland with the six foster children they were caring for. We traveled for days by rail and foot to the border, but they turned us away, claiming our papers had expired. I felt we had been turned away because they were caring for so many of us. Mr. and Mrs. Half went to the consulate to get the papers, and we were left together, a motley crew of seven children.

"After unsuccessfully trying to board a train to the French interior, our group was found crying and totally desolate by a young German soldier at the railway station. Alice Half, who was seventeen, told him we were separated from our parents and needed to get to a town just across the border from occupied France.

"We just stood there, and listened to them. We had no idea what the young soldier would do. Did he know we were Jewish? He went to make inquiries, brought us some food, and told us that he had made arrangements for us to take a train to the border. I never knew his name but if he is alive—and I hope he is—he has the eternal gratitude of seven young Jewish girls who owe him their survival."

Lotte went into many little details since she has, as I do, almost total recall of the events of those unbelievably difficult and dangerous days. Travel was difficult in Occupied France because everyone demanded papers. Alice's father had given her Swiss francs, so they rented a room from a farmer. It took six months, but somehow Alice managed to get us permission to cross the border into unoccupied France to stay at a Jewish children's home near Perrigieux."

Then, when Lotte heard that the Jews of Mannheim had been shipped to Gurs on the French-Swiss border, she finagled permission to get there, so she could find our parents. She arrived there on their 20th wedding anniversary and found them, in filthy, unsanitary conditions.

"When they saw me, they couldn't believe their eyes. It was undoubtedly the most beautiful anniversary present they could have received."

"What did they look like? How did they live?" It was the first time I heard she had seen them in Gurs.

"They lost weight and looked bewildered. Mud was everywhere. They aged. Yet, they tried to make the best out of a miserable situation. Oma looked like a ghost. Her clothes were filthy, mere rags. She was eighty-seven years old, living in an unheated barrack in the cold winter. She did not recognize me, and kept pleading: 'Give me a little piece of bread, a little piece of bread.' It was devastating."

Lotte stayed almost a week, sleeping in a barn in a nearby village, and visited our parents every day. There was nothing to do for them. Several thousand Jews lived in that camp from May, 1940 until deportation to Auschwitz in October, 1942. Oma died a few weeks after Lotte saw her and is buried near Gurs. She was spared the final indignity and fate of those who arrived in Auschwitz.

"Did they know where I was?" I asked.

"The last they knew was that you were working in a labor camp."

Lotte, 12 years old, realized that this was probably the last time she would see our parents. She had to return to Perrigieux. Letters from them stopped coming in 1942. They'd been deported to Drancy and from there, to Auschwitz.

We both fell silent, caught up in memories of our parents and the fate they suffered.

Lotte spent the next three years in various orphanages. The children knew they were surviving on donations from American Jews. She didn't realize until later that I worked for the organization who kept her and thousands of other Jewish children alive.

In 1943, there were selections and the older girls were sent to Auschwitz. One morning five nuns appeared at the home and took charge of 24 girls, including Lotte.

I could only imagine the rageddy procession through the French countryside, drawing the stares of the locals. Lotte found her new surroundings, filled with crosses and pictures of Jesus, very alien. But she is forever grateful to the Catholic nuns who snatched her from the hands of the Nazis. The girls were not pressured to convert. To the contrary. As much as possible, the dietary laws were observed and candles were lit on Friday night. In exchange, the girls helped the Sisters with their work.

"In June, 1944, Sister Jeanne Francoise told us to get ready to leave. The next morning, word came that our departure would be delayed. The Allied Armies had invaded France."

A month later, they were moved to Toulouse. By the time they reached the Pyrenées near the Spanish border, there were more than 100 boys and girls gathered, all about the same age. We later learned that the entire operation was organized with funds provided by the Joint Distribution Committee, and handled by Sally Meyer, a Swiss silk merchant who negotiated with the Germans for the children's release.

Before the children began their difficult march over the mountains to Spain, Youth Aliyah took them under their wing, distributed their rations and led them through the treacherous alpine passes. Soon they were out of food and had to discard what they brought with them. As the climb became tougher, Sami, another of the children, helped Lotte.

"I always tell Sami I couldn't make it without him, but really I was the one who took care of him!"

We agreed to call it a night. Lotte had prepared a small bunk in the hut next door. Despite my fatigue, it took me a long time to fall asleep. I was an American with a wife and daughter in Los Angeles, at the beginning of a professional career in the American Jewish community, and here was my sister, an Israeli kibbutz member, married with two children and a third on the way.

Fifteen years ago, we were two scared German-Jewish youngsters with no idea what the future had in store for us. Our parents were gone. It was up to us to build our own families and create a new future for ourselves.

After Shabbat was over, Lotte and I continued to talk. Her alpine hike lasted nine days, until, exhausted, and with only the clothes on their backs, the children reached Andorra and were taken by truck to Lerida, across the Spanish border. There they met other children who also climbed the Pyrenées to safety. One group didn't make it. No one knew what happened. They went to Barcelona, then to Cadiz, where they boarded a small ship and arrived in Palestine in October, 1944. Together with those who were with her on the journey, Lotte and Sami had built the kibbutz they lived on and created a home and family.

"We are now more than one hundred families and there are more than two hundred children. This is home, for Sami and me, our first real home. This is where we plan to live and to help to build this country so that what happened to us will never happen again. Then we were helpless victims. Today it is totally different."

Lotte's voice had taken on a new ring, one I had never heard from her. My sister had made up her mind to live here, far from any large city, in a desert, a mile away from the enemy. She was determined to build a life for herself and her family. I have enormous admiration for her.

The Mississippi Sheriff

XXII

IN 1958 I WAS promoted to Director of UJA's Community Development, and invited to join the National Executive Staff in New York. Suzanne packed up the kids, we bought a house in White Plains and became suburbanites in Westchester County, one of the bedroom communities outside Manhattan.

My job was to oversee the Fundraising Campaigns in more than 800 small towns and cities in all fifty states. These were places with small Jewish populations, which had no professional leadership. They were as diverse as Walla-Walla, Washington; Bozeman, Montana; Huntsville, Alabama; Greenville, Mississippi and Honolulu, Hawaii.

Because of my modest fundraising success in the west, my bosses felt that I should train a staff and increase the fundraising results in the smaller communities.

Suzanne kept the homefires burning and cared for our children while I traveled across the United States. The four years I spent in charge of the department offered me a challenging task which I enjoyed very much.

Often I was the guest speaker and I realized early on that the smaller the Jewish population, the easier it was to get everyone together for the traditional UJA annual function. Later, as I developed greater experience and worked in some of the larger cities, I learned that the larger the city, the smaller the number of Jewish families who contribute to the annual UJA-Federation campaign. This is quite understandable. In Bozeman, Montana, with a dozen Jewish families, the participation is 100%. In the city with the largest Jewish population, New York City, the participation is 25%. In Bozeman you can't hide. In New York, you can. Those are the facts of life. Besides, in large cities, competition from Jewish and non-Jewish charities is so much fiercer.

I'm very proud of my fellow Jews, who, over the years, have raised record numbers of dollars for charitable causes and especially for the UJA. By tradition and upbringing we are asked to be more generous in our giving. In one town, a local businessman and generous contributor who gave thousands to the UJA, was asked to donate to the United Way Campaign. His UJA contribution was generous but not extraordinary. After some thought and consideration, he sent the United Way a check for $500.

A week later he was wined and dined by the local United Way Chairman, who was well-known in the community. During the course of the meal he mentioned that he had already sent in his donation, and was told that that's what they were celebrating—he was being thanked for his outstanding generosity. His donation was one of the largest individual gifts in the town. Two years later, he became Chairman of the United Way and raised the largest amount ever.

I've never been satisfied with the results of any campaign I've worked on. And while I try to be objective and admit that Jewish giving is truly generous, not just to Jewish causes, but secular ones as well, my theory is that we are this way because we have been persecuted through the ages and we could only count on ourselves for assistance when we were in need. Jewish relief organizations exist in every land of the Diaspora. When I was growing up, every Jewish home, no matter how poor, had a pushka, a little charity box, in which coins would be dropped, usually before the Sabbath candles were lit.

I think there are three major reasons Jewish giving reached the level it has since the end of World War II.

1) The Holocaust, and the subsequent need to resettle and rehabilitate the survivors.

2) The establishment of the State of Israel and the permanent threat and hatred of its Arab neighbors.

3) The need for growing domestic institutions to provide essential social, educational and medical services to the American Jewish community.

While I canvassed the small towns around America, the turbulence of the civil rights movement—the sit-ins, the protests—was beginning to make itself felt, particularly south of the Mason-Dixon line. One of my staff, responsible for the smaller southern towns, asked if I would speak at the annual UJA dinner in Greenville, Mississippi. Since it fit into my schedule, I accepted.

A few days later I received a call from the local UJA chairman in Greenville. He read my biographical material, and was delighted that I agreed to speak at their annual dinner.

"But that's not what I called you for," he continued. "I'd like to ask to you do me a personal favor and address our local service club during lunch that day."

He felt that what I had to say was important in that moral climate, and told me a bit about the club, which consisted of the town's white leadership, the leading local businessmen and city officials. It sounded interesting, and since I hadn't spoken to a non-Jewish audience for a long time, I agreed.

Thirty years ago, Greenville was a real red-neck town. It was totally segregated, two-thirds black, one-third white. The whites ran the show. Twenty-five, maybe thirty men, attended the luncheon meeting, including the mayor, the sheriff, the local banker, and some other business and professional men.

I decided to talk about how it felt to grow up in Mannheim, and about the discrimination I faced as a Jew and the Nazis' attempt to murder all the Jews. I didn't draw a parallel between the situation in Germany with that of the African-American struggle in the South. However, the audience clearly understood what I referred to when I used the sentence: "This is what discrimination against Jews led to under the Nazis. This is what discrimination can lead to."

My local chairman squirmed in his seat, and I noticed that the sheriff got up and walked out. When the meeting was over, there was only perfunctory applause. My chairman escorted me back to my hotel and didn't seem very pleased.

"I think you went too far," he commented as we drove to the hotel. "These are sensitive times in this part of the country, and I think you antagonized some people, especially Bubba Jackson, the Sheriff."

Before I could reply, I noticed a man standing in the middle of the street whom I immediately recognized as the sheriff, the one who had walked out of the meeting. He held up his hand, indicating that we should stop.

"Oh no!" My chairman looked at me. "Look what you got yourself into! He can hold you and throw the book at you!"

We both got out of the car. There was nothing else to do. Bubba Jackson took me by the arm and led me across the street into his office in the City Hall.

I was scared, almost as scared as I was when I was picked up after wrecking Henry's car in Chicago. Only this time, I knew about lawyers and about my right of free speech as an American. Bubba Jackson did not say a word until we were sitting in his office. I tried not to show how afraid I was, but I was sweating.

"Scared ya, didn't I?" he gloated. Then he smiled, "Relax!"

Bubba Jackson was the prototypical Southern Sheriff. He was red-faced, heavy set, over six feet tall, and had huge hands. In his sheriff's uniform he was intimidating.

Jackson took a grimy, worn wallet from his desk drawer and put it on the table between us. "I'm gonna tell you a story." By this time I was totally confused. I had expected, at best, a severe reprimand, for what, I had no idea. I envisaged spending the night in jail. Maybe he'd order me to get out of town before sundown. Instead, Bubba Jackson was telling me a story.

"I was in the Air Force during the war. We were stationed in England. Our squadron flew thirty-six bombing missions over Germany. Of those, most had as their target, the town you come from: Mannheim."

I couldn't believe this was happening. Bubba Jackson hesitated and then continued:

"We bombed the shit out of that town and destroyed all the factories, the railroad, the bridges—just about the whole city. I've never been back there, but I know that city well, from a few thousand feet in the air. You're the first person I know who comes from there. I listened carefully about what the Nazis did to you and your family. I heard about that before, but never knew someone like you. I often felt sorry for the people in that town. But now I don't feel so bad. The bastards!"

He picked up the wallet and held it in his hands.

"When I left Greenville to join the Air Force, my mother gave me a wallet. This is it. I never had a wallet before. My mother put a few coins in it and told me to carry it with me at all times. It would protect me, she said. I kept that wallet. It went with me on all the bombing missions over Mannheim. Lots of guys didn't make it but I never got a scratch. So this wallet is my good luck piece."

He opened it. It was one of those simple wallets, a coin purse. There were a few coins in it: a quarter, a few dimes, some nickels and pennies. Most of them were green with mold.

He lifted a dime from the wallet and carefully placed it on the table.

"Ernie, I want you to keep that dime. I believe it kept me from getting hurt. It came with me on thirty-six missions over Germany. It will bring you luck, too."

I sat dumbfounded. There were tears in my eyes. Bubba was moved, too.

What could I say? Should I take the coin that clearly meant so much to this unusual man? That belonged to a man I had greatly misjudged?

"I can't accept this, Sheriff. It's too much. I know what it means to you."

"I insist. I won't accept no for an answer."

There was nothing to do but assent graciously.

I embraced Bubba Jackson and we held each other for a long time. As I left his office, he put his arm around me.

"Ernie, the South is not Germany. There will be changes here. And when you get back North, you can tell 'em about Bubba Jackson, the cracker sheriff who scared you to death and then told you a story."

Bubba Jackson, I don't know if you'll ever read this, but you gave a Jewish boy from Mannheim a lot of faith in this country.

I still have your dime.

XXIII

The Lindsay Story
PART TWO

WHEN I WAS BACK in Port Huron, in 1947, during my regular luncheon speeches to the service clubs of the Midwest, I ran into a man who asked me if I'd ever been to Wilmington, Delaware.

Wilmington, Wilmington—why did that sound so familiar? I wracked my brain...Wilmington...Lindsay...Affidavit...

Wilmington! Of course! My pen pal Robert Lindsay! I hadn't thought of him in years. I remembered how I came upon his father, lost in Mannheim, and how generous he was to get an affidavit for me. It certainly wasn't his fault it didn't work.

I went back to the office, stumped. For the life of me, I couldn't recall Mr. Lindsay's first name. I felt the compelling need to get in touch with him and let him know I was all right, that I had survived. I couldn't think of how I could begin my search for him, but resourceful newsman that I was, I soon had my hands on the Wilmington telephone directory.

Easier said than done. There was more than a full page of Lindsays and calling all of them long distance would have been prohibitively expensive.

I decided to use the local Wilmington newspaper to help me hunt for Mr. Lindsay. I wrote to the editor, briefly telling the story of how Mr. Lindsay had attempted to save my life by getting me an affidavit, and I sent it off with my high hopes. Less than a week later, there was a phone call for me.

"Is this Ernst Michel from Mannheim?"

"Yes. Why?"

"This is Herbert Lindsay."

"Mr. Lindsay! I'm so glad I found you!"

"So am I. So are all of us. You don't know how hard we tried to find news of you and your family after the war. It all came to nothing!"

It was really gratifying. He had never given up. He tried so hard to help, even though he hardly knew us.

"Mr. Lindsay, how is Bob? Is he home?"

"No. Ernst, Bob is in the Navy. He's a doctor, serving in the Pacific. Of our five children, three are in the service." We chatted for a long time. Mr. Lindsay told me the newspaper printed my story on a prominent page and that he was thrilled when he saw it, thrilled I was alive and well. After I told him that my parents were deported to Auschwitz and that Lotte was living in Palestine, he made an astonishing offer.

"Listen, young man. My wife and I have been talking, and we want you to know that what I wrote to your father so many years ago still stands today."

I could hardly believe it.

"We want to open our home to you and give you a chance to get an education. Maybe you're a few years behind, but we want to send you to the University and help you to get the right start. What do you say?"

What could I say? This man was a Christian, in the true sense of the word. He hardly knew me, yet he was offering to spend thousands of dollars to send me to school. How could I respond?

I promised I would think about it and get back to him. He gave me Bob's address because I wanted to write to him immediately and tell him my story since my last letter in 1939.

I decided that I wouldn't accept Mr. Lindsay's generous offer.

A few days later, I called Mr. Lindsay at home and told him my decision. He was very gracious.

I stayed in touch with the Lindsay family. When we transferred to New York I finally met Bob, my pen pal, and his family. He set up his medical practice in Worcester, Massachusetts, about 300 miles from New York City.

I'll never forget the Sunday afternoon in 1960 when we came to visit the Lindsays for the first time. As I drove up the long driveway of Bob's ranch home, his whole family was lined up on the porch, impatiently waiting for us. They all knew my story, and the important role the Lindsays played in my life.

Bob is a big, warm, tall and blond friendly person with a ready smile and easy personality. Ginny, his wife, immediately made us feel welcome and all eight children had no problems getting along.

We both cried as we embraced.

"Finally," he said. "It's about time we caught up with each other."

After an authentic American barbecue, Bob asked me to join him in the den. "I want to show you something that I'm sure you'll appreciate."

"Ernest," he looked at me as he slowly opened a small package, "you have no idea what effect you have had on me and my family. When we corresponded before the war it was through you that I was aware of the events in Europe. When we thought you were lost, it was as if a member of our family had died."

With that, he handed me the open package which contained, in order, all the letters I sent during the years of our correspondence. I silently looked at my letters, beginning with the first one dated October 29, 1937.

> *"Dear Robert,*
> *I know you don't know my name. Let me tell you, how I come to your address. Some weeks ago, and I drove with my bycicle to shool, there I saw standing at a corner a fine motor car, and many people were standing round this car. I went to it and saw a few men, speaking English. I kould understand some of their words, than I learn English one and half year. I looked to this car and ther a man of this people came to me and asked me, 'Do you speak English?' 'Yes,' I said. 'How old are you then?' I answered in English natural, forteen and a half year. (I have birthday on the first of July). This man was your father. He*

asked me all in English, weather I will write to you. I was very quickly and he gave me your addresse. I wrote my name in his copybook and some minutes afterwords I went away to school.

Now I am sitting at my writing table, and think about that, what I can write to you.

At first, I must tell you, that I am a Jewish boy. I have still a sister, ten years old. I am still in school, but next Ostern I go out of school. I don't know, what I shall make, if I come out of school, but I shall see all ready.

February 14, 1939
My dear friend Bob,

My best thanks for your last letter. Please will you excuse for my not writing such a long time. But I had to do very much. For the time being I learn English 5 to 6 lessons in day, for I can, if I come to AMERICA very much. In our course, we have 3 lessons of l hour, and at home I lern still with a friend 2 to 3 hours. Isn't it very much? Besides that, we can't make any-thing more, we can't go to the pictures, we can't go to the playground or looking to a football-game, we can't go into another performance or something else. All is forbidden for us. We must stay at home and can't do anything. Isn't it frightful?

It is very honest of your father, that he troubles him so much for me, and I hope, I can ever thank you and your father, what you did for me. It is very fine, that Kennett Square is lying only 12 miles from Wilmington. There we can see and speak us very often, than with the cycle it is only a short hour, isn't it? I'll take my cycle with me to the U.S.A. Shall I do so? Please, will you give me you advice.

On the 10th of November our flat here in Mannheim was destroyed. At this time, I lived still in Bruchsal, and there it was too. But I won't write more about this theme. I believe, you know this 'nice' things."

Bob kept quiet as I reread my letters. I thought about the years since I wrote them and was amazed that, despite the hardships I lived through, there was a tone of optimism in all of them.

"Every member of our family has read your letters," he told me. "We all are proud to know you. You've enriched our lives in ways you will never know."

Bob and I are still close. He and Ginny now live in retirement in Colorado. His father died many years ago. Before he died, I had the chance to meet him in Wilmington and thanked him for being the only person in the world who brought a ray of hope and humanity into the lives of my parents when they were in total despair.

As I conclude this chapter, I can't help but reflect that Lotte's life was saved by the selfless Catholic nuns in France, and that the only family that tried to rescue me was a deeply religious Christian family in the United States.

There is some reason for hope in this world. Perhaps there is a chance, after all, that we can all learn to live together.

XXIV

A Meeting with President Eisenhower
at the White House

ON MARCH 20, 1960, the first nation-wide dinner of survivors of the Auschwitz-Buna concentration camp was held in New York City. It brought together some 600 survivors and their families, and was the first function of its kind ever held in the United States.

Four days later, because I chaired the dinner, I was among five men invited to visit President Dwight D. Eisenhower in the White House. This is how it happened.

A slave laborer from Auschwitz had decided to sue I.G. Farben, the giant chemical combine, for forcing us to work as slaves in the deplorable conditions of Auschwitz. He was the man behind these two related events. I.G. Farben took advantage of the unlimited supply of "low-cost" Jewish labor, and built the huge factory near Auschwitz to manufacture synthetic rubber called Buna. That's where Walter died, and where I worked until I got hit in the head with a rifle butt for looking at an SS guard. Over 130,000 camp inmates, 90% of them Jews, died of starvation, disease, beatings, and gassings, in the process of building the plant, which was never completed and was eventually dismantled at war's end. The slave's name was Norbert Wollheim.

Norbert was born in Berlin and was one of the youngest members of the German-Jewish community leadership. In 1943, he, his wife and three-year old child were deported to Auschwitz. His wife and child went up the chimney with the others. He landed in Buna.

An extremely articulate, courageous, and determined man, Wollheim, liberated in Bergen-Belsen, decided to sue I.G. Farben in 1950. He claimed that he was forced to work for two years to build the Buna factory; that he was starved and beaten and never received any payment for his labor. He believed he had a good case. It took guts to single-handedly sue one of Germany's giant companies. With no funds or support from any Jewish organization, he engaged a sympathetic European-born lawyer, who took the case, pro bono.

In 1950, the case of 'Wollheim vs. I.G. Farben in Liquidation' was filed in a district court in Frankfurt, Germany. By that time, the Allied High Commission decided to break up I.G. Farben permanently. The company was worth billions of Deutschmarks.

Wollheim and his lawyer contended that the conditions under which camp inmates labored in Buna were known to the heads of I.G. Farben and asked for a token DM 10,000 (less than $2,500) in compensation.

The case lingered in the courts for years. I.G. Farben realized that if Wollheim succeeded, thousands of other survivors would file similar claims. It was estimated that some 6,000-7,000 survivors throughout the world were still alive.

In 1959, after exhausting one delaying tactic after another, I.G. Farben settled for distributing 30 million Deutschmarks to all the Buna survivors, on condition that no further individual claims be filed. The case received international attention, and was taken over by the United Restitution Successor organization, which handled the often difficult and prolonged negotiations.

Wollheim, who succeeded in forcing the great German combine to admit its share of the responsibility for war crimes, recruited a few former camp inmates to help him with the paperwork. I was among them. We voluntarily evaluated thousands of applications filed by survivors who claimed to have been inmates of Buna. Similar committees were formed in Israel, South America, Canada and other countries where survivors had settled.

Each survivor would receive 5,000 German marks or $1,250. In 1960, for many of us, that was a lot of money. We were just getting over the effects of the years in the camps and we were beginning to earn a living. Many we talked with during the lengthy process of checking claims, were in sad shape. Some suffered from recurring nightmares. Others were under constant medical care as a result of the beatings, malnutrition and similar illnesses.

We also encountered a number of survivors who refused, although they could have used the funds, to accept any compensation from Germany.

We usually met in the modest offices of URO in downtown New York City, where we evaluated the hundreds of claims from Buna survivors. Most were legitimate. Some made the honest mistake of confusing Buna with Auschwitz or Birkenau. We found only a few who tried to cheat. Between us, we were able to determine whether the claimant had actually been in the camp.

I don't remember who had the idea, but we decided to ask all the recipients of the I.G. Farben compensation to agree to make a one-time contribution to establish an Auschwitz-Buna Scholarship Fund. The money would enable a son or daughter of needy survivors to attend college.

Our small committee, led by Norbert, all agreed to contribute something from our own Farben checks and the fund was launched.

Then we decided to organize an Auschwitz-Buna Memorial dinner. Norbert was elected chairman of the Auschwitz-Buna Memorial Scholarship Fund and I was elected dinner chairman.

Invitations were sent to all Auschwitz-Buna survivors throughout the United States. It explained the goals of the Scholarship Fund and asked survivors to come together for a dinner in New York, the first of its kind, to celebrate our survival and launch the Fund. More than 600 survivors and their spouses made reservations and donations. Even I was surprised at the overwhelming response. The dinner was held at the Concourse Plaza Hotel in the Bronx, in an atmosphere of joy and remembrance.

It was the first time many of us, the alumni of Buna, had seen each other since the death march in January, 1945. Scenes of reunion took place at each table and in each corner. Emotions overflowed.

"Aren't you..." and then we'd fall into each others arms, laughing and crying.

Many who came found fellow inmates they had believed dead. One met a cousin he was sure had perished. These dramatic meetings were worth the exhausting hours we spent organizing the event. The cocktail hour stretched to two. People were too excited to sit down.

The main speakers were Nachum Goldman, President of the World Jewish Congress and a premier leader of world Jewry, and U.S. Senator Jacob Javits. I wrote to Sherman Adams, President Eisenhower's Chief of Staff, to ask the President to designate an individual to accept a specially prepared citation addressed to him, the Congress, and the People of the United States.

The citation, signed by all those attending the dinner, eloquently expressed our feelings towards the Five-Star General who led the Allied Forces to victory and liberated us. In his reply, Mr. Adams informed me that the President had asked Senator Javits to accept the citation on his behalf.

A special scroll of appreciation was also presented to the United Jewish Appeal. It expressed our gratitude for their aid and assistance—for making it possible for us to emigrate to Israel or America and start our lives.

Also on the program were Rabbi Herbert Friedman, head of the UJA, Rabbi Herschel Schachter, who, as U.S. Chaplain helped liberate Buchenwald; Yossele Rosensaft, President of the Bergen-Belsen Survivors Association, and the Consul-Generals of Poland and France.

The speakers, caught up in the emotion of the evening, ignored the time table, and the final speaker didn't begin his remarks until well past midnight. Most of our guests stayed to the end. For all of us, it was an unforgettable, emotional evening—and we raised $30,000 for the Auschwitz-Buna Memorial Scholarship Fund. (The funds were eventually turned over to Bar Ilan University in Israel, which is administering the scholarships in perpetuity.)

I sat next to Senator Jacob Javits. Moved by seeing so many survivors gathered for the first time, he passed me a note written on the outside of an envelope. "I'll call the White House tomorrow and suggest you and your committee make the presentation to the President personally. Stay in touch with my office."

Two days later we received confirmation from Senator Javits's office that the President would receive us the following Thursday at 12:30 p.m.

A meeting with President Eisenhower at the White House!

I immediately called the members of the Committee to plan for this extraordinary development. What would we say? How do we make a presentation to the President?

Haskel Tydor, the oldest member of our small group and an Orthodox Jew, proposed that we offer a prayer in the Oval Office in honor of the President.

"But, Haskel, we can't do that," one of us replied. "We can't turn a meeting with the President into a religious ceremony."

"There is a prayer in our religion which is said in the presence of a Head of State. It is a brief prayer and totally appropriate," Haskel answered.

We agreed to call Arthur Settel, Senator Javits's key aide, for his opinion. He wasn't much help. He suggested we play it by ear.

We took the morning train to Washington and went to the White House. Our names were listed with the sergeant at the gate and shortly after noon we were sitting in one of the waiting rooms on the ground floor, nervous about the forthcoming meeting. Shortly before 12:30 Senator Javits joined us. He would introduce us to the President. Norbert and I would make the presentation.

We were very quiet as we waited to be taken to the Oval Office. Soon we would be in there, in one of the most famous rooms in the world, in the presence of the most powerful man in the world, the symbol of our hope and of our liberation.

Did we ever imagine, in our wildest dreams in Auschwitz, in Buchenwald, during those years of horror, that we would survive and meet the man who personified everything America represented?

My thoughts were interrupted when a White House aide entered the room: "Gentlemen, the President will see you now." We followed the aide, led by Senator Javits, into the Oval Office.

The President came around his desk to greet each one of us. The first thing I noticed was that he had a small spot on his lapel.

"Mr. President," Senator Javits began the presentation, "last Sunday I attended, on your behalf, a most unusual dinner in New York."

He then described to the President the circumstances and asked Norbert and me to present the scroll. We both lifted it onto the President's desk. At that moment I felt a poke in my back. Senator Javits, accustomed to Washington photo opportunities, noticed that I was standing behind the scroll, almost totally obscured, while the White House photographers snapped the pictures which would forever capture this historic moment. I stepped forward. Good that I did. Otherwise I wouldn't even have a photo as a souvenir.

While all this was going on, Haskel Tydor put on a yarmulke and asked President Eisenhower if he could recite a prayer.

I gasped. How could he do this? We wanted to ask the President about his visits to the camps. He had come face to face with survivors, and was shocked by what he had seen.

But Haskel was undaunted and, first in Hebrew and then in English, recited the prayer while we all stood silently.

"Thank you very much," the President said, obviously moved.

The President, who had just come from a meeting with British Prime Minister Harold MacMillan, asked about Auschwitz, our liberation and our new life in the United States. The President was warm, informal and helped us to be very much at ease.

We spent at least half an hour in the Oval Office, and it was only when an aide reminded the President about his next appointment that we took our leave. He again shook hands with each of us and wished us all good luck. We thanked him for receiving us, and as we left the Oval Office, the President said "This beautiful scroll will eventually be placed in the Presidential Library in Abilene."

I told my kids, who were still a little young, the significance of their father's experience that day. I sat down and wrote the story of our meeting with the President. I submitted it to the Reader's Digest where it won the First Person's Story Award for that month.

Here, with permission of the Reader's Digest, is the story, as it appeared in the December, 1960 issue:

From Hitler's Germany to the White House! But even the author could not realize how far he had come until an unexpected incident caused it to be revealed on the face of the man standing behind the President's desk.

A Reader's Digest $2500 "First Person" Award

MY LONG JOURNEY TO EISENHOWER
By Ernest W. Michel

I had been to Washington, D.C., and on the flight home I wondered how I would tell my family about this day, the most remarkable in my life. My children were young and perhaps they wouldn't understand its significance, but I so wanted them to.

When I arrived home I kissed my wife, then turned to my three young children standing in their pajamas, faces scrubbed, eyes shining in anticipation of the nightly story. "Tonight I'm going to tell you a true story," I said. "Part of it is very sad, but it ends happily." I paused a long moment. Then I began:

Once upon a time there was a boy—we'll call him Ernest—and he lived in Mannheim, Germany. He loved to play soccer with his best friend, Kurt. But when he was ten years old a wicked man named Hitler seized power in Ernest's country and began to make people hate instead of love. Especially he tried to make people hate Jews. Ernest was a Jew.

On a warm spring day in 1935 Ernest and his friend Kurt ran out onto the soccer field, but the coach stopped Ernest and said, "You can't play soccer any more. You are a Jew." Ernest expected that Kurt would stand up for him. But he didn't. And the following day Kurt arrived at school dressed in a Hitler Youth uniform and he never spoke to

Ernest again. It wasn't that Kurt suddenly hated Ernest; he just wanted to be like everyone else. He didn't have the courage to say what he really felt.

As time went on, Ernest found that he couldn't go to the sports arenas, or to the movies, and finally even the public parks carried signs that read: "No Jews or dogs allowed." Then, on the night of November 9, 1938, many synagogues in Germany were dynamited and destroyed. That night Hitler's Storm Troopers broke into Ernest's home, ransacked the place and slapped his mother. Ernest couldn't understand what made normally decent men suddenly act like gangsters.

War began in September, 1939, and six days later Hitler ordered all Jewish youths in Mannheim between the ages of 16 and 20 to report for slave labor. Ernest was just 16. When he left, his father and mother were very brave in front of him, and he was very brave in front of them. Ernest did not know that he would never see his parents again, that they would soon be among the millions of Jews to be killed in Hitler's gas chambers.

For four years Ernest was starved and beaten until he was a skeleton of 85 pounds. Now he was of no more use as a slave; so he was sent to the notorious Auschwitz concentration camp. There the numbers 104995 were tattooed on his arm. These figures indicated the order of his death in the gas chamber. Each day Ernest waited to hear them called.

Then in the spring of 1944 something crept into the concentration camp—it was hope! Eisenhower had invaded Europe! Now Ernest prayed for life for one more month, one more week, one more day... until Eisenhower could arrive to free him.

Early in 1945 Ernest was moved to another horrible camp, called Buchenwald. But as Eisenhower came closer, Ernest and hundreds of other prisoners were marched northeast, away from Eisenhower, away from liberation.

And each day the guards methodically murdered two dozen men.

Ernest and two friends decided to try to escape. Late one afternoon as the straggling column breasted a hill, Ernest saw a dense stand of hemlock. He knew that this small forest would be their salvation or their grave. He signaled his two friends and they ran for the forest.

Soon each breath became agony; he crashed into trees but reeled on. At last he fell and could not get up.

But he had escaped. For the first time in six years he wept. Slowly his strength returned and he picked himself up, found his two friends and they all turned west, toward Eisenhower.

A few weeks later the war ended, and the next year Ernest came to the United States. He became a citizen of this great country, and he married a beautiful American girl and he had three wonderful children and a house and a good job. America gave him more than he ever dreamed life held.

But Ernest never let himself forget those terrible days in Germany, nor did he want the world to forget. So he and others who had survived created the Auschwitz-Buna Memorial Scholarship Fund for children of the victims of Nazi brutality. They also decided to thank Eisenhower publicly. They ordered a beautiful big scroll expressing gratitude and loyalty to the United States, and Ernest and five friends went to Washington to present it to Eisenhower, who had become President.

They arrived in Washington and Ernest took a walk. He gazed at the Lincoln Memorial, the Jefferson Memorial and the Washington Monument, and he thought of the wisdom of the founding fathers. And he was a part of it all! He felt very proud.

He returned to the hotel to meet his friends and discuss what they would say to the President the next day. One man, Haskel Tydor, being very religious, proposed to say a Jewish prayer for the President when they met him.

The others objected. Ernest was afraid the President might be embarrassed; after all, he was not a Jew. Also, Ernest had just stood proudly before the Lincoln and Washington monuments as an American citizen, and he wanted to act like an American before his President; he wanted to leave the old rituals back in the old country. So he and his friends told Haskel Tydor not to say the Jewish prayer for the President.

At the White House next morning they were ushered into a reception room outside the President's office. Ernest was nervous. He sat, he stood, he paced the floor. He still hadn't been able to decide how he should speak to the President. Suddenly a door opened and a man said, "Gentlemen, the President is ready."

Ernest straightened his coat and his necktie, and his mind raced back through the long journey he had taken to arrive at this door: the years of slavery, the hell of concentration camps, the nightmare of the long march when the very name Eisenhower had made him cling desperately to life. He felt a moment of panic; he didn't want to see the man in person, he preferred to keep him safe in imagination. But it was too late to turn back.

Behind a large desk sat the President. The first emotion Ernest felt was shock of recognition. There was the face he had seen in thousands of pictures; but now it was real and alive and looking straight at him.

The President grasped Ernest's hand firmly and gave him a smile, and Ernest felt himself blushing with emotion. Then in a warm compassionate voice the President asked Ernest and his friends to tell him about the concentration camps.

As Ernest spoke he suddenly realized that all nervousness had left him; he knew that he was in the presence of a man who cared deeply about his fellow men. When Ernest finished, the President recalled grimly his own shock at the horrors of the death camps and denounced those who had looked the other way and had denied responsibility for such inhumanity. He expressed pride that so many victims who escaped had come to America.

The scroll of appreciation from the Auschwitz survivors was presented and the President read it carefully. It was time to go. But, without warning, Haskel Tydor spoke up: "Mr. President, we Jews have an ancient prayer that calls God's blessing on the head of our government. I would like to call that blessing upon you."

Ernest and his friends gasped. Ernest was furious. Haskel Tydor kept his eyes on the President and said, "Do I have your permission?"

"Indeed you have," the President said. He had been leaning against his desk but now he stood erect and bowed his head in reverence.

Haskel Tydor put on a skullcap and opened a prayer book. He recited the ancient prayer in Hebrew, and the President listened to the alien words. Then Tydor repeated the prayer in English, and this time the President could understand. He heard the words, "Blessed be Thou, Lord our God, King of the universe, Who has given of Thy glory to mortal man."

Ernest saw tears in Tydor's eyes. Then he looked at the President and saw that he, too, was deeply moved. The President said in a low, emotion-filled voice, "Thank you very much."

Now Ernest realized how wrong he had been and how right Haskel Tydor had been. It was wrong to think that they should leave part of themselves in the old world. Here at last they could be whole men, Jews and Americans at the same moment. That was what Washington and Jefferson and Lincoln had said, but Ernest hadn't felt its true meaning until he saw it revealed in the face of the living President, Eisenhower.

And that was the end of the bedtime story. As I put my son to bed he reached up and ran his fingers over my left arm, over the Auschwitz numbers, 104995.

"Daddy, did the President see your tattoo?" he asked.

"He knew it was there," I said.

"When I grow up will I go to see the President of the United States?"

"If you do, my son," I answered, "it will not be because you carry on your arm the death numbers of Auschwitz."

Copyright © 1960 by The Reader's Digest Assn., Inc. Reprinted by permission.

As far as I know, our meeting with President Eisenhower was the first time that a group of Holocaust survivors had been received at the White House. It was one of the most memorable moments in my life.

Here I am in 1947 at the wheel of my new car.

Above: Herman Goering in his cell at Nuremberg, 1946.

Right: My official press card from the Nuremberg War Crimes Trial, 1946.

Top Left: With President Chaim Herzog of Israel in his office in Jerusalem, 1987. Top Right: Ludwig Jesselson presents German President von Weizsaecker a Menorah at the conclusion of our 1988 meeting. Middle: With Prime Minister Shimon Peres at a UJA-Federation meeting in New York, 1986. Bottom: With Israel Likud Party leader Binyamin Netanyahu, with my wife, Amy, looking on, in Washington, DC, 1988. *(Photo by Robert A. Cumins)*

Of all the Hollywood stars I've worked with over the years, two of
the kindest and most generous were Harpo Marx (top left), seen here
with me at a UJA dinner in Denver, 1956, and Jack Benny (bottom,
photo by Henry Kierstead) seen here at a UJA meeting in Long Beach,
California, 1958.

Top Right: With violinist Yitzhak Perlman at a New York UJA-
Federation luncheon, 1981. *(Photo by Jerry Soalt)*

Top: Our meeting with President Eisenhower in the Oval Office, June, 1960. Sen. Jacob Javits is on the far right. Next to me is Norbert Wollheim, and on the far left is Harkel Tydor.

Left: Baron Elie de Rothschild and me after a reception at City Hall in Paris, 1968.

Below: General Moshe Dayan, legendary Israeli leader, New York, 1972.

Top: One of the few pictures ever taken of David Ben Gurion, the first Prime Minister of Israel, in a tuxedo.

Right: Israeli President Yitzhak Navon with Ben Meed and me after the World Gathering of Holocaust Survivors at a reception at his residence in Jerusalem, June, 1981.

Below: With Golda Meir in New York, 1973.

Top: With Jerusalem mayor Teddy Kollek walking in Old City, 1976.

Left: With William Rosenwald, one of the Founders of UJA and Chairman of its annual campaign. *(Photo by Herbert Bennett)*

Bottom: Yitzhak Shamir, then Deputy Prime Minister of Israel, with me at a UJA-Federation meeting in New York, 1985.

Scenes from the final session of the World Gathering of Holocaust Survivors in Jerusalem, June, 1981.

Top: Prime Minister Menachem Begin addresses the crowd.

Right: Some of the 6,000 candles lit in memory of the 6,000,000 killed during the Holocaust.

Below: The final session at the Western Wall.

Through my work I have met some of the biggest names in American politics. Clockwise from bottom: Former President Jimmy Carter (Irving Bernstein, National UJA Executive Vice Chairman is in center); Then New York Mayor Ed Koch *(Photo by Joan Vitale Strong)*; New York Governor Mario Cuomo (In center: Morton Kornreich. *Photo by Robert A. Cumins*); Former President Gerald Ford; Senator Alphonse D'Amato. *(Photo by Jerry Soalt)*

Return to Mannheim

XXV

ALTHOUGH I SWORE I would never set foot in Germany, on July 1, 1960, my thirty-seventh birthday, I was in Mannheim. I was curious. Suzanne and I had arrived the previous day from Israel. I wanted to show Suzanne where I was born and see what happened to the town of my birth since 1946.

We used the money I got from the I.G. Farben settlement of the Wollheim class action suit. I wanted to find my two closest childhood friends, Kurt Hess and Heinz Manz, the two boys who became members of the Hitler Youth, and who never spoke to me again after I was thrown out of school. I wanted them to know what had happened to my parents.

I made reservations at the Hotel Mannheimer Hof, the best hotel in the city, and specified that I wanted the suite where Adolf Hitler stayed when he visited Mannheim in the 30's. I still recall that visit and how the whole town lined the streets to welcome the Fuehrer. We had stayed home the whole day, afraid to be seen.

It gave me a perverse feeling of satisfaction to be staying in the same room, to be sleeping in the same bed that the fallen dictator occupied twenty-five years before. He was dead. I was alive. The 1,000 year Reich was ashes. This was a new Germany. I was an American citizen. My publisher from Heidelberg, Theodor Heuss, was now the President of Germany.

First I went to Kurt Hess' house. I told Suzanne that I had a mission I needed to carry out alone. I found the address in the phone book, and decided to walk. The house was damaged but inhabited. I rang the doorbell. An old, grey-haired woman answered the ring. I didn't recognize her.

"Does Kurt Hess live here?" She looked at me, perplexed.

"Who are you?"

"I am Ernst Michel. I lived. . ."

Her mouth opened in surprise.

"You are Ernst Michel?! You are alive?!"

She started to cry and I had to hold her or she would have fallen.

"I recognize you. The face, a bit older but it is you!"

She invited me in. By now I knew that this old woman was the attractive, elegant mother of my boyhood friend.

"Mrs. Hess. Where is Kurt? Does he live in Mannheim?"

She shook her head, her eyes moist.

"Kurt is dead. He was killed in Russia during the war. That is all I know. I don't even know where he is buried."

I sat silently, thinking of my parents and their end in Auschwitz. What irony! Here was the mother of my best childhood friend, and she couldn't visit his grave.

I told her about my life and my family's fate since my deportation from Mannheim in 1939. Most of the time she listened silently, shaking her head.

So Kurt was dead. Killed in the war. There would be no confrontation. He was dead. I was alive.

Next, I sought out Heinz Manz. I found a shop named Manz on the main shopping street. I called the store and asked for Heinz. When the receptionist wanted to know who was calling, I hung up, certain I'd found him. I wanted to see his face when he saw me.

Manz was a beautiful gift shop, probably the finest in town. I walked around a bit, then asked for Mr. Manz. What would he look like now? What would I say?

I recognized him immediately, a second before he recognized me. He hadn't changed much. Of the three of us, he was the smallest. I didn't say a word.

"Ernst! Is it really you?"

He didn't seem too surprised to see me, because, as it turned out, he'd read my articles about the Nuremberg Trials and knew I was alive. He also knew that I was living in the United States. We had dinner together that evening, Suzanne, Heinz and myself. His wife, he told me, had a serious debilitating illness and was bedridden. He intimated that she wasn't expected to live very much longer.

Heinz served in the German Army, and was taken prisoner. He knew Kurt was dead. But whenever I tried to bring up the way he and Kurt cut me out of their lives, he stonewalled me.

"Ernst, that was long ago. We had no choice. We were good, patriotic Germans. We only followed orders."

I'd heard that excuse often at Nuremburg. Everyone in the Nazi hierarchy used it. However, I believe human beings always have choices.

"There are more important problems to talk about," Heinz huffed. "Together we have to fight Communism. That is the danger we face today."

He flatly refused to deal with my reason for coming back to Mannheim. He wouldn't allow me to confront him about the way he hurt me and my family.

I really don't know what I expected from the encounter. Was I naive enough to believe Heinz would apologize, and that he would accept responsibility as a German for the atrocities committed against us? Other Germans were participating in the national denial of guilt and responsibility. Why should he be different.

By evening's end, I realized that I had made a serious mistake in seeking him out. I couldn't wait to get back to the hotel. The next morning, before Suzanne and I left for the airport in Frankfurt, we took a long walk to the places I remembered so well. The city was almost new. Although over 90% of it was destroyed during the war, little trace of destruction remained.

Our apartment building on Richard Wagner Street was totally rebuilt. The whole street was new. Every house was rebuilt. My old school was still there, renovated, the playing field which I loved so much was there. Only the people who were part of my life were all gone. No one was left.

Our final stop was the spot where our synagogue had stood. It was an empty lot. There was nothing left. Very tidy. Nobody would ever know that for almost 100 years, a house of worship, a sanctuary and the center of our lives as Jews in Mannheim stood in that place. Suzanne left me alone to dwell in my thoughts.

From my earliest childhood, my father had brought me to synagogue every Shabbos morning and every Jewish holiday. I remember when I grew out of "short" pants and was given my first pair of Shabbos knickerbockers. Papi would wear his best suit and tie. Mutti would wear a lovely dress and matching hat. I remember the dark wooden pew we sat in, with its prayer books and "talleysim," the prayer shawls, neatly folded in their velvet and satin bags.

As a bar-mitzvah boy, I accepted my obligation as a Jew in its sanctuary. Inside, I learned the beauty of being Jewish. Even though we already lived in the shadow of Nazism, I remember how lovely it was that day, when my parents, Lotte, Oma and I walked to synagogue with Uncle Willie and Aunt Paula. For the first time, I sat on the Bima, facing the congregation and waiting to be called to recite my portion of the Torah. I remembered seeing Lotte and Mutti smiling in the balcony.

My thoughts were interrupted by a man in his fifties who walked by and gave me a strange look.

That spot, there, is where I stood on the morning of November 10, 1938, watching the smoldering ruins. Was he part of the gloating crowd that night?

Before leaving, I walked into the now empty lot, touched the wall of an adjacent building and silently recited Kaddish, the Hebrew prayer for the dead. Then, with dry eyes, and deep in thought, Suzanne and I walked away.

I was ambivalent when I left Mannheim. I felt empty, cheated. My visit hadn't produced what I expected, but what should I have expected in the first place? It was too strange. There were only tiny traces of the past. The Germans succeeded in Mannheim. It certainly was Judenrein.

I had no business being there and I was sorry I'd come back.

XXVI

France

IN 1962, THE UJA promoted me to Regional Director of West Coast operations in charge of eleven states. Good bye, Westchester. Hello, again, Hollywood.

The kids returned to school and did their homework. I went to work and took care of the lawn. Suzanne was our anchor, our custodian. For five years, we lived the suburban life.

In early 1967, Charles Jordan, an erudite, cosmopolitan gentleman, national director of the Joint Distribution Committee, asked me to see him after a meeting in L.A. I'd known him for 20 years, and I knew about the JDC since 1945, when I met Abe Laskove in Germany. He'd spoken at many of the conferences and dinners I had helped organize, and we had established a warm, cordial relationship.

"Ernie," he said even before we sat down for coffee, "I have a proposition for you."

"I'm listening."

"You know the French Jewish community. You speak German and French."

"Not really, Charlie," I interrupted. "German, of course, and French, only a little. I understand it, but I'm far from fluent."

"That's good enough," he continued. "More important is the fact that you were born in Europe and understand the European

211

mentality. Equally important is your expertise in fundraising, which I've seen you do so well."

He offered me a job with the JDC. I was flabbergasted. He was asking me to leave Los Angeles and my job with UJA. Our three children were all at a difficult age. Lauren was 14. Joel was 12 and Karen, 11. How would Suzanne adjust to living in Europe, starting all over again, learning new customs, learning a new language? These thoughts raced through my mind as Jordan continued speaking.

"Since the war and the recent massive immigration of Jews from North-Africa, the French Jewish Community has grown to 700,000. It's the only European country that, because of this influx, has more Jews today than they had in 1939. The French are bad at fundraising. It's done poorly and it shows. Few give anything at all.

"The JDC spends over one million dollars on Jewish education in France. That expense should really be the responsibility of the French themselves.

"Knowing you, I think you can help them and us. You're the only American professional who has the background and I think you're the only one who could do this job."

I listened carefully. From Charlie's point of view, it made sense. As for me, I could see enormous problems, personally and professionally. What would I do about my house? What about schooling for the children? How long would this assignment last? I never thought I couldn't do the job. I had confidence in myself. Rather, I was worried about logistics.

"Charlie, have you discussed this with anyone?"

"Only with the French. I discussed it with the top professional of the FSJU, Le Fond Social Juif Unifie, the equivalent of our local Federation, and with Baron Elie de Rothschild, the President of the organization. They'd like you to visit Paris for a few weeks to talk to them and explore the possibilities."

That evening I told Suzanne about the offer and was surprised at her positive reaction. She'd always seemed wary of change, yet the idea of living in Paris appealed to her. She also felt it would be a great learning experience for the kids.

A few weeks later I was in Paris. As promised, Jordan had discussed the offer with Herb Friedman, my boss at UJA. Herb called me and told me that, if I accepted it for a two year period only, he would guarantee my old job. That seemed fair.

I'd been to France once, on a stopover on my way to Tel Aviv. This time it was different. It was no sightseeing trip. I knew that what happened here could determine my future career.

I brushed up on my French during the weeks prior to the trip, but I realized that I was far from fluent. I tried, but after a few sentences, the men and women I met switched to English. I found out that many of them spoke better English than I spoke French. But I didn't stop trying, and after the first week, I could converse.

One of the first dignitaries I met was Baron Elie de Rothschild. His office was on the top floor of the Rothschild Bank on rue Laffite, in the financial district.

If we Jews have anything like royalty, the Rothschilds are it. Without a doubt, they are the most famous Jewish name in the world, going back seven generations to the founder of the dynasty, Meyer Amshel Rothschild of Frankfurt.

It was quite an experience. A butler in a morning coat and white gloves received me and asked for my card. It was a good thing I had cards with me. He placed mine precisely on a silver tray and asked me to wait in a private reception room. Moments later he was back.

"Monsieur Michel, the Baron will see you now. Please follow me."

I followed him through one beautifully and tastefully arranged office after another, to Elie de Rothschild's suite.

"Monsieur Ernest Michel from New York!" announced the butler as I was led into the Baron's presence.

Elie de Rothschild was then in his mid-fifties. He was tall and distinguished looking. He had the air of a man who knows what he wants and gets it.

I saw a warm smile and shook a friendly hand.

"Well, Ernest, I understand that you want to teach us how to raise money in France."

Thus, the Baron got right to the point, which established an informal tone, and I decided to follow it.

"Not today, Elie. This is just a get-acquainted visit. I haven't yet decided whether or not I'll accept the JDC's offer. I'll make up my mind after I've had a chance to talk with you and other leaders of the Jewish community."

He spoke perfect English, so I didn't have to stumble through my fractured French.

The Baron turned out to be a great source of information. He left France during World War II, to join the British Army. He told me that all the Rothschild properties were seized by the Nazis and returned to them after the war, looted and damaged. He spoke candidly about the Rothschild fortune.

"Much of it is exaggerated," he said with a smile. "That doesn't mean we plead poverty. But there are Jewish families in France who are wealthier than we are."

We established a good rapport and he invited me to his house for dinner. I enjoyed the dinner immensely, but committed a major "faux pas" by refusing to taste the Chateau Lafitte. I ordered a Coca-Cola instead. The servants gasped, Elie laughed, and I, the American, explained that Coke was the wine of my country.

I timed my visit so I could attend and observe the most important fundraising event of the French organization, which was held in the famous Conciergerie, the historic building located on the banks of the Seine in the center of Paris. It's where Queen Marie Antoinette was imprisoned before she was guillotined. It was gorgeous. It was stunning. This was the single most beautiful UJA affair I ever attended in my life. But from the fundraiser's point of view, it was a total disaster.

Some five to six hundred of the wealthiest Jewish families were present. The women wore beautiful gowns, and the men were in black tie.

The reception began at 7:30 p.m. and dinner was served at 9:00 p.m. I wondered when and how they would conduct the fundraising. That, after all, was the purpose of the evening.

The dinner was a six course affair which lasted until 11 p.m. There was no program. There were no speakers. I was getting nervous. Soon, the people would leave. When were the leaders going to make the appeal?

A little after 11 p.m., Elie de Rothschild left his table and went to the end of the long room which was obscured by many huge columns. He mounted a small platform and began to speak. The audience, with the exception of a few people, mostly staff, I later learned, didn't listen and couldn't have cared less. Conversation continued undiminished. The Baron spoke briefly of the need to support the campaign and asked those present to fill out the envelopes on their tables. Some probably did, although I saw many empty envelopes scattered about the tables after the hall emptied.

This was fundraising? Envelopes on the table? Hardly anyone listening? My surprise turned to disbelief when I later learned that the whole evening—which must have been costly indeed—was paid for by the organization, and not the attendees.

That made up my mind to accept the offer. From what I learned during my stay, I was sure I could bring about better results. They certainly couldn't be worse.

After weeks of escalating threats against its survival, in a pre-emptive strike on June 6, 1967, Israel pulverized the air forces of Egypt, Syria and other Arab countries. Then they quickly overran the Sinai. When Jordan's King Hussein ignored a warning to stay out of the war, they chased his Army across the Jordan, liberated Jerusalem and the entire West Bank and Gaza.

Jews around the world were euphoric. David had slain Goliath. The mortal danger to Israel was over (for the time being). No Jewish community in the world was as deeply affected as the French.

The event was the Six Day War.

Because it was the largest Jewish community in Europe, due to its proximity to Israel, and because the French remembered the Holocaust and the loss of several hundred thousand of their own, there was an outburst of pride in the Israeli victory that astonished the usually staid French. Discussions began to create a unified French Jewish Fundraising organization, serving both the needs of the growing local community, as well as Israel. No such combined drive existed anywhere outside of the United States and Canada.

It was in this atmosphere of excitement that my family and I left for Paris aboard the S.S. France. Jordan and I made arrangements to meet the day after my arrival. I was anxious to discuss the affect of these recent developments on our plans. On the third day of the voyage, the ship's bulletin carried the report that Charles Jordan, the Director-General of the JDC, had disappeared in Prague. There was concern for his life.

Upon our arrival in Paris on August 20, we were greeted with screaming headlines in the French newspapers. Jordan, the man responsible for my being in Paris, had been found dead in Prague's Vlatava River. I was stunned. I couldn't believe it.

Months later it was learned that Jordan had arrived in Prague on August 14, from Rumania. As a prominent Jewish leader with top level contacts in Eastern Europe, he was trailed by Palestinian guerrillas throughout his trip.

On the evening of August 16, he left his hotel room, telling his wife that he was going out for cigarettes. When he didn't return, his wife notified the concierge. They had seen him walk out of the hotel. The next call was to the American Embassy, who called Czech State Security. The search went on for four days. Then his body was found floating in the Vlatava River.

Although the Czechs claimed that Jordan had committed suicide, an independent autopsy established the fact that traces of drugs were found in his pancreas. Jordan had been murdered.

Shortly after leaving his hotel to buy cigarettes, he was abducted by four swarthy men, who dragged him into a car and sped away. This was in full view of three carloads of Czech security men, who watched Jordan and did nothing. They assumed he was an Israeli spy. The speeding car halted at the Egyptian Embassy and Jordan was carried inside. Czech security observed the entrance with an infra-red camera.

In the early morning hours, a group of men were observed carrying a body into a car. They drove the short distance to the riverbank and tossed in the corpse. They then returned to the embassy.

The Czechs were now in a dilemma. The Egyptians were allies. How could they denounce them and try them for murder? In the end, the situation was handled diplomatically. The secretary of the Czech's Communist Party Central Committee summoned the Egyptian Ambassador. An agreement was reached whereby the murderers would leave the country immediately.

The sordid affair ended the life of one of the finest, ablest Jewish professionals in the world. It was a severe blow to me personally and it was also a tremendous loss to the Jewish community. As I began my work in Paris, I missed him.

We rented an apartment near the Champ de Mars, directly overlooking the Eiffel Tower. Our children were enrolled in a bilingual school. We made friends. Life in France was enchanting. We traveled a lot and took advantage of everything Paris had to offer.

In the aftermath of the Six Day War, the French Jewish community was unified in their support of Israel, and our efforts to organize the Appel Unifie Juif de France were well met. Individuals from old French families and those who only recently came from North Africa were willing to become involved. The fundraising situation had changed.

As a result, our fundraising campaign tripled the results of the previous year. I was given credit for these results and, while modesty has never been one of my strong traits, I can honestly say that it was the post-Six Day War climate which was responsible for the success.

With an enthusiastic French staff, we changed some of the Frenchmen's outdated fundraising methods, and organized real fundraising events throughout the country. We made French Jews more aware of their responsibilities towards Jewish causes, both in Israel and at home.

I received permission to complete a third year in France and we were raising more than three times the amount which was raised prior to the creation of the Appel Unifie. It had been the right move at the right time, and I was fortunate to have made it.

Professionally, I couldn't have asked for more. It was exciting to be involved in something totally new. As the only American-Jewish professional active in Europe, I visited many countries on behalf of Keren Hayessod, the world-wide fundraising arm of

Israel. I traveled to England, Switzerland, Germany, Belgium and Holland to address the leadership on effective fundraising.

There was one major philosophical difference between the American way of Jewish community organization and the way it was done in Europe. In the States, the fundraising professional was part of the leadership. He was involved, more often than not, in taking the initiative, in running the affairs of the community. He was accepted totally, even socially, by the leadership of his organization or community. Not so in Europe. Here the professional was treated like a secretary, ordered to carry out the decisions of the lay leadership. It was most often "Oui, monsieur" instead of "Non, monsieur." The professionals were underpaid and undervalued.

The three years went by like a dream. At the end, my family and I were anxious to come back to the States and pick up our lives. Laurie, our oldest, was ready for college.

When people heard I was returning to the States, I received several interesting offers. Once again I was faced with a dilemma—which offer to accept. It boiled down to two. I could go back to my old job on the West Coast or accept running the UJA Campaign in New York, with a staff of 500, and an annual goal of over $60,000,000. It was the most important Jewish fundraising position in the world.

XXVII

Executive V.P. UJA-Fed
GREATER NEW YORK

I WAS IN NEW YORK. The meeting in Morris Levinson's spacious Park Avenue office lasted almost two hours. When it was over, the three men excused themselves briefly. When they returned, they offered me the position as CEO of New York UJA.

I floated out of that office on a cloud. I was 46 years old and had been in America for 23 years. I had no formal education, but Auschwitz had taught me well. I was able to choose the field of Jewish fundraising as my profession, and keep the promises I made to all those who died. My work was extremely satisfying and I enjoyed being involved in what I felt was an important time in Jewish history.

I was lucky to be in France when tremendous changes took place, and I was a beneficiary of those changes. I knew fundraising and the American Jewish community. I knew my strong points and my limitations. Was I biting off more than I could chew?

With all my self-confidence, I wasn't sure I had the background to run an organization with a staff of 500, a budget of $5,000,000 and a total annual goal of more than $60,000,000. I'd never done anything like that before. Neither had anyone else, Irving Bernstein, second in command at National UJA, told me when I confided in him. I had worked with Irving for years.

I took six months before I finally decided to accept the offer. In September, 1970, as the Jewish New Year began, I came to New York.

On my very first day in the office, Herb Rose, UJA's attorney, called and told me I could go home, that I had already earned my first day's pay.

"How did I do that?" I wanted to know.

"Well, I just received a call from the attorney handling a very large estate. He let me know the will provided for a payment of $3 million to UJA in recognition of the help given to a family member many years ago. Congratulations, you're off to a good start."

On a whim, my secretary looked up the deceased's annual contributions in previous years. I couldn't believe my eyes. It was $100.

At UJA New York, I found 235 people dedicated to raising money for the needs of the world community of Jews. There was a fundraising staff of over 150 men and women, an executive staff of 40 people, a public relations department with 20 professionals, and a separate women's division with 25 professionals. The organization was broken down into hundreds of separate trades and professions, each one with its own chairman and committee.

We covered them all. The smallest division was the one for Jewish detectives. The largest division was the Wall Street division. There was one for bridal gown manufacturers, one each for category of lower priced, medium priced and high priced dresses; pest control and policemen, and more. In conducting highly detail-oriented, citywide campaigns in the Greater New York area, the staff ran an incredible total of some 7,000 meetings a year—an average of 20 meetings a day every day of the year.

The UJA is a highly sophisticated organization which can call on thousands of volunteers. They spend an inordinate amount of time conducting the very serious business of raising money. Overhead is low—less than 10% of what is raised. This is because the thousands of volunteers make things work.

Through experience garnered over the years by doing fundraising in the small towns and hamlets across the U.S.A., the

UJA developed a highly effective method which, while often ridiculed and attacked, was responsible for the large amounts raised throughout the country. It's called card-calling. Here's how it works.

At each division function—breakfast, lunch, dinner—a speaker would tell the "story," and describe the current needs. Then the division chairman would stand up after the speaker was through, and say, "Well, friends, now you know what's going on. It's clear we're going to have to do our share. Business has been good. So let's do what Jews have been doing for generations. Let's respond as generously as we can."

The chairman would then tell the audience how much he or she has given personally and would publicly call on every person in the room to get up and announce what he or she would contribute that year. The staff carefully prepared the name cards for each attendee, showing how much he or she gave the previous year. This would then prompt an appropriate response from the chairman. Not everyone liked the method, originally conceived by Joseph Willen, one of the most innovative fundraising professionals in the business. But there's no doubt it increased the amounts raised very substantially. It made UJA-Federation the recognized leader in fundraising.

Of course there were exceptions. If an individual came to the meeting and didn't want his name called, the staff immediately marked the card DNC—Do Not Call—and respected the person's wishes.

Another effective method was the role played by the senior campaign leaders before an event. This is how it works.

At a reception, which usually preceded the event, one of the overall campaign leaders, carefully prepared by the staff, would pull aside one or two of the prospects and, over a drink, would try to get him to increase his contribution. The prospect was often flattered to be personally approached by one of the senior leaders, usually a well known businessman. More often than not, the prospect agreed to the increase, helping to set the stage for the actual fundraising, which always took place after the entree and before dessert.

Over the years, I must have attended hundreds of these functions and never failed to admire the role played by our leadership. In addition to their own substantial financial contributions, the amount of time and energy they gave to us was enormous. That dedication, more than anything else, accounts for the ever-increasing totals raised in successive campaigns.

When one of the senior UJA officials was asked what the formula is for such great success, he replied, "First you need 2,000 years of Jewish suffering." He had a point.

There's no doubt the Holocaust and the establishment of the State of Israel, the dramatic wars forced upon the young nation, other political and military events, and the huge influx of immigrants from more than 100 different countries, inspired Jews from all walks of life to respond generously. Added to that were the growing needs of the Jewish communities in the United States. There was also the pride Jews felt for maintaining a huge network of institutions covering these needs.

I found my work exciting and fulfilling. Time was meaningless. I had meetings around the clock—early morning meetings, receptions, dinners, Sunday functions. There was no time to think. Sixty, seventy hours were the norm per week. I worked with men and women who reached the pinnacle of success in their fields and were willing to take on leadership roles in the organization. This wasn't Hollywood. This was major league.

I'm going to indulge in a bit of name dropping. Among the powerhouses I was privileged to meet were people like Gus Levy, the legendary Wall Street figure; Charles Revson of Revlon; Larry Tisch, originally head of the Loew's Corp., and now president of CBS; Alan Greenberg of Bear Stearns; Ludwig Jesselson of Philip Brothers; Burton Resnick, Eugene Grant, Jack Weiler and Bob Arnow from the real estate industry; Jim Weinberg and Bill Wishnick of WITCO, to name a few.

These men were demanding. They had no time to waste. As busy as they were, they always found time to work closely with our staff and help build the organization into the major fundraising institution in New York.

And then there were the flukes, the strange things that happen. Like the dead man's estate, sometimes things just fell into my hands. One morning I read an article in the *New York Times* about a man who had just won the Nobel Prize for science. The article said that he was brought to America as a youngster, before the war, through the efforts of a Jewish relief organization.

The story intrigued me. There but for the grace of the exit visa, went I. Lotte was saved by relief organizations, too. On a whim, I sat down and wrote the distinguished scientist a letter, congratulating him on his achievements.

Two weeks later, I received a note in response.

"Dear Mr. Michel:

Many thanks for your kind letter. May I ask a favor? I would like to donate some of my prize money to your organiza-tion, and return some of the debt for bringing me from Germany in the 1930's and placing me in a United States home.

Could you tell me to whom I should address this, as well as a bank account number? Is UJA-Federation tax deductible?

Many thanks in advance."

I wrote back telling him that of course, his donation was tax deductible and gave him the information he asked for.

The return mail brought his check for $25,000.

The first real challenge came with the Yom Kippur War. Early on the morning of Saturday, October 6, 1973, the holiest day in Judaism, as Jews all over the world were preparing to go to syna-gogue, I heard the news of the Egyptian surprise attack against Israel. There was mention of considerable casualties. The news got worse during the day, and it became obvious by the hour, Israel was facing an invasion from both Egypt and Syria.

When I came home from synagogue, I called Sanford Solender, the executive head of the New York Federation of Jewish Philanthropies.

I met Sandy when I started in New York. At the same time I started at UJA, he started at Federation. Until we came to New York, there was only minimal contact between the top professionals of the two organizations. Federation dealt exclusively with the needs of the New York Jewish community in the areas of education, health, and social services, while UJA's responsibility was to support Israel and Jews in need throughout the world.

We had separate buildings, separate boards, even separate times for our annual fundraising activities. UJA campaigned in the spring, Federation in the fall. That year, the opening dinner for the annual Federation campaign was set for Monday, October 8th, two days after the outbreak of the war.

"I was expecting your call, Ernie." Sandy's voice came over the phone. "Do you have any more information than we get on the air?"

"Not yet, although I'm in touch with the Israel Consul General."

"You know, of course, we've scheduled our opening dinner for Monday. Obviously we'll have to cancel. With Israel in danger, I can't see how we can proceed with business as usual."

"That's why I'm calling you," I replied. "We have to do some creative thinking to rally the whole New York Jewish community in an emergency fund drive for Israel."

The next morning, Sandy and I met. I had already discussed some possible options with my current president, Larry Tisch, while Sandy spoke to his president, Larry Buttenweiser.

The understanding we arrived at was that UJA and Federation would jointly launch a city-wide Israel Emergency Fund campaign. The two professional staffs would be merged and the fundraising campaign would be coordinated at UJA. Regardless of how much was raised, the needs of the local Jewish agencies would be protected, and they would be guaranteed the same total net amount Federation received during the previous year. Everything else would go to help the people of Israel.

The agreement was simple, clear and clean. Everyone understood it. Eventually, it was unanimously endorsed by the boards of both organizations.

The next step was to select the best possible person to lead this special emergency effort. We all agreed that Israeli-born

Meshulam Riklis, now a prominent American businessman, would be an ideal choice to head the campaign.

I met Rik when I first came to New York. He was young, energetic, charismatic and generous. Rik was also outspoken and had the proven ability to get things done. He was a natural leader, and served previously as the city-wide UJA Chairman.

When I met him, he told me that he was packing, getting ready to leave for Israel. He simply couldn't stay in the States, he said, while Israel was in peril. However, he did agree to breakfast with me the next morning. His flight was leaving that night.

"Rik," I opened the discussion, knowing that he was under pressure, "there are two things I want to ask of you. We want you to serve as chairman of the city-wide Israel Emergency Fund."

There was not a moment of hesitation.

"Done. I accept. What's number two?"

I swallowed and hesitated a moment.

"We want you to set the pace for this campaign with a $5,000,000 gift."

I knew I was playing for high stakes. I also knew that Rik would understand better than anyone else, the importance of that kind of giving at this particular time.

"Five million," he repeated.

I nodded.

"How much time will I have to pay it?"

"Right now I need your commitment," I replied. "That's the important thing. As far as payment is concerned, this is October, 1973. I would hope that you could pay it off in a year, possibly two."

We were both silent for a moment. Then Rik looked straight at me.

"There is nobody who has a deeper feeling for Israel than I do. I am leaving tonight for Israel to be with them. I don't know when I'll be back. If you can get a few of the other key givers to join me, I'll make that commitment to you now with the understanding that I need time to pay off that pledge."

I had to hug him. It was the single largest solicitation I have ever made and it took less than two minutes. Both Rik and I knew instinctively that only this kind of giving would show the Jewish community in New York and the rest of the country what was expected.

Because of Rik's commitment, three other families in New York joined us by pledging the same amount. The outpouring of concern was unlike anything we had ever seen. People came to the office with cash, jewelry, checks. Within a few days the Jewish Community in Suffolk County organized a mass rally which was attended by 4,000 people. Through the efforts of a few dedicated individuals, we ran two telethons on behalf of the Israel Emergency Fund which brought in millions of dollars. We broke all records.

Immediately after Rik's return from Israel he addressed a major gifts rally. Men who had never been to a UJA function sat in the audience, and the outpouring of pledges was truly awe inspiring. They were led by Larry Tisch, Herbert Tenzer, Leonard Block, Jack Weiler, William Rosenwald and Charles Revson, who, in addition to their own substantial contributions, spent hours on the phone and at meetings, where they solicited other members of the community.

We worked eighteen-hour days. It was exhilarating, one of the greatest experiences I had in my professional career.

XXVIII

David Ben Gurion and Pinchas Sapir

PEOPLE OFTEN ASK about the Israeli leaders I've worked with. While I know and have worked with many great men and women, two stand out in my mind as being extraordinary.

The first, an obvious choice, is Prime Minister David Ben Gurion, the Founding Father of the State. He was the dominant figure in the years preceding statehood, during the war of Independence and during the early years of Israel's existence.

The first time I met him was in the mid-60's. My group visited his office for a photo opportunity and to hear a few words. Short of stature, with a flowing mane of white hair, he had a high pitched voice and spoke English with a heavy accent. Just looking at the man gave me the shivers. I remembered that he visited some of the DP camps in Germany shortly after the end of the war.

The second time I saw him was in Los Angeles. He and his wife, Paula, attended a number of meetings and bought books. No matter where he was, he made regular excursions to bookshops, to browse and to buy. He had an insatiable appetite for books, especially history books.

He was also an impatient man, with no patience for small talk. He played the cocktail party-dinner circuit game because it was expected of him, but he clearly didn't like it. At one function he was supposed to put on a tuxedo. Being rather short and stocky, it wasn't easy to find one that would fit. He hated to wear it and couldn't wait to get out of his "penguin suit."

I spent time with him because we had arranged for him to meet individuals who had made substantial contributions to major educational projects in Israel. He went through the motions of being interested in them, but it was obvious that his heart wasn't in it. He spent most of his time in his suite, writing. At that time, he was finishing his monumental history of the creation of Israel. To this day, it remains one of the important historical works about the development leading up to the Declaration of Independence and the first two decades of the new State.

The third time I met him was in Paris in the late 60's, after he had resigned from the post of Prime Minister for the second time. He was staying at the Bristol Hotel and I was among those planning his schedule in Paris. It included some official as well as private functions, including a dinner hosted by Baron Guy de Rothschild for some prominent members of the French government.

That was when I was working in Paris for the Appel Unifie Juif de France. Lauren was 15 and Karen was 12 years old. And so one day, after I brought BG, as they liked to call him, back to his hotel, I got the courage to ask him if I could bring my two daughters to meet him. He readily agreed, and I told Laurie and Karen that they would have a chance to meet one of the great men in Jewish history. I don't think they were as excited about it as I was.

The next morning, I brought them to the hotel. They were dressed in their best outfits. When we entered the suite, Mr. Ben Gurion was at his desk with his back to us, writing.

Discreetly, I waited for a while and finally approached him.

"Mr. Ben Gurion, you told me yesterday that I could bring my two daughters to meet you. They just want to say hello to you."

Ben Gurion didn't say a word. I stood there not knowing what to do next. He kept on writing. We just stood. The girls looked at me. I looked at them and then at Ben Gurion's back.

After what seemed like an eternity, but could not have been more than a minute or two, he turned around in his chair and asked the girls two questions, in Hebrew: "Do you speak Ivrit (Hebrew)?"

When neither one could answer, he asked in English:

"Are you planning to make Aliyah to Israel?"

Both girls, although they'd been to Israel and knew about the country, didn't know how to answer.

After looking from one to the other for a moment or so and not getting a reply, he turned to me, and with a brief gesture dismissed them: "Tell them to learn Ivrit."

Then he turned back to his writing. There was nothing for me to do but leave.

I must admit that it was one of the most embarrassing moments in my life and far different from what I had expected.

There's more to the story. Not long afterwards, on another UJA Mission to Israel, we went to Sde Boker, a Kibbutz in the Negev, where Ben Gurion made his home. His dream was to develop the Negev, the barren southern part of Israel, which is almost two thirds of the whole country, and since he felt strongly about it, he went there to live and to work.

After we spent a few minutes with him and just before taking our leave, he took me by the arm.

"Michel, how are your daughters?" And with a twinkle in his eye, "How is their Hebrew?"

"It's improved since the last time you saw them," I answered, amazed that he remembered that brief encounter in Paris.

He died in 1973, just before Laurie made Aliyah to Israel. I wish I could have told him about it—I'm sure he would have been pleased.

Ben Gurion was one of the great figures in all of Jewish history, and while my personal relationship with him was superficial, I considered it among the great privileges of my work to have been able to meet him.

Then there was Pinchas Sapir of the Jewish Agency, the quasi-governmental agency that distributes UJA funds in Israel.

In personality, looks, and in his relationship with people, he was totally different from Ben Gurion. Tall, bald, heavy set, with no formal education, he was one of the greats of the Jewish State, and I proudly worked with him during times of crisis.

Sapir was first treasurer, then chairman of the Jewish Agency. He had an uncanny knowledge of facts and figures, most of which he took down in his little black book. Only he could decipher it. The whole budget of the quasi-governmental body, names, addresses, the giving potential of the people he met over the years, were all in that little black book.

One spring day, when I was on the West Coast, I received a telegram from his office to let me know he would be arriving in Los Angeles on June 5, 1967. He would spend a few days in special meetings before going to South America.

The news from Israel was ominous. Nasser had closed the entrance to the Red Sea to all Israeli shipping. His speeches were inflammatory and an Arab invasion of Israel seemed to be only days, if not hours, away.

Sapir arrived in Los Angeles on June 5, as scheduled, and I met him at the airport. A jovial person by nature, he was not his usual self. On the ride to the hotel, he asked me to set up his schedule and, looking in the black book, ticked off the names of those he wanted to see.

The next morning, June 6, war had broken out between Israel and its Arab neighbors. Fighting was heavy and the Arabs claimed that the Israeli Army was suffering heavy losses. There were reports of air battles on all fronts.

I was at the hotel with Mr. Sapir. We set up a command post and made his calls. No one refused to see him. The Los Angeles UJA and Federation leadership, men like Victor Carter, Joe Shane, and Larry Weinberg, stayed at the hotel to make phone calls and line up appointments.

Eventually, our quarters looked like a doctor's office. We set up a waiting room, where we put the people on their way in to see Sapir, and they watched the news on TV. Everyone knew why they were there. Sapir asked them for large amounts of money for the UJA-Federation campaign. Gifts were earmarked especially for the needs in Israel.

While every contributor knows that funds contributed to UJA and Federation can only be used for social and humanitarian needs and not for arms and related material, it was equally clear that

Israel was in mortal danger and that huge amounts of money would be needed.

Mr. Sapir held brief discussions with each contributor. We allowed 15 minutes per meeting, not more. I'd bring in each person and make the introductions.

"Mr. Sapir, this is Mr. X. He's been a constant supporter and..."

"I know him. You're in the food business," Sapir said, shaking his hand and asking him to sit down. And then he ticked off everything he knew about him.

Sapir would get right to the point. "We need your help, now more than ever. While we, the Israelis, will pay what is necessary to win this war, in money and in lives, we need your help to take care of the social needs, the flow of immigrants, the old, the sick and the young."

The response was unbelievable. Men agreed to make huge sums available by going to their banks for loans, by emptying bank accounts and selling their wives' jewelry. Some sold their real estate holdings.

Sapir, who had been on the phone all night with Israel, was very tired but kept going. Sometimes he saw people alone. Other times he'd see them in groups. He always used the same approach. We need your help. Now. Today.

Sometime during the afternoon of the first day of the Six Day War, I took an urgent phone call for him from Israel. It was from his office and made my heart stop. They'd just been informed that his oldest son, Amos, had been severely injured in one of the early battles. Sapir was just beginning one of his solicitations. I told the person on the line to hold the phone while I went into his room.

"Mr. Sapir, I need to see you for a moment."

He looked at me. "Not now."

"Mr. Sapir. It's urgent. Please."

I took him aside and as gently as I could, told him about the call. He swallowed hard and gave me a private telephone number in Israel.

"Call this number and let me know when you have it." Then he went back to his business. As it turned out, Sapir's son, Amos, was injured in a tank battle in the Sinai and was evacuated to one of the hospitals. He was seriously injured, but eventually recovered.

After I got his wife on the phone for him, and reassured that his boy would be OK, Sapir kept up the killing pace until late that night. By that hour, the news from Israel was that the Israeli Air Force had wiped out almost the entire Egyptian and Syrian air forces and had taken over the skies. Israeli ground forces were advancing into the Sinai, pursuing the Egyptian army. Despite Israel's warning to Jordan to stay out of the war, King Hussein joined in the war with tragic consequences for him and great ones for us. In a few days he lost Jerusalem and all of the West Bank.

At 10:00 p.m., I took a physically and emotionally exhausted Pinchas Sapir to the hotel dining room, just to get him out of his suite, which was bedlam.

I ordered a steak and a salad for him, but before I could cut his meat, he put his head on the table and fell fast asleep. I had a little trouble getting him to his room. But when I looked for him early the next morning, he was already on the phone, getting the latest news from Israel.

Pinchas Sapir could have become Israel's Prime Minister but he said he wasn't interested. He said others were better qualified.

He died of a heart attack in August, 1975, as he carried a Torah scroll at a dedication at Moshav Novatim. When it happened, he was walking with Yitzhak Rabin, who later became Prime Minister.

Pinchas Sapir, in my opinion, will be remembered as one of the greats of Israel. With Shimon Peres, Golda Meir, Levi Eshkol, Moshe Sharett, Yigal Allon and others, he was part of a team of men and women who created a nation; they brought about the realization of a 2,000 year-old dream.

Among my prized possessions is a beautiful family Haggadah designed by the Jewish artist Arthur Szyk. In that book, I've collected the autographs of all those men and women who will forever be part of our history, beginning with Ben Gurion. My wish is that this priceless book will become a Michel family heirloom, passed on to my children and to their children with the knowledge that it was started by a grandfather who survived the Nazi concentration camps and played a small role in building the Jewish nation.

President Sadat's Historic Visit to Jerusalem and the Signing of the Israeli-Egyptian Peace Treaty at the White House

ON SATURDAY, NOVEMBER 19, 1977, I was in our New York apartment watching television, tears running down my face, as I witnessed the approach of a Boeing 707 marked "Arab Republic of Egypt." It was bringing President Anwar Sadat from Cairo to Jerusalem. The balance of my world was about to change. I suspended disbelief. The time was 7:59 p.m. Israel time, and the plane rolled to a stop on the tarmac at Lod. It was one minute early. The first person to reach its door was Rechavam Amir, Chief of Protocol of the State of Israel.

The door opened. A few seconds later, the familiar figure of President Sadat appeared. Thousands of people, anxiously awaiting this moment, broke into spontaneous applause. Men and women cried openly as they watched something they thought would never happen.

This truly historic visit, which brought together the Prime Minister of Israel, Menachem Begin, with the President of the largest country in the Arab world, had its genesis in an unlikely place, the Rumanian capital, Bucharest.

On a visit there in August, three months previously, Menachem Begin told Nicolae Ceausescu, the Rumanian President, that he "would be delighted to meet with any Arab leader, anywhere, anytime."

233

In October, 1977, President Sadat visited Bucharest. During his talks with Rumanian officials, the subject of Israeli-Egyptian relations came up. Shortly after he left, Israeli officials were informed that Sadat expressed interest in Menachem Begin's statement.

On his flight back to Egypt, Sadat made the decision to go to Israel. "It came to me like some divine inspiration" was the way he explained it later. "I believed, without any doubt, that this was the only way in which the problem could be solved."

In his speech at the opening session of the Egyptian Parliament, Sadat publicly declared what he had shared with only a few of his closest advisors. He was going to Israel. He dropped a bombshell.

"I would go even to the home of the Israelis, to the Knesset, to discuss peace with them."

The rest is history. After both men were interviewed by Walter Cronkite, Sadat stated his readiness to go to Jerusalem and Begin replied that he was ready to meet him "any time, any day." The formal negotiations were conducted through the U.S. ambassadors in Tel Aviv and Cairo. It happened so fast, people doubted it would really happen.

On my TV screen Sadat walked down the gangplank. He was greeted by Israel's President Ephraim Katzir and Menachem Begin. The entire Israeli cabinet was there. Golda Meir, Moshe Dayan, Ariel Sharon. All of them. Sadat had a special greeting for Mrs. Meir, "Madam, I have waited a long time to meet you" and kissed her. Golda Meir replied, "And I have waited a long time to meet you, too."

After a formal twenty-one gun salute and the obligatory passing of the honor guard, the motor cavalcade made its way to Jerusalem, where thousands of people lined the streets waving Israeli and Egyptian flags, shouting, "Shalom, Sadat!"

As an Arab diplomat described it later, "In one stroke, Sadat recognized Israel as a State and Jerusalem as its capitol, something not even Americans would do."

The next day, Sadat and Begin addressed the Knesset. It was a very emotional thing for me to watch the two former enemies talking to each other.

One of the statements by President Sadat said it all, "You would like to live with us in this region of the world, and I tell you in all honesty that we welcome you among us. I proclaim to the whole world that we accept to live with you in a lasting and just peace."

In early March, 1979, I received a telegram from the White House.

"Mr. and Mrs. Ernest Michel. The President and Mrs. Carter request the pleasure of your company at dinner in celebration of the signing of the Egyptian-Israeli Peace Treaty on Monday, March 26, 1979 at 7:30 o'clock, The White House. The Social Secretary, The White House."

Once again, my job allowed me to experience history as it was being made.

We began our day on the lawn of the Rose Garden, where the Peace Treaty would be signed. After we passed through security, we found two good seats right behind those reserved for members of Congress. I could see MPs on the roof of the White House, and in other strategic places.

Promptly at 2 p.m., President Carter, President Sadat, and Prime Minister Begin took their seats at a table in front of the White House, which faced the audience. All three men were dressed in dark suits and white shirts. Carter was in the middle, flanked by Sadat and Begin. There were a few brief speeches, then they signed the official documents, which were passed from one to the other by their respective aides.

We stayed to explore the White House grounds, snapping photographs. Everyone had a camera, even the Senators and Congressmen. Everyone knew that this one moment would be important history.

As an autograph collector, I used the opportunity then, and later in the evening, to get the autographs of the principal participants, Israelis, Egyptians and Americans. I met the Egyptian Ambassador, Mr. Ghorbal, Mrs. Sadat and one of their daughters. Walter Cronkite, who played an important role in bringing the two men together was there as was Barbara Walters.

I was very proud of the fact that Suzanne and I were invited to participate in such an historic event. I never dreamed it could happen when I wrote to the White House as a child. I was becoming a "White House Regular," but this occasion was very special.

We mingled, we gossiped, we gawked. The White House was open to all visitors, and we wandered through the rooms. A dinner for a thousand guests was arranged in two tents adjacent to the White House. We were assigned to a table with Senator and Mrs. Packwood.

I don't remember the food that evening. I was too busy walking through the tents and watching the two Presidents and the Prime Minister and their wives, the Secretaries of the cabinet and other celebrities.

During the formal part of the program, President Carter proposed a toast. Both Mr. Sadat and Mr. Begin replied. Itzhak Perlman and Pinchas Zuckerman entertained us.

It was an exhilarating evening.

We left Washington the next morning, and I, like many others, hoped that this was just the beginning, and that from this signing of a peace treaty between two ancient enemies, there would come a new understanding among Arabs and Jews. I hoped that in my lifetime, there would be permanent peace in that troubled part of the world.

I wish they'd hurry up. I'm not getting any younger.

An Aborted Meeting
with President Sadat

THE EXHILARATION that followed the signing of the Camp David Accords didn't last long. As part of the agreement, Israel gave the Sinai back to Egypt—it was an area almost three times as big as all of Israel. What did the Israelis have to show in return? A signed peace treaty, the first with any Arab state. At least it was a beginning, a very slow beginning. As far as the Israelis were concerned it was a cold, cold, peace.

During the first few months, thousands of Israelis visited Egypt. They went by plane, by car, and bus. Travel agents could not keep up with the demand for reservations. On the other side of the border the Israelis waited in vain for the first Egyptian tourists. Few came. Cultural exchange, which was part of the peace agreement, never materialized. Israeli artists weren't going to Cairo and no Egyptian artists made an effort to come to Israel.

Egyptian government officials pointedly refused to meet their Israeli counterparts. Then the autonomy talks broke down and everyone was busy blaming the other side.

American Jewish organizations organized trips to Egypt and were most cordially received. The Egyptians went out of their way to make them welcome and subtly asked the American Jewish leaders why the Israelis were so difficult to deal with.

Then I had another one of my "brilliant" ideas. Why not arrange a UJA-Federation Mission to Egypt and Israel? After all, the nations were at peace. Both countries had exchanged Ambassadors and trade between the two countries was growing.

We scheduled a mission to Israel for October, 1980. The only problem was to figure out how to deal directly with the Egyptians—to take care of the logistics. I talked it over with Stephen Peck, one of the outstanding Wall Street division leaders. He was a former member of the Board of Governors of the New York Stock Exchange, and he agreed to chair the mission. He's a young, successful, level-headed, and extremely articulate businessman, and I trusted his judgment.

When I proposed adding Egypt to the Israel mission, Steve, characteristically, focussed on all sides of the issue. It was a tricky idea with a very sharp edge.

"The idea has merit. Lots of it. It's a first for us and will attract—I believe—several hundred of our leadership. With the peace treaty signed, there should be no objections to adding Egypt to the program.

"Now, let's look at the downside. One, how will the Israelis react? Two, should UJA-Fed be the first to send a major group to make such a trip? Three, will it help our fundraising effort?"

I thought Steve had some cogent points which needed to be explored before we made a final decision. Then I floated the idea with a few of the officials at the Israeli Consulate in New York. No problem. When we sounded out key Board members, we found virtually unanimous support. Everyone wanted to go.

I'd met Ashraf Ghorbal, the affable Egyptian Ambassador to the United States, at the signing of the Israeli-Egyptian Peace Treaty a year ago. I phoned him, and after I explained what we what we wanted to do, he quickly agreed to discuss it with Steve Peck and myself. We flew to Washington to meet him at the Egyptian Embassy.

Ambassador Ghorbal is an extremely able individual—and an erudite and knowledgeable diplomat. He was involved in all of the difficult negotiations between the two countries, and was aware of the role UJA played in America and in Israel. He was also personally acquainted with many American-Jewish leaders.

Ghorbal liked the idea and offered his full cooperation. Steve and I were jubilant. We decided to make this the best mission we had ever organized.

A few days after our visit, Ambassador Ghorbal called me from Washington.

He confirmed our arrangements, and then he surprised us. He had contacted Cairo and explored the possibility of having our group meet with Egyptian President Sadat.

I was dumbfounded.

What an exciting idea! Our mission meeting with Anwar Sadat!

Steve was equally excited. As soon as the word got out reservations poured in. In a few weeks, more than 200 people signed up.

I stayed in touch with Mr. Ghorbal's office to discuss things like security, protocol and all the other details which go into meeting a Head of State. The trip was scheduled for October. In June, Steve and I were in Israel for the annual assembly of the Jewish Agency, the organization charged with the spending of the funds raised world-wide by the Jewish communities.

We went to the Foreign Ministry to spend some time with Joseph Ciechanover, the Director General. We'd promised to keep Yossi (as he's called) informed of our "Egyptian Mission" plans. When we told him that the Egyptians had arranged a meeting with President Sadat, he was startled.

"How did this happen?" he asked. And I saw immediately that he wasn't very happy.

Steve and I told Yossi about Ambassador Ghorbal's phone call and the New York leadership's decision to accept the offer to meet with Mr. Sadat.

"But why?" Steve asked. "You knew of our plans to go to Egypt and there was no objection then! So why now?"

"Very simple. It is one thing for New York UJA leaders to visit Egypt and see the country. It is another thing for you, the leaders of the largest Jewish community in the world, to meet with President Sadat."

Yossi hesitated a moment.

"Look, Steve and Ernie. I think we have a problem. You know that we have serious difficulties in working out the details of the peace agreement. As far as we are concerned, the Egyptians are dragging their feet."

He then outlined the problems, some of which we were aware of. Others were new to us.

"I want to make it clear," he continued, "that we are not telling you that you should not meet with President Sadat. That is your decision in New York. The only thing I can do is to make you aware that you are in a no-win situation and will be right in the middle of some very sensitive and extremely difficult negotiations between our two countries."

We realized, of course, what Yossi was talking about. Israel and Egypt, despite the peace treaty signed in Washington the previous year, had not been able to iron out their differences on issues which both countries considered to be of major importance.

Steve and I listened to Yossi's arguments. He was convinced that Sadat would use us to make the Israelis look bad. He continued. "Sadat will use this meeting to convince you of his good intentions and make us look like the villain. You will have no opportunity to question him, nor to make any comments. It will be a perfect opportunity for the Egyptians to state their side of the story on world-wide TV and you will be helping him to achieve his objective."

While we realized Yossi's argument might be valid, we were terribly disappointed because we knew that canceling the Sadat meeting would, without a doubt, cause a large number of participants to cancel the mission. We left Yossi's office deeply troubled but assured him that we would convey the Israeli point of view to our leadership. I promised that I would come back to him with our response as quickly as possible.

Before I left for New York, Ciechanover called me at my hotel to tell me that he had spoken with Moshe Dayan, then Israel's Foreign Minister, about our plans. Mr. Dayan made it clear that he did not want to interfere with our plans but stated, as conveyed by Ciechanover, that it would be against Israeli interests at that delicate stage if we were to meet the Egyptian President.

We left for New York still deeply troubled. After all, the arrangements had been made and confirmed. How could we get out of it?

Steve and I went over it again and again. This was a serious and unexpected development. In the end, we decided to call a special meeting of our board. When I called Ciechanover with this information he asked if he could attend. After hesitating a moment, I told him that he was certainly welcome, that his participation would only help us come to the right decision.

After returning to New York and discussing the latest developments with some of our colleagues on the Board, we concluded we had to cancel the trip. There was no justification for going through with it.

I hated to admit it, but our Israeli friends were right. There was more involved than whether we would have 100 or 250 people on the mission. The stakes were too high, and it was simply unthinkable for us to go against Israel's best interests.

"How do we get out of it?" I asked, talking more to myself than to the committee.

"Well," Yossi said, noting my distress. "You got yourself into this. You'll find a way to get out!"

"Thanks a lot."

Steve and I stayed after the others had gone, to kick it around some more. How were we going to tell the Egyptians that we couldn't go through with it? Should we write a letter? Make a phone call? Go back to Washington?

The longer we talked, the clearer it became that writing a letter was the coward's way out. The Egyptian Ambassador had been a gentleman from the beginning. A letter would add insult to injury. The same with a phone call. There was only one way to do it. We had to face Ambassador Ghorbal in person.

The Ambassador greeted us warmly.

"Are your plans coming along? We're looking forward to your visit."

Steve and I looked at each other. I was first to face the music. Steve, as the Mission Chairman, would make the case for our decision.

"Mr. Ambassador," I began, after clearing my throat a few times, "we asked for this meeting because of some recent discussions among our leadership."

Ghorbal's smile slowly faded. He was now all business.

I continued by telling him that our leadership was concerned about the tone of the ongoing negotiations between Israel and his country and that we were afraid of being innocently drawn into an area that we shouldn't be in.

I will never forget Ghorbal's face. He did not say anything to us but picked up his phone to speak to his secretary. The tension was awful. I wished there was a trap door in the floor. A few seconds later, a member of the consular staff joined the meeting, pad and pencil in hand.

"So I understand that you are rejecting the invitation from my President?" He looked at Steve and then at me. He was angry. His demeanor had changed. If I could have found a hole to climb into I would have preferred it. My heart was pounding so loudly I could almost hear it. How did we get ourselves into this? Me and my bright ideas. I should have thought about this more carefully.

Our lame answer did nothing to satisfy Mr. Ghorbal. There was really nothing else to say. We were sorry. We apologized.

He waved the sorries and explanations away as his assistant took notes.

The Ambassador rose from his chair. "There is really nothing else to say. Under the circumstances, you might want to reconsider your entire visit to Egypt." He did not shake hands.

Steve and I didn't talk much on the way back to the airport. We agreed that, as difficult as it was, we'd just gone through our only option. Then we canceled the Egyptian part of the mission.

It was the most unpleasant professional experience in my career.

XXXI

The World Gathering of Holocaust Survivors

IT WAS 1977, and I was in Israel again. As usual, I visited Kibbutz Nezer Sereni, which is one of hundreds of settlements in Israel. Some were founded more than 100 years ago; Nezer Sereni was founded by Holocaust survivors, and it's located halfway between Tel Aviv and Jerusalem. My friends from Paderborn and Buna were here. They got here right after the big war and then picked up guns and fought in the War of Independence in 1948.

Many kibbutzim exist on income from agriculture. Others make furniture, machinery, leather coats, or plastics. Some make frozen soy products, others make microchips, some do a few things at once. A few are even in the tourism business.

I make it a point to visit Nezer Sereni every time I'm in Israel. Piese and Onny both live there. They were both with me in Buna on Passover in 1943. Hilde, Piese's wife, was a member of the infamous Auschwitz orchestra which played Vienna waltzes as the inmates were marched to the gas chambers. The book, *Playing for Time*, describes what the orchestra went through. It was made into a TV movie some years ago.

Usually we sit around the coffee table and shmooze, our conversations often interrupted by children and grandchildren. We talk about our families, our friends, and sometimes, not often, about the years in the camps when none of us really believed we'd survive.

243

This time our get-together was a little different. When we made the date, Piese told me they had something important to discuss with me.

The weather was hot and humid. We sat in front of Onny's house. Munzie, his wife, had baked a special cake for the occasion. We drank iced tea and soda. After we swapped news about family, Piese turned to me. "Ernst," he said, "we have an idea. It's not new, but we believe it's exciting."

Onny nodded. I had known him since Paderborn. He is a tall, gangly fellow with a ready smile. We worked together in the same *Kommando* unit, cleaning streets and sewers. We were in the same transport, experienced the same dreadful years in Auschwitz. Onny, whose family name is Ohnhaus, is number 105006, which is tattooed on his left arm, just a few digits after mine. Piese got there a few months before we did. He has a lower number. Both of them, like me, were born in Germany. Like me, they lost most all their families in the Holocaust.

"Ernst," Piese continued, "do you remember an evening in Auschwitz—I believe it was Passover, 1943—we were talking about trying to meet with other survivors if we indeed survived?"

I smiled. I remembered that Passover. No matzoh, no nothing, just a dream of liberation, of freedom.

"Piese, did anyone really believe that any of us would come out alive from that hell?"

"Well, you did!"

He was right. I did remember. The game that we played was called "What if?" What would we do if we were lucky enough to survive. That Passover someone had suggested bringing all the survivors together. No one believed it could happen. No one believed we'd be liberated, either.

Munzie cut another piece of cake. They all knew about my sweet tooth. She looked at me.

"We have talked about that conversation and went to Jerusalem to see people in the government with the idea of organizing a survivors' reunion."

Onny broke in.

"You know what we got? A lot of tea and slaps on the back. Everyone thought it was a good idea, but nobody was willing to really help us."

"Who did you talk to?" I asked.

"Some friends in the Prime Minister's office."

"Why wouldn't they help?"

Piese got up and started pacing around the room.

"First, they said no one would come. They asked who wants to participate in a reunion of death camp survivors? The only thing you have in common are bad memories. Three: there's no money for something like that. Four: we've got more important problems to deal with. That's it."

There was a moment of silence while I thought about the idea. It intrigued me.

Piese looked at me.

"Ernst, you know survivors in the States. You have traveled in Europe and know survivors there. We know Auschwitz survivors here in Israel. Together we can get the names of several hundred people and their children and extended families."

"Who'll pay for this? It would cost money. It doesn't just happen."

"That's why we wanted to talk to you. You have more influence than we do."

"Where would you want to hold the reunion?"

"Here in the kibbutz."

"When?"

"In a year?"

"How many survivors do you think will come?"

"Maybe a few hundred."

"What kind of program were you thinking of?"

He hesitated a moment.

"We have some ideas, but nothing specific. We first wanted to hear what you thought about the whole project."

We spent the better part of the afternoon dissecting the idea, batting it back and forth. I tried to be the Devil's Advocate, raising objections, reacting to some proposals—all the while thinking whether or not this was something I wanted to get involved in. I didn't realize it then, but I really had no choice.

Instinctively and professionally, I knew that the logistics of such a reunion, especially if it involved people from various countries, would be mind-boggling. While there are some active survivor groups (among them the Bergen-Belsen Survivors Association, The Warsaw Ghetto Fighters organization and various landsleit groups) an international reunion of Holocaust survivors had never been attempted.

While Piese, Onny and some of the others were thinking of bringing together those who had been in Auschwitz-Buna, I began to think in much larger terms. Why not *all* survivors? Why not include those who had been in hiding, who had lived with false identity papers, who had fought with partisans? Why not make it something really big, pump up the numbers, invite a thousand or more? Why not make this a world-wide event?

The more I thought about it, the more I believed it had possibilities. There were still lots of questions and lots of hurdles, but I felt it was worth a try.

On the long flight back to New York, I made a list of those I needed to talk to. I realized that an undertaking of this kind would take a lot of time, and that I couldn't do it without the full support of the leadership of the UJA and my colleague Sanford Solender, my fellow Executive Vice President of UJA-Federation.

Sandy was the first one I spoke to upon my return to New York. He quickly sensed the scope of such a reunion and agreed that it had to be done on a large scale, if at all. More, it and must include survivors from all over the world. Not just camp survivors, but those who had been in hiding, those who had been partisans, those who left and joined military groups. It had to include any Jew who suffered at the hands of the Nazis.

"Sandy, where can we get the money that's needed?"

"There are foundations, I'm sure, which might respond favorably to this. I would think that UJA-Federation would support this effort as well."

I went to see Stephen Shalom, then the President of UJA. He, too, immediately sensed the unique purpose of such an event and agreed to let me use UJA-Federation facilities and allowed me to give it the necessary time. He went so far as to tell me that he would recommend the Board allocate a one-time contribution towards the budget.

As part of my preparation, I gave some thought to the cost of organizing the event, and realized that we would need several hundred thousand dollars. There was no mailing list, no staff, no organization—nothing. At the moment, it was just an idea born out of a dream in the hell of Auschwitz.

At a meeting with my colleagues, the professional heads of the major Federations from throughout the States, I presented an outline of the plan. All of them were born in America. They all went to college. They were dedicated. They were able, articulate, tough and accepted me with warmth and friendship after my appointment to head the New York UJA.

They asked some tough questions and I didn't have all the answers.

Who will run the show?

Who will handle logistics?

Who will have financial responsibility?

Will you set up an office?

How will you gather the names?

How do you plan to publicize the reunion?

When and where will it take place?

I also contacted the survivors in New York. Norbert Wollheim, who put together the Auschwitz-Buna dinner, agreed to play a role. His first wife died in Auschwitz, and his second wife had just died after a long illness. I called Sam Bloch, president of the Bergen-Belsen Survivors Association; also Eli Zborowski, Roman Kent, and others, all survivors and prominent in their various Jewish organizations. From Los Angeles there was Fred Diament and Sig Halbreich, and from San Francisco, Bill Lowenberg. They all agreed to join the effort.

One thing none of us were sure of. Would survivors come to Israel for an obviously highly emotional event? Would survivors be willing to face the past? Would they spend the money, several thousands of dollars for the trip and incidentals?

During that time I met Benjamin Meed, the President of WAGRO, the Warsaw Ghetto Resistance Organization. Ben, a small man with a round friendly face and penetrating blue eyes, was born in Warsaw, Poland, where his family had lived for many generations. He and his wife, Vladka, are both survivors of the Warsaw Ghetto. Ben, who does not look Jewish at all, became a courier in the Ghetto. He survived on the outside, posing as a Christian. Vladka is a true heroine. She fought in the Ghetto during the uprising and wrote a book about her experiences, *Inside the Wall.*

Ben became a successful businessman, but gave it up some time ago to devote himself full-time to perpetuate the memory of the Holocaust. He is a dynamic, imaginative, and driven individual whose total being is devoted to the Holocaust. The Meeds have two children, both doctors, and four grandchildren. Over the years, we became close friends.

At the suggestion of some of the men I had met, I invited Ben to join the fledgling committee. This turned out to be the best move I made. Ben brought a sense of dedication, an enormous zeal and a creative imagination to the project. He became my right hand, and he deserves a major share of the credit for the incredible success of what became known as "The World Gathering of Holocaust Survivors."

The second major move I made was hiring a young Israeli conference organizer by the name of Yitzhak Rogov. Born in South Africa, he immigrated to Israel in the 50's and went into the business of stimulating and running major seminars and conferences. Although we didn't have a nickel in the bank, and only uncertain promises of support, Yitzhak agreed to handle all technical and logistical details. He believed in the importance of the Gathering, as much as any of us. He did it for a minimum fee, and I am sure the Gathering cost him money. He didn't care. He felt the importance of our effort and put his entire organization behind it. Without him the Gathering could not have taken place. It is as simple as that.

The problem of how to finance the reunion was eased when we got financial commitments from the National UJA, The Jewish

Agency and most of the major Jewish Federations. My colleagues from the major cities came through and I will forever be indebted to them. Major funding also came from individuals I contacted and who responded as the plan gained momentum.

We were given office space at the World Jewish Congress and hired a small staff. We called fellow survivors all over the world and some of us traveled to many countries to personally enlist their cooperation. I went to France, England, Sweden and Germany. Others went to South America, Mexico and Italy. Word began to spread after we called a news conference in New York and set June, 1981, as the date for the four-day event.

Piese, in the meantime, organized the Israelis.

I was given the name of a young survivor, a woman living in Johannesburg, South Africa, by the name of Miriam Lazarus. I wrote to her explaining what we were trying to do and asked if she would be willing to organize survivors in her part of the world.

Miriam, one of the youngest survivors alive, was born in Poland in 1940. Her parents were able to find a Christian couple who agreed to take care of her as an infant. After the war, Miriam's father went to find her, her mother had been killed, but the couple would not give her up. After a lengthy court battle her father reclaimed his daughter and they went to settle in South Africa. Eventually, Miriam married and had three sons. She had little, if any, contact with other survivors and knew little about her own background.

One day I received a telegram from her.

"What right do you have to disturb me with the Holocaust? I had thought that I had put it out of my mind. Since receiving your letter, I have not been able to sleep. I am arriving in New York next week and want to meet with your committee."

She turned out to be an attractive, tall, blonde woman in her late thirties, full of doubt about the Gathering. The news of the planned event had shattered her tranquil life in Johannesburg. She simply could not understand why survivors wanted to get together, but after attending a meeting of the full committee and sensing the purpose of our plans, she became an ardent activist and went back to Johannesburg to organize the survivors living there.

Eventually, she brought more than sixty South Africans to the World Gathering. Miriam was given the honor of opening the program. For her, as for many others, the Gathering became a turning point in her life, as survivors were finally able to confront their past and, in doing so, could deal with it in a positive way and come to "closure."

The preparations for the World Gathering took more and more time. Evenings, weekends, holidays—every minute was taken up with the multitude of details involved in organizing such a momentous event.

Support came from many countries. Simone Veil of France, an Auschwitz survivor who became President of the European Assembly, joined us as Vice-Chairman. So did Elie Wiesel, the future Nobel laureate, and Stefan Grayek, head of the major survivors organization in Israel.

We stayed in constant touch with Piese and arranged for him to come to New York to participate in major decisions about format, agendas, speakers and so on. Things didn't always run smoothly. There were sharp differences, based on our varied cultures and lifestyles. While we all had shared the same hardships, we lived in different worlds and had different concepts of what the Gathering should be.

We did agree on most major points, among them our unanimous feeling that the event should not be a four-day memorial service. We wanted to show the world that we had become active, fruitful citizens in the countries where we lived and that, despite our past, we were able to lead productive lives. The Gathering would be a celebration of our survival and the strength of the Jewish people while, at the same time, we would remember, with reverence, our families and friends and all those who perished.

And so it came about that on June 15, 1981, 36 years (in Hebrew double chai—meaning twice life) after our liberation, some 6,000 survivors and their children and grandchildren, from 23 countries and four continents, came together in Jerusalem in an outburst of remembrance and emotion.

Four Days in Jerusalem

XXXII

JUNE 15, 1981 WAS a warm summer evening. The air was clear, the moon was full. That night six thousand survivors of the Holocaust gathered in the huge plaza at Yad Vashem, the national Holocaust memorial in Jerusalem, for the opening ceremony of the World Gathering. They brought their families—their children and grandchildren, aware that we were participating in a moment of grandeur and high drama. Born out of a chance remark by an inmate in Auschwitz in 1943, discussed over a coffee table in Kibbutz Nezer Sereni, and worked on by volunteers and survivors and the Second Generation (their children) for four long years, the magic moment finally arrived. It was the largest event in the history of the State.

I find it difficult, even as I write this, to put in words what it meant to me. I was torn between my responsibilities as chairman, thinking of all the big and little details that go into such an important event, and my emotions as a survivor whose dream was coming true. I thought of my parents. I thought of my friend Walter. I remembered the day of our arrival in Auschwitz and the agony of our helplessness. I saw the bodies, Leo, Jannek and Chaim on the gallows, and remembered Honzo and me taking them down gently. I saw myself on the death march from Auschwitz, and then relived our eventual escape. What had happened to us in our lives? How come I had survived and Walter, Felix and all those others I saw die in front of my eyes did not?

251

A fanfare interrupted my thoughts. Yitzchak Navon, the President, was arriving. We all stood up and I went forward to welcome him. He took the seat of honor and the program began.

Among the speakers were Dr. Yitzhak Arad, Chairman of Yad Vashem, himself a Holocaust survivor, and Gideon Hausner, Israel's prosecutor at the infamous Eichmann Trial.

Then it was my turn.

I stood up in front of that mass of humanity, and said many of the things I had said to the people in Port Huron and across the nation during my early years in America. But at Yad Vashem, on that day, my heart was full to bursting, and my words meant more to me.

"Like many of you, I had a dream. Mine was born in the darkness of Auschwitz, nourished by our liberation, and finally brought to life four years ago when a few of us met in Kibbutz Netzer Sereni. The dream was that one day—if we live—we, the survivors of one of the greatest tragedies in all of human history, would come and stand together to remind a world that would rather forget, not to let another Holocaust happen—to Jews or non-Jews. Once is enough.

I remember vividly my arrival in Auschwitz on a gray winter evening in 1943, after endless days in a cattle car, with the SS in their long leather coats, elegant, tall, clean-shaven. I remember jumping out of the car, hungry, frightened and whips lashing down. Then the line moving slowly forward until we came face to face with Dr. Mengele—the Angel of Death—and his thumb went up and down: Up, you live. Down, you die.

Since they have no graves where we can mourn, we have brought to Israel—in their memory—a piece of rock, a stone. Here is mine—it is a simple stone. On it are written the names of the immediate members of my family who perished. We brought these rocks from all over the world. Eventually they will be built into a monument here at Yad Vashem, so that our children and theirs, too, can have a place to mourn.

So here we are, all of us survivors, who came to Israel, sharing memories of a horrifying past, carrying the evidence on our bodies, but proudly standing together to tell a world: We have survived!

We survivors want to tell those who try to rewrite history and deny that the Holocaust ever happened:

Our eyes have seen;

Our ears have heard.

Our nostrils were filled with the acrid fumes from the gas chambers drifting over our camp. Day after day. Week after week. Year after year.

These hands have carried more corpses than I care to remember. Friends, families.

So don't tell us it never happened. We were there. To deny us that part of our lives negates our very existence. We are the living witnesses and we will continue to speak out until the last survivor is no more. After that, only faces on films and our recorded voices will be left to tell future generations.

My fellow survivors, touched by the madness of our nightmare, we have tried to live normal lives. Scarred by the acid of barbarous hatred, we have tried to give love to our children. Forgotten by a silent world, we have tried to avoid cynicism and despair.

Despite all we have known, we affirm life—despite the most ferocious of efforts to steal it from us. While we shall never forget, we will not live with hate. We assert faith and can hug and embrace each other goodbye.

We came to this place in a great burst of love for one another and for the ideals in which we believe—our Jewishness, our Israel, our ancient heritage.

When the final shofar of that closing ceremony sounds, we shall return home and most of us will never meet again. But we will leave with gratitude in our hearts for the miracle of our survival, for that of the Jewish people, and for the rebirth of the Jewish land. Go, my friends—go—knowing that history will tell our story forever."

The Gathering attracted radio, TV, newspaper, and magazine reporters from all over of the world. We were told that more than 700 media representatives were covering the Gathering.

Among them was David Schonbrunn, former chief CBS European correspondent. It was the first time that PBS had agreed to live coverage of an event outside the U.S. David, assisted ably by Laurel Vlock, brought the highlights of the four-day event to the United States every night at 10 p.m.

The most popular feature of the World Gathering was the Survivor Village. The Jewish Agency agreed to let us use Binyanei Ha'Umah, the Jerusalem Convention Center, as headquarters. One large room was designated as the "Survivor Village."

We knew that many survivors coming from different parts of the world had not seen each other since the years in the camps. Some hadn't seen each other since before the war, and would be searching for friends and relatives. In order to facilitate this search, we installed a computer system which was tied into the Israeli national system, including the records at Yad Vashem. All day long survivors queued up in front of the computer operators looking, mostly in vain, for long lost family members.

But there were also heartwarming scenes of recognition as men and women stared at someone.

"Aren't you...?"

"Were you not at Block 9?"

"Don't we know each other from...?"

At the conclusion of one of the meetings, a bald, tanned well-dressed man stopped me.

"Ernst—do you remember me from Buna?" I looked at him but couldn't place him.

Julius Paltiel from Trondheim, Norway, looked very different from the fellow in the striped uniform I had known in Auschwitz. He was one of the small group of Norwegian Jews deported to Auschwitz in 1943.

Of course, I remembered him. I just didn't expect survivors to come from Norway. I learned that Julius was now living with his family in Trondheim, that he was in business there, and that he had

PROMISES TO KEEP / 255

built the only Norwegian-style house in Israel. It was where he spent his summers.

Friends gathered from all parts of the world. Some even did find long lost relatives. We knew the emotional strain was great, and we were urged, by members of the Second Generation, to provide doctors, psychiatrists and nurses in anticipation of nervous breakdowns and heart attacks. It was a prudent move but none were needed. Not a single survivor needed medical attention. There were tears; yes. There were highly charged emotional moments. But it is a credit to our strength as survivors that not once during the entire Gathering was there even a minor incident to mar the drama of our being together.

On the second day, we broke into smaller groups and visited some of the kibbutzim founded by survivors during the years after the war. In addition to Nezer Sereni, where Piese was host, groups went to Lochamei Hagetaot, the kibbutz of the Warsaw Ghetto survivors.

Among those to address the survivors at Lochamei Hagetaot was the legendary Yitzhak 'Antek' Zuckerman, one of the last surviving leaders of the historic uprising of the Warsaw Ghetto. Those who were present will always remember the tall, dignified hero, as he sat quietly in the audience, listening to Elie Wiesel.

The next morning the radio announced that Antek had suffered a heart attack during the night and died. It cast a heavy pall on the Gathering as we paid tribute to his memory. He was a man who personified the strength, the willpower—the very best of our people.

Ben Meed and I talked for many weeks about the program for the last evening of the Gathering, the climatic event when we would meet at the Western Wall, the last remaining part of the Holy Temple, which was destroyed 2,000 years ago. Until it was liberated in the Six Day War, it was referred to as the Wailing Wall because, for hundreds of years, Jews came here to pray and to mourn the destruction and Diaspora of our people.

We invited Menachem Begin, the popular Prime Minister of Israel, and future Nobel Laureate, Elie Wiesel, to address the survivors that final evening. The Prime Minister had agreed, when

Ben and I met with him, to accept the role as Patron of the Gathering. He didn't commit to addressing the survivors, because he wasn't sure the pressures of his office would allow him to do so. We stayed in touch with his office as we got closer to the date.

There was still no final confirmation that he'd speak. I asked Yehuda Avner, Begin's advisor, for a meeting with the Prime Minister. Yehuda, who had been helpful and supportive from the beginning, came through again. The Prime Minister would see me for a few minutes on the day before the final event.

I was nervous when Yehuda ushered me into Begin's office. I didn't know what he was going to say. Yehuda told me the Prime Minister had a heavy schedule the next day, including his secretary's wedding in Tel Aviv. It didn't look good.

Begin was most cordial. He'd been following the Gathering through the media and remembered very well our last discussion concerning his appearance the next evening.

He told me he had promised to attend his secretary's wedding in Tel Aviv. Before I could feel deep disappointment, he added that he would make a brief appearance at the opening of the session, greet the audience and then leave for Tel Aviv. There was no way to get him to change his mind. We would have to rearrange the program, but at least the survivors would see and hear the Prime Minister.

When I came back to the hotel, Ben was making final preparations for what became one of the most memorable moments of that last evening. All the survivors would march en masse through the Old City to the Wall, carrying candles. Six thousand survivors and their families would carry 6,000 candles, each one lit for 1,000 victims.

It sounded good on paper, but the Jerusalem Police nixed it. Candles—No. The March—Yes.

Ben, undaunted, came up with another idea. The candles would be placed in front of the platform where the program would take place. All 6,000 of them. They would be lit by each survivor as they entered the Plaza facing the Western Wall.

And that's how it happened. Ben arranged for the candles. As the sun sank, Jerusalem took on that golden glow she is so famous for. The sky was a deep azure with purple streaks. The Mezzuin in the mosque above us sang his evening prayers, as below him, survivors and the Second Generation filed into the plaza, lit their candles and took their seats.

Then it was night, and the sight of the 6,000 candles flickering in the breeze, with a full moon lighting up the entire Plaza, left an indelible impression on all of us who were there. In addition to the survivors, the plaza was filled from one end to the other with thousands who stood in the back, and wanted to be part of this very special and cleansing moment in Jewish history.

At 7:00 p.m., the Prime Minister arrived in his motorcade. When he saw close to 15,000 people packing the courtyard, he seemed overwhelmed. I could see the astonishment in his eyes as he looked over the huge throng of survivors standing quietly in front of their seats. I saw him motion to one of his assistants. Ben Meed and I came forward to greet him. He turned to us and said, "You go ahead with your program. I will stay until the end."

Ben and I looked at each other. We couldn't believe the Prime Minister had changed his mind so quickly.

Immediately after Mr. Begin took his seat, the program got underway. In addition to speeches, there was one other major part of the program to which we had given a great deal of thought.

We wanted the Gathering to be more than a gathering of men and women who had survived the Holocaust. We wanted to leave a legacy which could be passed on from generation to generation, a reminder of the greatest tragedy to befall our people.

Elie Wiesel had agreed to draft "The Legacy of the Holocaust Survivors." It was read that evening by survivors from six different countries in six languages, English, Hebrew, French, Spanish, Russian and Ladino.

Fifteen thousand people maintained total silence. One could sense the emotion running through the crowd. There was an electricity, an unseen bond, as each of the six survivors, born in six different countries read this Legacy:

"WE TAKE THIS OATH! We take it in the shadow of flames whose tongues scar the soul of our people. We vow in the name of

dead parents and children; we vow, with our sadness hidden, our faith renewed; we vow, we shall never let the sacred memory of our perished Six Million be scorned or erased.

WE SAW THEM hungry, in fear, we saw them rush to battle, we saw them in the loneliness of the night—true to their faith. At the threshold of death, we saw them. We received their silence in silence, merged their tears with ours.

Deportations, executions, mass graves, death camps; mute prayers, cries of revolt, desperation, torn scrolls; cities and towns, villages and hamlets; the young, the old, the rich, the poor, ghetto fighters and partisans; scholars and messianic dreamers, ravaged faces, fists raised. Like clouds of fire, all have vanished.

WE TAKE THIS OATH! Vision becomes word, to be handed down from father to son, from mother to daughter, from generation to generation.

REMEMBER what the German killers and their accomplices did to our people. Remember them with rage and contempt. Remember what an indifferent world did to us and to itself. Remember the victims with pride and with sorrow. Remember also the deeds of the righteous Gentiles.

WE SHALL ALSO REMEMBER the miracle of the Jewish rebirth in the land of our ancestors, in the independent State of Israel. Here, pioneers and fighters returned to our people the dignity and majesty of nationhood. From the ruins of their lives, orphans and widows built homes and old-new fortresses on our redeemed land. To the end of our days we shall remember all those who realized and raised their dream—our dream—of redemption to the loftiest heights.

WE TAKE THIS OATH here in Jerusalem, our eternal and spiritual sanctuary. Let our legacy endure as a stone of the Temple Wall. For here prayers and memories burn. They burn and burn and will not be consumed."

Then, in response, six members of the Second Generation, our children, rose, one after the other to accept the legacy for themselves and future generations. It was a response drafted by the leadership of Second Generation on a sticky hot summer day in

New York, and I'm proud to say, my oldest daughter Lauren participated in the writing of it all the way from Israel. She stayed on the phone with her New York associates until it was done.

> *"WE ACCEPT the obligation of this legacy.*
> *WE ARE the first generation born after the darkness. Through our parents' memories, words and silence, we are linked to that annihilated Jewish existence whose echoes permeate our consciousness.*
> *WE DEDICATE this pledge, to you, our parents, who suffered and survived;*
> *to our grandparents who perished in the flames;*
> *to our vanished brothers and sisters, more than one million Jewish children, so brutally murdered;*
> *to all Six Million, whose unyielding spiritual and physical resistance, even in the camps and ghettos, exemplifies our people's commitment to life.*
> *WE PLEDGE to remember!*
> *WE SHALL TEACH our children to preserve forever that uprooted Jewish spirit which could not be destroyed.*
> *WE SHALL TELL the world of the depths to which humanity can sink and the heights which were attained, even in hell itself.*
> *WE SHALL FIGHT anti-Semitism and all forms of racial hatred by our dedication to freedom throughout the world.*
> *WE AFFIRM our commitment to the State of Israel and to the furtherance of Jewish life in our homeland.*
> *WE PLEDGE ourselves to the oneness of the Jewish people.*
> *WE ARE YOUR CHILDREN.*
> *WE ARE HERE!"*

The next moment was one that will forever be etched in my memory and I must admit I still get the chills when I think of it.

I stood on the platform and thought, less than fifty years ago, we were the victims of the Nazi death factory, with little chance of survival. Today we were alive and in the Jewish homeland.

Israel was created in 1948, to a large degree, because of the guilt of the western world, which stood by while millions of us were slaughtered. No other Prime Minister of Israel identified more with the survivors than the man I was about to introduce.

As I approached the microphone I felt the weight of the moment. The full moon was directly overhead and cast its glow over Jerusalem. Thousands of us were massed at the Kotel. It was a sight to behold. I realized then how far we had come, that out of the ashes of the Holocaust we were privileged to see the fulfillment of the ancient dream, the rebirth of the State of Israel.

My thoughts went back to my parents. How I wished they could be here to see this moment. But the knowledge that both their son and their daughter had survived was denied to them. (Lotte and two of her daughters stayed by my side for most of the four days.)

Perhaps here in Jerusalem, where miracles happened and prayers are answered, they joined with us in spirit. Perhaps the spirits of all those who had perished through the ages to sanctify His name, who died because they were Jews, were with us in Jerusalem on that solemn and important night.

I know today, that of all the events I have participated in, of all the things that have been part of my life since the escape on the transport from Berga, nothing will ever equal that magic moment when, full of emotion, I introduced Prime Minister Begin to my fellow survivors:

> *"And now the moment we have been waiting for. My fellow survivors from around the world: The Prime Minister of the State of Israel, Menachem Begin."*

I had tears in my eyes as I turned to shake hands with the Prime Minister. The entire audience rose as one in silence. There would be no applause at any time for any of the speakers—this was a once in a lifetime event that called for a different approach.

Begin began his address speaking without notes, with the following words:

"My sisters, my brothers, in pain, in persecution, in fate, loneliness, in bereavement, in orphancy. From the Baltic Sea to the Black Sea and the Mediterranean, including the island of Rhodes, from the Atlantic Ocean to the Dnieper and the Volga, millions of Jews lived for centuries in many countries.

Our fathers and mothers, brothers and sisters, our sages, some of the greatest in our history, philosophers, physicians, artisan, workers, good-hearted people, loving their families, devoted to their parents and their children, hospitable, G-d-fearing, believers in Divine Providence, loving Zion, believing in the coming of the Messiah and in Redemption, and among them a million and a half of our children."

There was absolute total silence as the Gathering listened to the Prime Minister conclude his remarks:

"Tonight let us say again, No, there will never be a repetition of the Holocaust. Never! This is our doctrine and our oath. Israel is strong and confident, stronger than the Jewish people has ever been since the days of the Maccabees. Israel is proud and humble, tempered by its experiences, struggles and commitments.

Israel will never allow an enemy to develop weapons of mass destruction to be used against the Jewish people, never again! The ultimate historic lesson of Masada is to learn how to prevent it. Never again downfall in heroism. Always, when the necessity arises, heroism and victory, so help us G-d!

As we take leave from one another, allow me to express on behalf of all the survivors from abroad, our profound gratitude to Israel for its very existence: we thank you for being here when we need you—and we always need you. We thank Jerusalem for surrounding us. We thank Jerusalem for enveloping us. My friends, had we met anywhere else, perhaps we would not have been able to resist the sadness that is part of our collective memories. It is thanks to the fact that we met here in Jerusalem that it was bearable at all.

And so, as we are about to bid farewell to our brethren in Israel and to friends elsewhere, let us pledge to one another our loyalty to Israel, our strength in friendship, our commitment to memory. We shall not give up, we shall not give in. It may be too late for the victims and even for the survivors, but not for our children, not for mankind."

Slowly, the survivors rose from their chairs and, holding hands, stood for one final moment of togetherness and memories, aware that we had shared a rare moment of Jewish history.

The Prime Minister, too, had risen from his chair and, after briefly speaking to one of his assistants, began to walk to the Western Wall, the holiest shrine of our people that has been in our minds and hearts for two thousand years.

I asked Mr. Begin's permission to accompany him and, receiving an affirmative reply, followed him the few steps to the Wall.

All around people stopped and, recognizing him, made way. Arriving at the Wall, he touched the ancient stones, bowed his head and prayed silently. I stood a few feet away, caught up in the emotion of that moment.

After a few minutes he turned, looked me straight in the eye and shook my hand. Not a word was spoken. That single moment, that silent handshake from the Prime Minister of the State of Israel, was a fitting climax to the greatest experience of my life.

Return to Auschwitz

MY LIFE AS A UJA executive was very hard on my family. Since 1948, I was very busy, traveling all over the world, dragging my family from coast-to-coast, continent to continent. There were overseas trips without the family, midnight phone calls, weekends taken with conferences, meetings, receptions, rallies; there was never any time to be a devoted husband and father. I was too busy. I needed to put community first. My job came first.

Suzanne, who had suffered the slings and arrows of such a marriage for years and years, began to show the strain when we moved to New York in 1970. I must admit she tried very hard, and always provided me with an impeccable home and hearth. But by 1979, she had enough, and I didn't blame her at all. The children were either in college or out on their own, and we decided to go our separate ways. We stayed close; in 1982, she was diagnosed with cancer, and I needed and wanted to support her through the tough times. Lauren and Karen were with her when she died in 1984.

A few months after the divorce in 1979, I was asked to appear on a radio program. I was with Elaine Winik, who is one of the outstanding Jewish leaders in the U.S., a past chair of the National UJA Women's Division and past president of UJA New York. My colleague, Sandy Solender was with me, too.

Amy Goldberg greeted us at the studio. She was utterly self-assured, confident and knowledgeable. She was also young, vivacious and attractive. I was intrigued and enchanted. I knew many women, but she really struck a high note. I was the quietest radio show guest in history. I let Elaine and Sandy do the talking while I sat there and studied her. I was trying to figure out a way to persuade her to have lunch with me, but I didn't have the nerve to ask.

A few days later, I saw her talking to Malcolm Hoenlein, a close friend and colleague who later became Executive Vice-Chairman of the Conference of Presidents of Major American Jewish Organizations. They were in the lobby of the UJA-Federation building, and I stopped to say "Hi" and left. When I was gone Amy asked Malcolm who I was. She didn't remember me. Wow. What a great impression I must have made!

The next day, I decided to call her. I used my involvement in the World Gathering as an excuse, and asked her if she would be willing to give me advice on handling the media coverage in Jerusalem. She was an assistant producer at NBC and knew the radio business. It might work. I asked her to meet me at Patsy's, my favorite Italian restaurant in New York.

Well, one lunch led to another, and we began dating. There were ups and downs as the two of us worked on our developing relationship. I, especially, had a tough time adjusting to our age difference, but we finally decided to take the big step. We were married in Elaine Winik's beautiful home in Westchester in the summer of 1988.

Amy knew what she was getting into. I had a history, and was well known in the upper echelons of the communities as being a total workaholic devoted to my job. There was no doubt that my job would come first. She also knew I came with the baggage a Holocaust survivor always carries with him—the commitment to the past.

In the spring of 1983, Amy and I were in the process of planning my 60th birthday party. Every birthday is meaningful, but as I get older I am more aware of how I beat the odds...

It was going to be a very special celebration. Besides close family and friends, I wanted my fellow survivors to be there to celebrate with me. Honzo and his wife, Martha, were coming.

In the middle of all of this excitement, I received a phone call from Bob Loup of Denver, the National UJA Chairman.

"Ernie, this is not an easy call for me to make, and I hesitated for a long time," he began. "I'm planning a national chairmen's mission to Auschwitz and Israel in July. The chairmen of many major and intermediate cities will be there. They are the highest caliber of Jewish leadership on a national scale. Now comes the hard part." He hesitated a moment, and I had an idea what was coming.

"I'd like you to consider leading the mission."

I assumed that was what he would ask. I didn't say a word, but I kept listening.

"Ernie. Don't give me an answer now. Give it some thought. If you feel uncomfortable about going back to that place, I'll stop right now. You know how much all of us think of you and what you've accomplished. I discussed this with some of the other UJA leaders, and we all feel that your leading the group would have tremendous impact. Nobody can tell the story the way you can."

I didn't say a word.

"Are you with me?"

"Yes, I am, Bob."

"I want to make it clear to you right away that the decision is totally yours. If you decide not to go, I will fully understand it."

I promised Bob that I would give it some thought. He was coming to New York in a week.

Back to Auschwitz! How could I do it? How would I react to seeing the train tracks where we arrived in March, 1943, the barracks, the remains of the gas chambers, the crematoria? Would anyone in their right mind want to do that? Could I do it? I remembered what happened when Suzanne and I went to Mannheim. There was no satisfaction in it. And a little piece of me wondered if I should allow myself to be used in this way.

I discussed it with Amy that evening. She thought it was crazy for me even to consider it.

"You're a strong person, but that's too much for them to ask."

She was right, of course, and yet I kept thinking about it. Bob had said that my leading that group would have a deep impact, and I believed him. It's one thing to talk about the Holocaust, about Auschwitz, in the abstract. It's another thing for someone to say: "I was here. This is where I stood when... This is where I fell... This is the place where Walter died. Here's where they experimented on Diana. Here's where they hung Chaim, Janneck and Leo."

I was sure I could handle it, but I wasn't so sure of how I would react.

What made the situation even more bizarre was the fact that the visit to Auschwitz was scheduled for July 1, my birthday.

It was absurd. But the drama of it appealed to me. I would be making a statement to myself and to all those on the mission. I would declare myself. I was physical and psychological living proof that despite what happened here 40 years ago, I was back, on my 60th birthday, to celebrate my survival in the place that tried to kill me.

So I decided to go. On June 28, 1983, together with 100 top national UJA leaders, chairmen and executives, I boarded a special El Al plane, the first ever to fly directly to Warsaw. The first two days were spent in the Polish capital, visiting the site of what used to be the Warsaw Ghetto.

We visited Mila 18, the headquarters of the heroes of the Warsaw Ghetto uprising, and, not far from it, the powerful monument created by the world famous sculptor Jacques Lipshutz in the Umshlagplatz, where they gathered everyone for deportation.

Early on the overcast morning of July 1, we flew to Krakow and took buses to Auschwitz. Now it's a museum and one of the most visited attractions in all of Europe.

I sat by myself, looking at the countryside whisking by, thinking of 1943, of the terrifying five-day train I took with Ruth and Onny and the rest, to this place. I thought about how I held onto Ruth one last time. I thought about the selections, the screams, the bodies, the hunger, the beatings. Little details came back to me. In my pocket I carried a letter to a baby boy who was killed in the flames. I would bury it under a barracks.

The bus went through the town of Oswiecum (Auschwitz), which I had never seen before. There was the railway station, there were people shopping, children playing. Did they go shopping while we were being killed a few blocks away? Were children playing then, too, while Jewish children were being gassed? Were these same people living here 40 years ago? Didn't they smell the fumes from the gas chambers? How could people lead normal lives while the biggest mass murder in history took place under their noses?

A few hundred yards beyond the center of town was a huge lot where dozens of buses and a large number of private cars were parked. There was a sign: 'Auschwitz Museum.' The buses had license plates from Germany, France, and all over Eastern Europe. There were hundreds of people milling around, many of them school children. All kinds of languages were being spoken. Tourists were laughing, eating, and children were running around. There was an ice cream stand, a book store, and another selling flowers. The atmosphere was Disneyland. It was so different from what I had expected.

Our mission was divided into groups of 25, each one accompanied by an English-speaking guide. Then we set off on foot. Nothing was as I had remembered it. In the museum, a movie theater showed a 20-minute movie of Auschwitz as it once was. The administration building had a place to change money, a vestiere to check coats, restrooms, a souvenir shop, and a cafeteria.

It was not until our group walked through the main gate with the inscription: 'Arbeit Macht Frei,' work makes free, that I knew I was back in Auschwitz.

Auschwitz was actually three separate camps within close proximity to each other. Auschwitz I was the main camp. This is where the SS commanders directed the systematic killing. It had 30 brick buildings, built for the Polish Army in the 1930s. Mostly non-Jews were kept there. It was also where Mengele conducted most of his medical experiments on twins. There was the death wall where prisoners were executed daily after being kept in punishment cells not larger than 3 x 3 feet. The cells are still visible today and give an idea of the terror methods used by the SS.

Auschwitz I also contains, behind glass partitions in several of the barracks, exhibits of the items brought to the camp by the doomed. There were suitcases, hundreds of them still marked with the names of their former owners. There were combs—thousands of them, shaving brushes, baby clothes, eyeglasses, crutches, prayer books, by the hundreds, by the thousands. Case after case, it was one of the most gruesome exhibits imaginable. Had some of these items belonged to my parents? I wanted to scream, but no sound came out.

The most horrifying case of all contained bales of human hair, blond, brown, black, white—all colors. The hair, bundled in large sacks, was then used by the Germans to weave blankets. Inmates at Bergen-Belsen were witnesses to this. Other items were used for the German war machine and industry. Nothing was wasted. Not even our ashes.

This was the first time I'd ever seen it. The guide, a young Pole, tried to explain to our group what took place here, never referring to the fact that over 90% of the victims were Jewish. He always spoke about Poles, Hungarians, and Czechs. He never used the word Jews.

I wanted to see Buna, where I spent most of my two years, but the guide explained that the camp had been totally bulldozed and erased. There was only a monument where our barracks once stood. The roll call place, the Krankenbau, the barracks—nothing was left.

The last place we visited was Auschwitz II, Birkenau, the greatest mass extermination center ever built, the place where four gas chambers and four crematoria worked 24 hours around the clock. This was where an estimated 1,500,000 men, women and children were put to death, sometimes at the rate of 20,000 per day.

Here was where we had arrived from Paderborn in March, 1943. The same train tracks were there, silent. Grass grew through the rails. A few wildflowers were popping through. Could grass grow in Auschwitz?

I closed my eyes to recall that scene 40 years before, the screaming, the dogs, the selection, hugging Ruth once more before she was torn away. I could hear the order of the SS: "Women to the left, men to the right."

The people on the mission left me alone with my thoughts, and I sat down on the tracks, not very far, I was sure, from where I jumped from the car that night 40 years ago.

It seemed so strange. When I was there I never realized how huge Birkenau was. Where row upon row of wooden barracks, hundreds of them, once stood, was a huge open meadow of sweet grasses. The only remnants were endless rows of chimneys, which stretched as far as the eye could see. Where once there was a sea of humanity in striped prisoner clothing, there was only silence.

The guard towers and the double rows of barbed wire still existed. The sign showing that one of them was electrically charged was still there. I remembered that wire very well. Almost every morning we would find the bodies of prisoners who committed suicide by running into it. Ludwig did that a few weeks after our arrival.

Why did I let Bob talk me into this? If I was smart, I would have been home celebrating my birthday with Amy, Honzo, my family and friends.

That evening, after we returned to our hotel, I told the group my story. I didn't have anything prepared. I shared some of my feelings about having come here on my birthday. As I spoke, I realized that coming back had been the right decision. I had survived. I had chosen to help build a Jewish future because I had been an inmate in Auschwitz. I was who I was because of what happened to me here, in this place.

When I finished, drained, Bob Loup came over and wordlessly threw his arms around me. Some of the other men also showed, by their response, how much it had meant to them to listen to an eyewitness account. There was no need to say anything at all. A handshake, an embrace, was all that counted.

My talk was a second catharsis, similar to my first speech to the students at the Port Huron Junior College in 1946. The world had changed a lot. I was no longer the same frightened, starving young prisoner. I was part of the leadership of the largest, strongest Jewish community in the world. I was respected, not for having survived, which was more a matter of luck than anything else. It was because I had kept my promise and accomplished many things in the memory of those who went up the chimney, by working for the largest Jewish philanthropic agency in the world, the UJA-Federation.

What brought it all home to me, early the next morning, was the sight of the blue and white El Al plane, with its Star of David logo on the tail, as it waited for us on the tarmac at the Warsaw Airport. It was taking us to Israel.

That's when my return to Auschwitz really hit me. The moment I saw the plane, I started to cry. Those were the first tears I shed on the trip, and I kept thinking that if there had been a Jewish State, a State of Israel in the thirties, Auschwitz would never have happened. There would have been a place for us to go. No affidavits would have been necessary. No visas. All the suffering would not have happened.

I've never appreciated the reality of the Jewish State and its role in our lives as much as I did that day. On July 2, 1983, when the El Al plane crossed the Israeli coast and landed at Ben Gurion airport, I walked down the gangway proudly, with a big smile on my face. I had survived to see Israel reborn out of the ashes of Auschwitz.

It was a great birthday present.

XXXIV
A Meeting with Rev. Jesse Jackson

I'VE ALWAYS CONSIDERED myself a liberal. I'll never forget my astonishment when, during my first speaking tour in Texas in 1946, I came across a drinking fountain marked "For Whites Only." I was appalled.

The first American soldier I saw in Germany was a black man. Black men had liberated Buchenwald and saved thousands of Jewish lives.

Because I suffered discrimination as a Jew, how could I be part of a society that discriminated against African-Americans?

I didn't take an active role in the civil rights struggle, but I supported it. Communally, this support operated on a two-way street. We supported them, and they supported us. Together we were very powerful. But even together, we weren't always able to overcome.

In the spring of 1985, President Reagan and German Chancellor Helmut Kohl went to Bitburg, despite the outcry of protest from Americans of all faiths and colors.

I was, personally and professionally, furious. What right did the President of the United States have to visit a cemetery where members of the Waffen SS, Hitler's elite storm troopers, were buried?

In order to show my anguish over this unfortunate and misguided diplomatic event, I accepted an invitation to join a group of forty Americans—Jews, African-Americans, Christians and clergymen, men and women—to fly to Munich when Reagan and Kohl went to Bitburg.

The trip was organized by the American Jewish Congress, led by its President, Ted Mann, and its Executive Director, Henry Siegman. With us were David Dinkins, the Manhattan Borough President, who was elected the first black Mayor of New York City in 1989, Wilbur Tatum, editor of the Amsterdam News, the largest black newspaper in the country, and Dick Gregory, the comedian and civil rights activist. Betty Friedan, the well known feminist and author, also joined us.

We chose Munich because it was the city in which a few courageous German students led a protest against the excesses of the Nazis in 1942. They were all caught. Some were sentenced to death and hanged. Others were sent to concentration camps. Joined by the handful of German survivors who belonged to the White Rose movement, we went to the cemetery where the dissidents are buried, to lay a wreath and pay our respects. This was where our President should have been. Not in Bitburg.

David Dinkins made a moving speech as we joined the members of the White Rose for dinner. As an African-American, he felt as deeply as I did the injustice and insensitivity of the President, and he expressed his feelings clearly and unequivocally.

Soon after we got back from Munich, I received a phone call from the minister of Trinity Church in New York. Trinity, which sits at the foot of Wall Street, is one of the oldest churches in the city. He wanted to know if I would be interested in sharing the platform with Rev. Jesse Jackson during services in observance of the Rev. Martin Luther King Jr.'s birthday. The subject of the joint lecture was "Celebrating our Differences."

"Are you sure Rev. Jackson will agree to share the podium with me, a Jewish Holocaust survivor?" I asked.

"Yes. He knows of you and is pleased to appear with you. He suggested that you go first and that he would follow you. After the two presentations we will have a rebuttal from each of you."

At the time, Jesse Jackson was not the most popular person in the Jewish community. Although I hadn't met him personally, I was familiar with his support of the PLO, his 'Hymietown' remark, and the fact that many considered him an anti-Semite.

On January 16, 1987, I stood at the pulpit of Trinity Church, next to Jesse Jackson. He was most cordial when we met in the Pastor's office, said that he had been looking forward to meeting me and was anxious to hear what I had to say.

The church was filled to capacity.

I spoke of the history of the Jewish people, the suffering we had endured over the years, and the similarity of these persecutions with those of the African-Americans. I quoted from some of the statements made by Martin Luther King, Jr., of his respect and admiration of the Jewish people and Israel, and voiced the hope that other black leaders would follow his example.

I acknowledged, with regret, the strains which were apparent between the African-American and Jewish communities. I concluded with a plea to work together more closely in the common interest and, by doing so, overcoming our prejudices.

Rev. Jackson, in his response, agreed that Jews and African-Americans had much in common and were equally beset by the "insensitivity" of a President who visited Bitburg while cutting social programs and vetoing sanctions against South Africa. These actions, he said, were part of the "spirit of racial disunity" that emanated from the White House.

We spent some time after the services talking about the rift between African-Americans and Jews and I sensed a willingness on his part to continue the dialogue in a more informal atmosphere. Since I've always believed in the value of open exchange, even where there are strong differences, I suggested to Jesse that we should bring together a few of my colleagues in the Jewish community who dealt with the process more directly than I did.

When I called him a short time later, I found him immediately receptive.

"But," I added, "no TV coverage, no press, no reporters, Jesse. Just a few of us around a table talking to each other to see if we have some common purpose in working together." He readily agreed.

We met a few days later on neutral territory, in the private office of a friend of mine. From the Jewish community, there were three senior executives of leading Jewish communal organizations. Jackson came with three supporters, two of them Jewish. I started off the meeting by talking about our Trinity Church encounter and my strong conviction that an informal, non-publicized discussion among people with the same common interest could only produce positive results.

I asked those around the table to put their prejudices behind them and see if we could find common ground.

The talks, regrettably, went nowhere. Jackson made it clear that he was tired of the constant "Hymietown" accusation and that he had apologized many times for his "unfortunate" remark. He felt it was time to put it behind him. He also made it clear that, while he took no responsibility for the anti-Semitic statements by the Rev. Farrakhan, neither would he repudiate him.

At that time, these two issues overshadowed any constructive possibilities. My colleagues, who had more experience in inter-ethnic community relations than I did, felt that unless Jesse made a clear unambiguous statement on these two points, there was no basis for further discussion.

We parted on friendly terms and agreed to continue the dialogue, but I knew that my efforts were not a glowing success. I felt badly about the outcome, but I've never regretted giving it a try.

As I write, Rev. Jesse Jackson has joined hands with Elie Wiesel and prominent rabbis in the New York Jewish community, and is bringing the story of the liberators, those heroic African-Americans who saved the lives of many survivors, to the African-American community.

The story has touched him deeply. He has made public statements to that say that African-Americans are bound to the history of the Holocaust and bonded with the Jewish people in that suffering. He showed the film "The Liberators" to a group of African-American and Jewish leadership at the Apollo Theater in Harlem. He admitted that if he had known this story as a young man, he would have been different. And he feels we need a Jewish-African-American coalition more than ever.

I hope he's right. It could lead to a new beginning.

"CBS This Morning" and the Mannheim Reunion

NOVEMBER, 1988

I worked closely with former U.S. Ambassador to Austria, Ronald S. Lauder when he served as Chairman of the New York *Kristallnacht* Commemoration Committee. A few days before the 50th anniversary of that infamous night of November 9-10, 1938, he asked me to appear with him on "CBS This Morning."

The co-anchors were Harry Smith and Kathleen Sullivan. Ambassador Lauder talked about the commemorations, which were going to take place all over the world, and addressed the importance of remembrance.

I talked about my memories of that tragic night in Bruchsal and Mannheim, and the fear that we felt. I had just returned to my office when someone at CBS called.

A gentleman from Dayton, Ohio claimed to have come from Mannheim and knew me from my school days. Did I want to talk to him? Of course, I said.

An excited voice with a typically German accent came over the wire. "Are you Ernst Michel from Mannheim?"

"Yes. Who are you?"

"I am Robert Kahn. Do you remember me? We sang in the synagogue choir together and we traded stamps. Now do you remember? I saw you on the CBS morning program. So I called

275

the CBS station here in Dayton and they put me through to New York. I didn't know that you were alive!"

Robert Kahn. Yes, I remembered a Robert Kahn, although that was over 50 years ago and so much had happened since then. We chatted for a while, exchanged addresses and phone numbers, and agreed to get together as soon as we could.

The more I thought about the call, the more it came back to me. Sure, I had always been interested in stamps, having inherited that passion from my father, and Bob and I had traded duplicates. We also played soccer together.

The next day the producer from CBS called again.

"Ernie, we put the Robert Kahn story, his seeing you on 'CBS This Morning,' on the wire services, and there's a great deal of interest. We want to bring him to New York from Dayton and have the two of you meet on the show. Would you be willing to come back?"

Of course I would. A few days later, Robert and his wife, Gert, arrived in New York. CBS put them up at the Essex House, where Amy and I met them for lunch the day before we were to appear on the show.

Bob said he still remembered me, although I didn't recognize him. After all, both of us were now in our sixties. He was able to leave Germany with his parents just before the war. They settled in Dayton, Ohio and, after serving in the Army, he became an interpreter. Eventually he became a civilian employee at the Wright-Patterson Air Force Base near Dayton. He raised a family and, like me, was now retired. We spent a lovely lunch together and spoke about Mannheim, our youth, and what had happened to us over the years. We also discovered we are both ardent tennis players and agreed to get together on the courts as soon as we could.

Bob was in touch with many former Mannheimers and brought up the idea of a Mannheim get-together. To me it seemed like deja vu, another World Gathering of Survivors on a much smaller scale. To my surprise, the issue came up again the next morning, during the TV program. Kathleen Sullivan asked if we had ever thought of getting together with some of the people we went to school with.

When Bob replied that we had vaguely discussed the possibility, Harry Smith concluded the segment with the promise that, if there was going to be a reunion, CBS would cover it. Well, it didn't happen quite that way, but the reunion did, and it astonished all of us.

Before he and Gert flew home to Dayton, Bob and I talked a bit more about trying to get the names of a few former Mannheimers to see if there was any interest. Since Bob admitted that it was difficult to plan such an event from Dayton, I agreed to bring together a few former Mannheimers in the New York area to discuss it.

The initial letter brought an overwhelmingly positive response. We chose Kutsher's Country Club in the Catskills as the best location, because many were observant Jews and would only eat kosher food. With the enthusiastic support of a small committee, we established a master list of over 500 names from all over the world. Then we began the difficult task of planning a program and handling the details which are always part of an event like this.

In June, 1989, 350 Jews from Mannheim, Germany came together for a four-day reunion that none of us will forget. Many of us hadn't seen each other since we were children in the 1930's. Some came from as far away as Australia, South America, Israel, Germany, and every corner of the United States.

I was strongly reminded of the World Gathering in Jerusalem. This time we asked all the participants to attach photos of themselves as children to their name tags. When people recognized each other, the scenes were unforgettable and moving. All of us met school friends we never would have recognized without the identifying photos.

The most remarkable part of the reunion was the participation of the two Rabbis who served the Jewish community in Mannheim before *Kristallnacht*. Rabbi Karl Richter was the rabbi in Mannheim during *Kristallnacht*. Rabbi Dr. Max Grunewald served the community from 1927 until his emigration to the United States in 1937. Rabbi Grunewald was the revered leader of the Jewish community of Mannheim while we were growing up. I'm sure no other Jewish community in 1989 had two living rabbis whose service went back seventy years. Rabbi Richter was in his late 80s and Rabbi Grunewald was in his 90s. (Rabbi Grunewald passed away at age 93, just before this book went to press.)

Our beloved Rabbis conducted a special Friday night service, aided by the last Cantor of the Mannheim synagogue, Cantor Erwin Hirsch. He was in his late 70s.

It was poignant to see these three elderly, yet vigorous men, sing the same ancient melodies, read the same ancient prayers, they read in our synagogue until that night in November, fifty-one years ago.

Rabbi Grunewald delivered the sermon. He spoke in a firm voice without any notes. We sat mesmerized as he evoked memories and obligations, our losses and the miracle of our survival. It was a Shabbat service unlike any other, and we knew there would never be another like it.

Rabbi Grunewald was the last living member of the 'Reichsvertretung der Juden in Deutschland,' the central governing body of the Jews of Germany. Its last president was Rabbi Leo Baeck, who survived the Theresienstadt concentration camp and came to America after the war. The Leo Baeck Institute was created in his memory, and its purpose is the study and commemoration of Jewish life in Germany. Today, I am privileged sit on its executive committee.

On a very personal note, Mrs. Emma Major, 93 years old, one of the oldest Mannheimers attending our reunion, came to see me on the first evening and to tell me a story about my parents.

"Do you know how your parents met?" she asked. I admitted I didn't.

"Let me tell you the story.

"Your mother came to Mannheim from Norden because she was offered a very fine position at the well-known department store, Hirschland. She was a beautiful young woman, and we became friends.

"She lived, at first, in a boarding house, but didn't like it very much. I knew a man, a bachelor, who had a cigar factory and owned a big apartment. This was your father. I arranged for your mother to have a room there, properly chaperoned by servants.

That is how your parents met, so I guess I had something to do with your being here. They were married in 1921. I was at the wedding reception."

I was fascinated. It was very remarkable to hear the story of how my parents met from a marvelous old lady, Mutti's girlfriend from Mannheim.

Should We Go To Germany?
A Meeting with the President of Israel

THE TRADITION OF annual *Kristallnacht* commemorations in New York began in 1978.

That year marked the 40th anniversary of *Kristallnacht*, the night the Holocaust began.

We planned, many months before, to use *Kristallnacht* as the theme for the opening dinner for the annual UJA-Federation Campaign. It turned out to be one of the most dramatic functions we ever held. The program brought me together, for the first time since 1938, with Rabbi Richter (who was the last rabbi in Mannheim and participated in our Mannheim reunion two years later) and Rudi Appel, a schoolmate of mine who was sent by his father to warn the Rabbi of his imminent arrest by the Nazis.

The highlight of the evening was the moment Rudi unwrapped a small velvet cloth containing a simple rough piece of stone. Everyone in the audience had their eyes riveted on him as he lifted the stone and showed it to them.

"This stone still shows the black burns of fire on one side. It is the only piece left of our synagogue in Mannheim. My father, who was a Board Member of the synagogue, picked it from the rubble the day after *Kristallnacht*. He brought it to America on one of the last ships leaving Germany before the war."

Turning to Rabbi Richter he said, "My dear Rabbi, although the synagogue no longer exists, this stone, a symbol of what hap-

281

pened to us Jews in Germany, should remind future generations never to let this happen again."

The stone will eventually be placed in the Holocaust Museum in New York, together with other mementos and exhibits from that agonizing period of our lives.

In early November, 1978 the "Zionism is Racism" resolution was introduced by the Arab countries during their annual diatribe against Israel in the General Assembly of the United Nations. The permanent representative of Israel to the U.N. was Ambassador Chaim Herzog, a member of one of the most distinguished Israeli families.

His late father, the Chief Rabbi of Israel, had also served as Chief Rabbi of Ireland. His brother, Yaacov, served as Ambassador to Canada and Director-General of the Prime Minister's Office, as well as in other prominent posts.

Prior to his appointment as Israel's Ambassador to the U.N., one of the most difficult and thankless jobs any diplomat could ask for, Chaim Herzog served as Military Commentator for the Israel Broadcasting Authority during the Six Day War. He was widely-known internationally.

In my role as Executive Vice President of UJA-Federation, I often had the opportunity to meet with him. I learned that he enjoyed an occasional tennis game, so I invited him to play and enjoyed our cordial relationship. He was an excellent competitor.

During the week of the "Zionism is Racism" debate in the General Assembly, we shared the dais at a dinner of one of the major Jewish organizations. Ambassador Herzog was to give the main address. My role was to bring greetings from UJA-Federation.

We all talked about the ongoing U.N. debate and the forthcoming speech by Mr. Herzog. "When are you speaking?" I asked him.

"On November 10," he replied.

I looked at him. "What a coincidence—November 10! The 40th anniversary of *Kristallnacht*! The exact date! It was the night our apartment was ransacked, the night my father was arrested and my mother was beaten."

After a brief moment, he turned to me.

"Ernie, you've given me the opening of my speech at the General Assembly!"

And that is exactly what he did.

In one of the most electrifying speeches in the history of the United Nations, and following the sad vote in the General Assembly, equating Zionism with Racism, Ambassador Herzog, rose at the rostrum in the G.A. Hall, and said:

"It is symbolic that this debate, which may well prove to be a turning point in the fortunes of the United Nations and a decisive factor in the possible continued existence of this organization, should take place on November 10. Tonight, thirty-seven years ago, has gone down in history as Kristallnacht, the Night of the Crystals. This was the night in 1938 when Hitler's Nazi storm troopers launched a coordinated attack on the Jewish community in Germany, burned the synagogues in all its cities and made bonfires in the streets of the Holy Books and the Scrolls of the Holy Law and Bible. It was the night when Jewish homes were attacked and heads of families taken away, many of them never to return. It was the night when the windows of all Jewish businesses and stores were smashed, covering the streets in the cities of Germany with a film of broken glass which dissolved into the million of crystals which gave that night its name. It was the night which led eventually to the crematoria and the gas chambers, Auschwitz, Birkenau, Dachau, Buchenwald, Theresienstadt and others. It was the night which led to the most terrifying holocaust in the history of man."

Ambassador Herzog concluded his remarks as follows:

"For us, the Jewish people, this is but a passing episode in a rich and event-filled history. We put our trust in Providence, in our faith and beliefs, in our time-hallowed tradition, in our striving for social advance and human values, and in our people wherever they may be. For us, the Jewish people, this resolution is based on

hatred, falsehood and arrogance, and is devoid of any moral or legal value."

At this point, in a dramatic gesture in front of the Assembly, he tore the resolution in half.

The resolution was repealed on December 16, 1991 on the initiative of the United States.

In 1982, Chaim Herzog was elected the fifth President of the State of Israel. He was re-elected for a second seven-year term in 1989 and served with distinction until 1993.

As the 50th anniversary of *Kristallnacht* approached, I had another one of my "patented, brilliant ideas." Instead of an event in New York, why not commemorate *Kristallnacht* in the country where it all began, in Germany?

In October, 1987, my secretary came rushing into my office. "You won't believe this—Ernie, Dr. Ruth is on the phone. She wants to talk to you!"

Dr. Ruth? The sex expert? What could she want from me?

"Put her on."

In a moment I heard the well-known, high pitched voice of Dr. Ruth.

"Are you Ernest Michel, who was born in Germany?"

"Yes, I am."

"I must meet with you right away. Are you free this afternoon?"

"Hold it, hold it." It was hard to get a word in edgewise. "I have no sex problems, Dr. Ruth. What is it about?"

"I'd rather tell you in person. It's important, and I'm convinced you can be very instrumental in bringing it about."

By now I was intrigued, and we made a date for the following day. My secretary had, of course, alerted the whole office that Dr. Ruth was coming to see her boss.

"I didn't know she made house calls," was one of the more generous remarks I heard that day—others were much worse.

The diminutive, four foot eight bundle of energy, with a big smile on her face, greeted all the office staff who lined up to say hello. When we sat down in my office, she was all business. I knew

Dr. Ruth was born in Germany, but I didn't know her personal background. In many ways, it resembles that of my sister Lotte.

Born as Carola Westheimer in Frankfurt, which was only a short distance from Mannheim, her parents sent her, as a young child, alone, to Switzerland. All the members of her family were killed. She survived and eventually arrived in Palestine, where she joined the army shortly after the War of Liberation.

"I was in Frankfurt on *Kristallnacht*, 1938, and saw our synagogue burn to the ground. I have never forgotten it." Dr. Ruth continued her story while I listened attentively. There was something compelling about that small woman, so full of energy and determination.

"I came to you because I know that you, too, came from Germany and survived the Holocaust. I have given this a great deal of thought. We must do something to keep the memory of that tragic night alive. I need your help on this. You know the American Jewish community, and they know you. I am convinced that if we put our heads together we can come up with a program which will effectively commemorate *Kristallnacht* in this country."

Dr. Ruth had not known, of course, that I'd been thinking along those same lines. What she said made a lot of sense. I felt instinctively that a program could be developed which would appropriately remind the world of the events almost 50 years ago.

Dr. Ruth, through her own extensive contacts in the television industry, engaged a producer to begin plans for a TV documentary, but she needed the funds to put it together. I was convinced that it wouldn't be too difficult to obtain the necessary funding for the program, and I was sure that I'd find support among the UJA-Federation leadership. Together we established a working committee composed of many segments of the Jewish community, who pledged their total support for our ambitious undertaking.

We then joined forces with Ambassador Ronald Lauder, who, we learned, had the same idea and was independently producing another, though totally different, one-hour TV special.

While I was engaged in these plans, I was also busy with the notion of commemorating *Kristallnacht* in Germany itself. I felt strongly that the presence of prominent American Jews in the country where it all began, would bring this event to the attention of the German public. They needed to be reminded of what happened on their own soil.

The subject of organizing a UJA-Federation sponsored visit to Germany aroused some strong emotions in the leadership. While a good number supported the idea, others were violently opposed to it. "It's too early to go to Germany as a group. We have no right to do that a mere 50 years after these events."

The discussions remained inconclusive, so I decided to consult Israel's President Herzog, who had just returned from a state visit to Germany. I remained in contact with the former Ambassador, and he had been gracious enough to receive me when I went on official visits to Israel.

I made arrangements to see Herzog at his official residence in Jerusalem. Chaim Herzog, now in his sixties, looks like a President. Perfectly groomed, with gray hair and a warm smile, he greeted me as I entered his office.

"Well, how's your tennis these days?" he asked.

"Not as good as it used to be, Mr. President."

We talked about the intifada, which had just begun and then I came to the point. I described the proposed commemorative visit to Germany.

"I appreciate your wanting to discuss this with me," the President replied, "and I will tell you my reaction to my recent visit."

The President then described his emotional visit to the Bergen-Belsen concentration camp, accompanied by the German President, Richard von Weizsaecker. He told me about his discussions with the German President and his reception by the government of the Federal Republic, and the people of Germany.

"The visit to Bergen-Belsen was a particularly difficult one for me," he continued. "I remembered clearly the first time I came to that hell-hole, in the spring of 1945, as a young officer in the British Army, and how appalled I was by what I saw. I'll never forget the sight. The bodies. The living skeletons looking at me with those empty eyes. The degradation. The filth. As a Jew, as a human being, I was revolted by the sight. 'How could this happen?' I asked myself. I was also aware of the reaction of the German President. He was as moved as I was."

President Herzog then spoke about Germany and its growing, close relationship with Israel.

"After the United States, Germany is our most important partner. More Germans visit Israel today than American Jews. It is ironic, isn't it?"

What I found especially meaningful was his description of the evidently warm relationship which had developed between him and his German counterpart. It was his deep conviction that he was dealing with a President who firmly believed in accepting German responsibility for the crimes committed during the Nazi era, who was eager to support the growing contact between their two countries and heal the wounds caused by the almost total destruction of German Jewry.

One ironic footnote in history is that this President was the son of the State Secretary of the German foreign office in the 1930's who gave the eulogy for Herschel Grynspan's victim at a State funera. He was Hitler's personal representative for the occasion.

The elder von Weizsaecker was eventually tried by an Allied Tribunal in 1949 as a war criminal and sentenced to seven years in jail. His sentence was commuted to five years, and by order of General McCloy, the German High Commissioner, he was released in 1950 after serving only one year.

It is one of the ironies of history that his son became the moral voice of the new democratic Germany, leading his nation in facing its past openly and honestly. Since he was elected, President von Weizsaecker has indeed been that voice. On many occasions, in many public forums and private meetings, he has acknowledged Germany's guilt for the crimes committed by the Nazis with the solemn assurance that this would never happen again.

When I left his office, I felt great about being a Jew in Israel, I felt great about surviving, I felt great about having done as much as I could in the Jewish community. On an impulse, I shook hands with the guard at the gate and told him: "Do you know what it means to be received by the President of Israel in your country?"

He just looked at me, shaking my hand and wondering, I was sure, about the crazy American.

When I got back to New York I called a meeting of our leadership and shared President Herzog's reaction to our proposed trip. I made it clear that Herzog's feeling that a visit by the New York Jewish leadership to Germany to commemorate *Kristallnacht* was indeed appropriate and timely.

One of our most respected leaders, the chairman of our board, Joseph Gurwin, was born in Lithuania and left just before the war to come to the U.S. He made a most moving statement which had a deep effect on all those present.

"I fully recognize and understand the position of President Herzog. He speaks as an Israeli who knows the reality of the world in which we live. I have never, and will never, set foot in Germany. I can never forget what the Germans did to our people and to those of my family who perished during the war. That is my personal point of view and I will never change it. However, I am also a realist and know that such a visit can have an effect in Germany, as well as here in the United States. It is because of this that I withdraw my opposition and support the decision for the UJA-Federation Mission to go to Germany."

When he finished, there was a brief silence. There was nothing anyone could add. The meeting concluded with the vote to go ahead, although there were a number of abstentions. We proceeded with plans for the first UJA-Federation mission to Germany.

Had I done the right thing to push for it?

XXXVII

The Meeting with the President of Germany

WE WERE ONE hundred New Yorkers, major contributors and leaders of the UJA-Federation of New York who made a memorable and highly emotional trip to commemorate the 50th anniversary of *Kristallnacht* in Germany. Our first stop was Munich. We chose that city so we could visit Dachau. The camp is a typical German reminder of the horror that once was. It is clean and sanitized. Two barracks are all that remain. All the others have been torn down. There is gravel on the ground where they once stood. Signs explain the various sites.

There's a museum, describing in clinical and excruciatingly horrifying detail, the story of that grand daddy of all of the Nazi concentration camps and the tortures committed on the unfortunate victims. It was built by the Nazis in 1933, immediately after they came to power, to deal with those they considered anti-social elements.

Communists, priests, Free Masons, union leaders, all kinds of groups the Nazis wanted to eliminate, were sent to Dachau. Jews began arriving only after November, 1938, when the Nazis arrested most Jewish males over the age of 16.

We held a memorial service in the Jewish chapel. We did the same at the Olympic Village, the site where the Israeli athletes were taken hostage during the Olympic Games of 1972. We stopped where the main synagogue of Munich once stood. A simple stone, inscribed in German and Hebrew, tells the story.

It was all done very correctly and appropriately for the occasion. Our activities were duly noted in the German press, usually in a brief, buried paragraph on page 17 or 19. For the average German, it was part of a past they would prefer not to acknowledge.

Munich was, after all, the birthplace of Nazism, where Hitler led his Brownshirts on a march which eventually engulfed the world in flames and resulted in 50 million dead. We participated there in three special events which left a lasting impression on all participants.

The first was a memorial service in the Munich synagogue, conducted by Rabbi Richter. The service was especially written by him for the occasion. It was poignant, meaningful and very moving, especially when the Cantor sang the El Mole Rachamim, the prayer to those who died a martyr's death. There wasn't a dry eye among us when the last notes resounded in the synagogue.

The second event was a reception and luncheon, given in our honor by the Mayor of Munich in the beautiful, old City Hall. The Mayor spoke in German about remembering the past, the loss of the Jews of Germany, and concluded with an emotional plea towards understanding and forgiveness.

The final event was rather special. We met with the members of the White Rose, the surviving dissidents of the only organized German resistance against the Nazis during the war. They especially protested the ongoing extermination of European Jews.

To this day, they remind Germans of their past and guard against any sign of undemocratic tendencies. The head of the movement is Franz Mueller, a man my own age, with a heavy mustache, an outgoing personality, and as decent a man as I have ever met. Franz tirelessly travels all over Germany, speaking about his own past as a warning to all those who would listen, especially students.

Franz addressed our group, recalling his youth. "I would do it all over again," he concluded. "It was the only answer to Hitler."

In my reply, I referred to the fact that both he and I, a Christian and a Jew, had suffered a similar fate. Hopefully, from our experiences we would develop a different relationship between Jews and Germans.

This was all a prologue to the one event I anticipated with a great deal of trepidation—meeting the President of Germany. The arrangements were made through the Foreign Office in Bonn, and while I hoped von Weizsaecker would meet the entire group, I understood he preferred a more intimate setting.

That's how we became a delegation of twelve men and women, waiting in Villa Hammerschmitt for the arrival of the German President.

The room was tastefully decorated and had been prepared for an informal meeting. There were place settings for each of us, with the place at the head of the table reserved for the President.

After a few minutes, the door opened and the impressive figure of the President appeared. Tall, with a full head of white hair, piercing eyes, and a friendly smile, he greeted everyone personally as I made the introductions. It was obvious that he had been carefully briefed. He asked about our program and the impressions we had of his country. He spoke perfect English. In some ways, he reminded me of President Herzog and I could easily understand why the two men hit it off.

After a few minutes, von Weizsaecker asked us to sit down. The moment I had been so anxiously awaiting had arrived. I was face to face with the President of Germany, 50 years, almost to the day, since *Kristallnacht*.

"Mr. President," I spoke in English for the benefit of my colleagues. "This has been a difficult visit for all of us, especially me."

Then I spoke of my background as a young Jew growing up in Nazi Germany, of *Kristallnacht* in 1938, of the loss of my family and my miraculous survival. I spoke about my emigration to the United States and how difficult it was to decide whether or not to undertake this mission. I concluded:

"We came here for two reasons. First, to remind ourselves of what happened almost a half century ago and to affirm the need to keep that memory alive for all time to come.

"Second, we came to remind the German people of the events which took place in your country, so that future generations, as well, shall never forget. This is why we appreciate the opportunity to meet with you, Herr Bundespraesident, the leader and conscience of your people. We ask you to remain vigilant and to make sure that the horror we endured will forever be part of the German psyche. To forget what happened would be the ultimate tragedy. We believe in the special relationship which exists between your country and Israel, and we know that this will continue.

"Fifty years ago I would not have dared to believe that I would meet face to face with the President of Germany, here, in your home, and to address you in this open and direct manner, but times and circumstances have changed."

The President listened carefully, nodding every once in a while, without trying to interrupt. I had difficulty controlling myself as I spoke, and von Weizsaecker knew it. My colleagues, fully cognizant of what this meeting meant to me, listened attentively.

When I finished, von Weizsaecker waited for a moment before replying. He spoke of his own feelings as a German, about the Nazi period and the fact that Germany would for all time, carry the stigma of those years. Recognizing the suffering of the Jewish people at the hands of the Germans, the injustice and persecution, he assured our group that there could be no forgetting.

His tone was serious, his voice firm. The President clearly spoke from his heart as he spoke of the new democratic Germany, where human rights were sacred.

The discussion then became less formal and he gave everyone in our group an opportunity to express themselves.

We spent an hour with the President. Before taking our leave, Ludwig Jesselson, who, like me, was born in Germany and had ably chaired the mission, rose to address von Weiszaecker. The president rose, too.

"Mr. President," Jesselson said, "on behalf of all of us on this mission, we would like to present you with a gift."

He then gave him a beautiful contemporary Chanukah menorah, and explained its meaning to the President. "This eight-branch candelabra is lit by Jews throughout the world every year," he said, "to commemorate the victory of the Maccabees over Antiochus in the year 164 B.C.E. This was our first successful battle for religious freedom, a victory of good over evil."

After a final handshake, we rejoined the other mission members. The next morning we took off via El Al, for the second part of our mission, our trip to Israel.

This visit to Germany brought me full circle. There was no catharsis or resolution. It brought me face to face with my past and rounded out five decades of one man's uniquely felt experiences. I consider myself a very lucky man. Not only did I survive, but I did so against all odds.

More than anything else, I'm proud that I never gave up hope and that I was given the chance to rebuild my own life and participate in a meaningful way in the Jewish community.

I couldn't ask for anything more.

Epilogue

IT IS A COLD, CLEAR, beautiful winter morning as I sit down to write the last lines of my life story. Writing it has awakened many memories. I have become even more aware than I had thought of the unbelievable circumstances which brought me to this point.

I will be 70 years old this summer. I was not quite 20 when I arrived in Auschwitz and 22 when I escaped on that final march in April, 1945. I am one of the youngest living survivors. Many of us are in the 80s and even older. Our numbers are shrinking, and we often meet at funerals. In another generation, maybe less, there will be hardly any survivors left to tell our story; there will be only be books, tapes and film to document our past.

I have been given a gift—so far fifty years worth of a full and satisfying life. It hasn't always been easy, but it has always been exciting.

I appreciate America, and I am grateful to her. I came off the boat in 1946, a greenhorn, carrying a battered suitcase. I couldn't even speak English. But America gave me the opportunity to do everything I ever hoped for.

And I was allowed to observe the events of the 20th century from a unique perspective. Without a doubt, this has been the most dramatic century in the long history of the Jewish people— which incorporates six seminal events.

The first was the Exodus from Egypt. The second was the destruction of the two Temples in Jerusalem followed by the Diaspora. The third, in 1492, was the expulsion from Spain. Then, in the 20th century, we experienced the Holocaust, the rebirth of the State of Israel and the Ingathering of the Exiles. I was a participant in all three of these, and it affected me deeply.

Reflecting about Germany is an ever-recurring part of my life that is filled with contradictions and emotions. Germany's actions during the Second World War will forever be remembered. The Holocaust is unique. It was the lowest point in human behavior, when the Nazi government made a systematic effort to completely destroy the Jewish people.

I should hate Germany and everything German. But one can't waste one's life on hatred. I have come to recognize that the Germany of today is different from the Third Reich. The German people have a democratic government. More than one million German protesters crowded the streets in dozens of German cities to protest Neo-Nazi and skinhead violence. The Holocaust is on the school curriculum. German leaders publicly apologize and acknowledge responsibility for the persecution and murder of the European Jews. The German people are trying to make amends.

So while I do not hate, I am still uneasy about Germany and Germans. It is subjective, of course. But I ask myself, "Can people change in a generation or two? Do they really understand their own past and how and why Nazism developed? Do they know how the world sees them when there are outbreaks of anti-ethnic violence and anti-Semitism in their homeland?"

In the words of the German president, "Our country will have to live forever with the guilt of what happened on our soil, in this century."

Nothing can erase the memories of my youth. I cannot forget and I cannot forgive. No one can. No one has that right.

WHERE ARE THEY NOW?

The reader may wonder what happened to some of the people who have been part of my life.

My daughter Lauren lives with her husband Chaim and her three children in Jerusalem. Chaim is an architect, Lauren works part time with emotionally handicapped children.

My son Joel lives in New York. He is divorced and has a son, and is working as a limousine driver.

Karen, my youngest daughter, is married to Rabbi Brian Daniels. They have two daughters and live in McAllen, Texas.

Honzo Marek has remained one of my closest friends. He stayed in Prague until the Soviet takeover and came to the U.S. in 1951. He and his wife Martha, also a survivor, live in Long Island. When he first came to the States, he worked as a counterman in a delicatessen. Then he and Martha became caterers. Now retired, they are planning to move to Virginia to be near their daughter and her family.

Every year, on April 18, we get together with our wives to celebrate the anniversary of our escape from the death march in 1945.

Franz and Lisa Kaufman from the Bruchsal cardboard factory, managed to leave Germany and came to Atlanta after he was released from Dachau. His stay in Dachau caused him to go blind. He died in 1986, Lisa died in 1992.

My closest childhood friend, Maxi Kuhn, was deported to Gurs and Auschwitz with my parents and all the other Mannheimers in August, 1942. Not one of them survived.

Bob Lindsay and his wife Ginny remain close friends. Bob was a civil rights activist concerned about the plight of migrant farm workers. The Lindsays are very devoted, active members in their church. They are retired and live in Colorado.

My sister Lotte and her husband Sami have four daughters and thirteen grandchildren and still live in Ein Hanaziv near Beit Shean in Israel. Sami was the manager of one of the largest dairies in Israel. Two of their grandchildren are already married.

Piese and Onny still live in Kibbutz Netzer Sereni with their families. Izzy, 87 years old, one of the heroes of Auschwitz, lives with his wife near Tel Aviv.

Stephan Heyman from the Krankenbau in Buna, the man who "hired" me for my calligraphy, remained a Communist. He returned to Berlin after the liberation and became Minister of the Interior of the first East German government. He died many years ago. I will forever be grateful to him for saving my life.

Dr. Solomon Samuelides from Salonika, Greece, who was in the Krankenbau in Buna with Honzo and me, survived and moved to France, where he started a new family. His first wife and children were killed in Birkenau. In his 80's, he is now retired.

Of the 100 plus Paderborners who arrived in Auschwitz that cold March in 1943, nine survived. Eight are still alive.

Arthur Tholen, one of the editors at the *Port Huron Times Herald*, is the only one from that first year who is still in touch with me. He's retired and lives in Denver with his wife, Ruth.

My close friend and mentor, Al Hutler, who found me in Mannheim and encouraged my involvement with UJA, is retired and lives with Lee, his wife, in San Diego. He's 83 and still plays tennis four times a week. He was also the first executive director of the Israel Tennis Center, which builds and supports tennis centers for Israeli and Arab children in eleven cities.

Rabbi Abraham Haselkorn, the first American Rabbi whom I met in Mannheim and brought me to Lt. Hutler's office on that fateful day in July, 1946, died some 10 years ago in Salinas, California, where he served as the local Rabbi.

After Honzo and Felix left the farming community of Lindenau the day after the war ended, I was only able to contact Honzo. Neither one of us was ever able to find Felix. We ran into dead ends, no matter what we tried. We assume he disappeared or was killed in the havoc at war's end.

Gerd Hartog, my close friend from Paderborn, became a kapo in Auschwitz-Buna. The last time I saw him was on the death march to Buchenwald in January, 1945. All efforts to find him have been in vain.

Dr. Josef Mengele, the death doctor from Auschwitz who did his horrible medical experiments on Diana and thousands of others, fled from Germany through the Odessa organization to South America and eventually drowned in Brazil. His remains have been positively identified.

Rudolf Hoess, the commandant of Auschwitz, was sentenced to death by a Polish court and executed on a site overlooking the camp where he had killed so many. Of 617 SS defendants tried in Polish courts, 34 were sentenced to death.